IS THERE A GOD?

QUESTIONS and ANSWERS
ABOUT SCIENCE
and THE BIBLE

ILLUMINATION
PUBLISHERS

JOHN M. OAKES, PH.D.

IS THERE A GOD?

QUESTIONS AND ANSWERS ABOUT SCIENCE AND THE BIBLE

Illumination Publishers
www.ipibooks.com

IS THERE A GOD?

Questions and Answers About Science and the Bible

©2006, 2023 by John M. Oakes, Ph.D.

Printed in the United States of America.

Cover and Interior design: Toney Mulhollan.

ISBN: 978-1-958723-11-1. Updated edition, October, 2023.

Unless otherwise indicated, all Scripture references are from the Holy Bible, New International Version, (c) 1973, 1978, 1984, 2011, by the International Bible Society. Used by permission of Zondervan Bible Publishers. Scripture references marked NAS are from the New American Standard Bible, (c) The Lockman Foundation, 1977. Used by permission.

Illumination Publishers International is committed to caring wisely for God's creation and uses recycled paper whenever possible.

About the author: **John Oakes** was a professor of chemistry at Grossmont College. John became a Christian while attending graduate school in 1978. He earned a Ph.D. in chemical physics in 1984 from the University of Colorado. That same year he married his wife, Jan. They have three adult children and reside in San Diego, California. John also serves as president of the Apologetics Research Society. John and Jan now serve as church leaders in a mission church planting in Merced, California. Some of his other books include: *From Shadow to Reality, Reasons for Belief, Daniel: Prophet to the Nations, That You May Believe, Field Manual for Christian Apologetics, Mormonism: What Do the Evidence and Testimony Reveal?, Golden Rule Membership* and *The Christian Story: Finding the Church in Church History.* For more information about John's schedule and ministry engagements, go to www.EvidenceForChristianity.org.

ILLUMINATION **IP** PUBLISHERS www.ipibooks.com

To Jan, Benjamin, Elizabeth, and Kathryn

I would like to express my thanks first of all to my wife, Jan, who never complained and always covered for me when I slipped out late at night or early in the morning to work on this book.

Keith Tabor was the one who convinced me to write this book and I am very grateful that he did. In addition, I would like to thank those who have encouraged me in this project. These include my good friends Gregg Marutzky and Gary Bishop, who urged me when I was a young Christian to use my training as a scientist to study and teach evidences related to Christianity and the Bible.

Thanks also to Douglas Jacoby, who gave great encouragement and much needed criticism, and serves for me as a model of a Christian writer. I would like to thank the editor and publisher of the first edition of the book, Rex Geissler, whose dedication to the project and willingness to challenge my thinking had a great effect on its final form. A special note of thanks to Illumination Publishers for this new edition of the book.

...THE GLORY AND GREATNESS OF ALMIGHTY GOD
ARE MARVELOUSLY DISCERNED IN ALL HIS WORKS AND
DIVINELY READ IN THE OPEN BOOK OF HEAVEN.

—GALILEO GALILEI
A LETTER TO THE DUCHESS CHRISTINA, 1614

The need for biblical evidences is greater in our generation than ever before. Secularism and humanism are rampant, the media and the educational system bombard us with half-truths and untruths about the meaning of life, and multitudes are confused about the fundamentals of human existence. So profound is the confusion today that many ask not, "What are the answers?", but rather "What are the questions?" We in Western society are in a bad way indeed! The need for scientifically current apologetics books— well thought out, well written, and well adapted to our generation—is great. I believe that, with this volume, you have acquired such a book.

For me it was fascinating to watch *Is There a God?* take shape, realizing what invaluable evidence John Oakes was bringing to light. Christians the world over will appreciate its careful treatment of science and Bible. My heart thrills at every piece of information, every perspective or new angle of entry into apologetic questions. During high school and university years my own faith was strengthened enormously through reading apologetic works, and it was through our mutual interest in apologetics that John and I first came into contact. Over the years I have built up a small library around the subject of evidences. I was proud to add John's book, *Is There a God? Questions About Science and the Bible*, to my collection.

Surely every reader will want to follow the flow of John Oakes' reasoning and master the arguments, in order to be better equipped to convince others about God's reality and the truth of his Word.

It is rare to find a man of high caliber and academic integrity serving the Lord both as university professor and disciple of Christ. Thanks to that precious combination, a superb new book has been authored, and to you I gladly commend both it and its author. I have every confidence that in this book you will find something to strengthen your faith in God's existence, wisdom, and power.

Douglas Jacoby,
Marietta, Georgia

TABLE OF CONTENTS

WHENCE IS IT THAT NATURE DOES NOTHING IN VAIN; AND WHENCE
ARISES ALL THAT ORDER AND BEAUTY WHICH WE SEE IN THE
WORLD?

—ISAAC NEWTON
OPTICKS, 1730

A few years ago on an episode of the ABC show "Nightline," a debate was held between Carl Sagan and Jerry Falwell. Sagan, then professor of astronomy at Cornell University, presumed to speak for all scientists as he propounded the view that the known laws of science are sufficient to explain the origin of the universe and all life on earth. Jerry Falwell, then president of the Moral Majority, presumed to speak for all "Bible-believing Christians" as he supported the view that the universe itself is only a few thousand years old, and that all scientific evidence supports this view. Who "won" the debate? Obviously Carl Sagan, a scientist who had thought through the issues, had a great advantage. He skillfully won the debate and made the "Christian" perspective on science appear to be intellectually questionable. Unfortunately, debates are not always won by those on the side of truth, but are usually won by the more eloquent and well prepared. A more important question than "Who won this classic debate between the atheist and creationist?" would be "Who was right?" The answer: neither was correct!

As a professor of chemistry and physics (my PhD is in chemical physics), I have often had the opportunity to help students struggling with questions on the interface between science and religion-questions which relate to the scientific reliability of the Bible. Having at different times served as a minister and a professor, I have often been asked whether I find there to be contradictions between my faith in the Bible and my knowledge of science. I cannot agree with the renowned evolutionist Niles Eldredge, who has said that we should "take the position that religion and science are two utterly different domains of human experience" and have "little in common."[1] If the Bible is a reliable source of truth, there would be profound implications in the realm of science. If the Bible is true, then there are implications for at least two of the most important questions scientists ask: "What is the origin of life?" and "What is the origin of the universe?" Clearly, both science and religion address these questions and others, although they answer such questions by different methodologies. Eldredge and others suggest that we should simply brush aside the obvious fact that many questions are asked and answered by both science and religion. For people who grapple with the fundamental questions of life, such as "How did I get here?" and "Why am I here?", ignoring the obvious points at which science and religion touch will not work.

Consider the case of Augustine of Hippo.[2] Augustine is thought by many to be the most influential Christian theologian of all time. When he was a youth, Augustine's mother was a devout Christian. She longed for him to follow suit, but Augustine was an independent thinker from an early age. He was attracted to the Manichaean religion. Manichaeism was a dualistic (good vs. evil) religion founded in the area of present-day Iran by a man named Manes. This religion had affinities with Gnosticism and Zoroastrianism. In studying the writings of Manes, Augustine discovered some statements about the cosmos which were contradicted by what he knew to be true from empirical evidence discovered by the astronomers of his day. None of his Manichaean teachers would even address Augustine's questions. To quote Augustine, "I was told to believe in these views of Manes; but they did not correspond with what had been established by mathematics and my own eyesight."[3]

There was one teacher widely regarded to be the greatest and wisest of the Manichaean sect. His name was Faustus. Faustus visited the city where Augustine was studying. As Augustine relates, he eagerly awaited the opportunity to ask Faustus the question that none of his other teachers would answer. He assumed that there was a logical answer to his questions. However, when he approached Faustus, the great teacher refused to answer Augustine's questions about the cosmology of Manes. In fact, he admonished Augustine for his lack of faith.

In the end, due to his encounter with Faustus, Augustine eventually left Manichaeism and was won over to Christianity.

This incident illustrates two of our previous points. First, it shows that religion and science can and do overlap. Pretending this is not so is untenable. Augustine was turned away from his Manichaean belief because he found that the scripture of that religion contradicted what he knew to be true from his study of nature. Second, it demonstrates the need for believers to provide honest, reasonable answers to those who are seeking the truth about science and the Bible.

Let us go back to the debate between Falwell and Sagan. Why were they both wrong (one in saying that natural laws can explain the origin of life, the other in claiming that science supports the belief that the earth is a few thousand years old)? Both Carl Sagan and the school of atheists he represents and Jerry Falwell and the creationists he represents had the same fundamental flaw in their thinking. They were simply not approaching the evidence as scientists are supposed to when processing data.

The first chapter of this book discusses the potential pitfalls for many atheists and creationists, and proposes a more open-minded approach to thinking about the fundamental questions arise at the interface between science and religion. Should creationism be taught in our schools? Should the atheistic explanation of the origin of the universe and life be the basis of the science curriculum? Should science instructors teach both views and then let the students decide for themselves? Or should we avoid the debate entirely? These questions can be ignored, but they will not go away.

Christians, and especially Christians who are students, will eventually be confronted with comments like "Do you really believe in Adam and Eve? Oh come on... that's a myth!" The believer might also be confronted with a statement like "It's a proven fact that man evolved from apes. Do you mean to say you don't believe in evolution? And you want me to take your belief in the Bible seriously? Right!"

REASONS TO NOT STUDY SCIENCE AND THE BIBLE.

Despite the importance of the scientific questions raised by the Bible, especially the question of origins, the majority of Christians devote little or no energy to providing reasonable responses. There are several reasons for this. First, many accept the Bible by faith, and that is sufficient for them. It is often hard for non-believers to understand this perspective, yet most Christians believe the entire Bible is God-inspired, true and reliable. They take at face value the flood account in Genesis chapter seven, as well as the account of Adam and Eve in Genesis chapter two, just as much as they take at face value the Bible's claim that Jesus Christ was a real person. Whether or not an individual Christian has done enough research and study to verify this belief for himself, inerrancy is clearly a claim of the Bible.[4] The fact that many followers of Jesus Christ accept the inerrancy of the Bible by faith is, paradoxically, one reason that they do not spend a lot of time testing the scientific accuracy of the Bible. It is easy to understand how unbelievers see this as intellectual inconsistency. One of the purposes of this book is to address this dilemma.

Another reason followers of Jesus tend not to spend a lot of mental energy on these questions is that they simply are not issues of importance in their daily lives. There are many issues that could be debated regarding Christianity and the Bible. When will Jesus come back? What about the people who never heard about Jesus? What about the "rapture"? The list seems to go on indefinitely. Practical believers should ask themselves: "Does this issue affect my or anyone else's eternal destiny?," or "Does this question affect how I live my life?" If the answer to both questions is no, then one has found an issue which is probably worth little concern or debate. In the words of Galileo, "Can an opinion be heretical, and yet have no concern with the salvation of souls?" [5] It would seem at first glance that one's view of the creation story in Genesis is not relevant to salvation, or to one's way of life. A case will be made in this chapter that these issues are nevertheless important enough for all believers to spend time thinking about them.

A third reason many believers do not focus on these questions is that most are not scientists. Even if followers of Jesus wanted to ponder these questions in an intelligent way, would they know where to begin? How do scientists answer questions? What is a reliable source for the answers they would be seeking? Because of these difficulties, it is easy to just ignore the issue or perhaps read a single book which agrees with one's own preconceived opinion, failing to carefully question the arguments put forth in that book. Granted, one's interpretation of the first chapter of Genesis is not a salvation issue, or even a practical matter affecting daily Christian life. Granted, most Christians do not possess sufficient scientific training in biology, chemistry and physics to sort out many of the highly technical questions relating science, God and the Bible without help. Nevertheless, ignoring questions relating to science and the Bible is a mistake. Some of these reasons will be addressed in this introduction. Questions about science and the Bible will inevitably arise, so why not deal with them now?

WHY I SHOULD STUDY SCIENCE AND THE BIBLE.

One reason disciples of Jesus need to think carefully about these questions is related in 1 Peter 3:15-16.

> *Always be prepared to give an answer to everyone who asks you to give the reason for the hope you have. But do this with gentleness and respect, keeping a clear conscience, so that those who speak maliciously against your good behavior in Christ may be ashamed of their slander.*

Here the followers of Jesus are told to be prepared to answer the questions of non-believers. Outsiders will want to know what they believe and why. If a sincere question is asked, such as "What is the your Christian response to Darwin's theory of evolution?" and a flippant response is given, that would clearly not square with this biblical command. If a person is ignorant on the subject, the best response is simply, "I don't know," not an attempt to deflect the question. For a person new to the faith, this is a reasonable answer. However, according to this scripture a Christian has a responsibility to work to become "prepared to give an answer," especially to the questions which come up most often. This book is an attempt to help readers move toward that goal.

Many believers have heard questions like, "What about evolution and the Bible?" or "How can you believe in the Genesis creation myth in view of what we know from science?" At times, questions like these are a smokescreen on the part of a person who is not yet ready to face up to the issues

God is exposing in his or her life. This sort of interaction is recorded in John 4:7-26. When Jesus confronted a woman about sin in her life, rather than talk about the issue, she immediately changed the subject to an important but safer, theological issue. On safer ground, she would not need to deal with her own sin. Jesus answered her question with gentleness and respect, just as believers are admonished to respond to questions in 1 Peter 3:15-16. This gentle, respectful approach may have been part of what led this woman to believe in Jesus. In similar situations, we will not always get the same results as Jesus. Some would rather debate abstract ideas than deal with the fundamental need for repentance in their lives. It is true that some people raise questions of science and religion more to argue than to seek answers. However, many who ask these questions are sincerely seeking the truth. Those who believe in the Bible must prepare themselves to give a carefully reasoned answer to such questions.

A second reason followers of Jesus need to be prepared to answer scientific questions relating to Christianity is for the sake of their children. It is a fact that as a matter of public policy as well as of general consensus, the atheistic approach to interpreting scientific knowledge is presented to students from grade school to graduate school. Parents cannot afford to sit back and say "*Que será, será.*" The faith of their children is at issue. Students tend to accept at face value the things they are taught. The information is accepted along with the assumptions that underlie how that information is presented. Parents must be prepared to discuss with their children the truth about the origin of life and the creation of the universe. They cannot afford to brush aside challenges to the Genesis creation account that their children will face. Where will our children find a reasonable alternative to the atheistically biased treatment of these questions if not at home? Rest assured, your children will ask these questions. A simplistic explanation from parents or church leaders, one that is not consistent with the accepted facts of science, will do more harm than good.

Children are very inquisitive. Younger ones tend to accept what they hear from their parents as authoritative. However, as they move into adolescence, a natural skepticism arises. Most teens are smart enough to see through shallow explanations that contradict the facts. Perhaps one day you will take a family trip to the Grand Canyon. Your child will notice that the explanations she is reading in the park brochures, describing the hundreds of millions of years required to create the geological features in the canyon, are in agreement with what she is seeing. Perhaps this child will have heard the claim at church or at home that "the Bible says" the earth is actually just a few thousand years old. This would seem to contradict the evidence of thousands of feet of sedimentary layers carved out by the Colorado River. It is vital for parents to be prepared to answer the questions children will inevitably ask. Will you be prepared to give a reasonable answer?

The quality of the answer may have a dramatic effect on the child. To the extent that it is possible, children must be presented the truth, not half-truths or parent's uneducated guesses, especially in areas where science and religion overlap. Respect for you will grow when your children realize that you have grappled with these challenging questions. An unprepared answer may have the opposite effect.

The third reason believers need to be prepared to answer the questions raised in this book is for the sake of their own faith! Our faith in the inspiration of the Bible will be challenged by the world. Surely the reader has asked himself how the details of the creation account in Genesis chapter one can be understood in light of what he learned in science classes. With our busy lifestyles, it is tempting to sweep questions under the rug, especially when finding the answers seems challenging. (And let's face it, questions about science and the Bible are in that category!) The problem is that questions and doubts may come back to bite us. It seems to be a common human tendency that when the spiritual life is going well, nagging questions disappear into the background. They appear to fade into insignificance. However, there comes a point in the life of anyone trying to live for God when struggles, temptations and discouragements will come up. It is at such times, when our faith seems to be at its lowest ebb, that the nagging questions we put aside suddenly come to the forefront of our minds. Unresolved doubts about the Bible and the challenges to belief which come from science are potential pitfalls that Christians cannot afford to ignore. The wise person will deal with such questions when things are going well, rather than at a crisis point in life.

We learn from the life of Jesus that Satan attacks at our most vulnerable points, in times of greatest weakness. This is described in Luke 4:1-12, where Satan chose to tempt Jesus at the end of a forty-day fast. Jesus was apparently in a vulnerable position, and Satan's strategy was to get him to question the authority of God's Word. Satan attempted to do this by using a dubious interpretation of scripture. Jesus was prepared and skillfully responded to his attack.

Jesus was prepared. We often are not, and the ideal time to build defenses is not when the battle is already raging. Fortifying one's faith with regard to difficult questions may well need to be a gradual process, but eventually unresolved doubts need to be nailed down with the truth!

There are many books written on the subject of God and science as well as on science and the Bible. I have read many of them and learned much from them. However, most of them are missing some important elements. There have been a rather large number of books published on the subject, yet I had difficulty finding readable *and* objective books on the two subjects I could recommend to friends. Some support the Bible, but do a poor job of presenting the science. Others discuss science and religion, but start from an assumption that the Bible is not the inspired of God. Still others do a fairly good job with justifying science and the Bible, but would be difficult for most people to understand. I felt that there was a need for another book which deals with the science in a simple and forthright way—one which addresses questions of science and the existence of God, which answers science questions raised by the Bible, and one which presents positive evidence for biblical inspiration from scientific information in the scripture.

There are three concepts I have tried to keep in mind in writing this book. First, I have assumed the reader is unfamiliar with the scientific issues involved. I have therefore provided a brief introduction to the relevant science on such important topics as the Big Bang theory thermodynamics, evolutionary theory, planetary evolution and so forth. Second, I have attempted to avoid the sarcastic tone I feel many authors writing in this area tend to slip into. It is unfortunate that many of the Christian writers can be as sarcastic in tone as the unbelievers they seek to refute. This is not acceptable behavior. As we have already seen, Peter encouraged those who seek to answer the unbeliever to do so with gentleness and respect. Third, I have taken pains to present scientific conclusions that are well-supported by the evidence. I have tried very hard not to let my theology influence my interpretation of the scientific evidence. This would contrast with the methodology used by many in the creationist and atheist camps, whose conclusions fit neatly with their beliefs about science and religion, but are only poorly supported by the scientific evidence. Although much science is presented, at times they make big leaps and state beliefs as facts. I will attempt to point this out when it happens.

It is impossible for anyone to be an expert in all the areas of science. Answering the full range of questions about science, religion and the Bible requires knowledge from cosmology to particle physics, from physiology to theoretical chemistry, from thermodynamics to evolutionary biology, from geology to medical science. Having a doctorate in chemical physics, I have taught modern physics, classical physics, astronomy, theoretical chemistry, organic chemistry and biochemistry. I have less formal background in geology, biology evolution and medicine. I have tried to emphasize the questions in which I have expertise and to make less strong statements regarding the areas in which I have less academic training. Where I have less background, I have provided suggestions for further study. It is my hope that this book will shine light on the important questions of science, God and the Bible.

John M. Oakes
Fond du Lac, Wisconsin
1999

INTRODUCTION TO
THE REVISED EDITION

In the past seven years since writing *Is There a God?*, I have done extensive study in the areas covered by this work. I have been honored to teach on the Bible, science and religion in more than a dozen countries around the world. I have received and answered hundreds of questions on the topic of Christian Evidences at my website. For the past five years I have been teaching a class on the history and philosophy of science. My good friend Richard Albert and I have taught an honors section of the class at Grossmont College in which we spend considerable time discussing science and religion. The sparks fly at times, but hopefully some light is shed. Both our agreements and disagreements of the subject have been fruitful in developing these ideas. Between all these influences, my thinking has developed enough that I decided a revised edition of this book was required. The new edition includes more teaching, an expanded bibliography and, hopefully, better writing.

Thanks go to Douglas Jacoby for further editorial comments and suggestions, as well as to Toney Mulhollan and Illumination Publishers for their hard work in producing this completely revised edition.

San Diego, California
January 2015

---

1 Niles Eldredge, *The Monkey Business* (New York: Washington Square Press, 1980), 10.

2 The story of Augustine's conversion is found in his autobiography, *The Confessions of St. Augustine* (New York: Penguin Books, 1963). Books V and VI contain the section about his conversion from the Manichaean religion to Christianity.

3 Ibid, book V, chapter 3.

4 See for (example), Psalm 12:6, Psalm 119:160, Proverbs 30:5-6, 1 Thessalonians 2:13, and 2 Timothy 3:16.

5 Galileo Galilei, excerpted from a letter to the Grand Duchess Christina, 1614.

CHAPTER 1

WHAT CAN BE ACCOUNTED FOR BY FEWER ASSUMPTIONS
IS EXPLAINED IN VAIN BY MORE.

NOTHING SHOULD BE CONSIDERED AS EVIDENT
UNLESS IT IS KNOWN PER SE, IS EVIDENT FROM EXPERIENCE,
OR IS PROVEN BY AUTHORITY OF SCRIPTURE.

—*WILLIAM OF OCKHAM*

HOW SHOULD I THINK?

One may ask, "Are you trying to tell me how to think?" Well, yes, in a way. I will suggest a way of thinking about scientific evidence which will dramatically increase the probability of arriving at reliable conclusions. This approach will work in almost any investigation, not just in scientific questions. Stated simply, when you seek the most reasonable explanation of the available facts, a reasonable, unbiased analysis of the evidence best leads to the answer. The greatest impediment to objective analysis is assuming the answer before investigating. The tendency to allow bias to affect one's interpretation of evidence is a part of human nature. Outsiders to the scientific community sometimes assume scientists are somehow immune to bringing their bias into their data analysis—that they are always logical in their analysis of scientific questions. Yet the history of science will prove this assumption is far from true. Perhaps the reader believes that he or she can easily ask questions of science and the Bible without wearing glasses colored by preconception. I think it is very difficult to overcome our preconceived ideas. Personal experience informs me that Christians can be just as biased in their thinking as anyone else.

In many hours of counseling people with a broad range of problems in their lives (both as a minister and as a college professor) I have found one phenomenon to be consistent. If an issue arises which threatens our sense of security, our sense of being loved, our sense of well-being, and sometimes even our desire to pursue pleasure, we will readily believe things that from a logical standpoint are obviously not true. For human beings, the emotional need for security and love trumps logical argument in almost every case. I have found this generalization to hold true for arguments about science and religion. It is helpful to keep this in mind when analyzing the arguments of atheists and creationists. It takes a well-disciplined mind to let logic and reason overcome emotion in attempts to discover what is true. "An alcoholic is a victim." "Premarital sex is helpful to establish a healthy long term relationship and to find out if we're compatible." "I could never get AIDS." "People can take advantage of each other and still be great friends." "A woman can change an abusive partner by loving him." "There's nothing wrong with cheating on our taxes, since everyone does it." "If you're feeling down, eating will make the problem go away." "Success in a career is the best way to be happy." Every one of these statements is untrue! When we watch another person telling himself such things, we recognize it for what it is. And yet how often, in similar situations, all of us have made such statements to ourselves. All of us have believed such untruths at one time or another. Why? It is difficult for us to accept the truth. The truth can threaten us intellectually or, more likely, emotionally. It would be wise for all of us to admit that we are prone to accept illogical conclusions for emotional reasons. Quite frankly, sometimes we don't want people telling us the truth!

Are scientists human? Of course they are! Contrary to a commonly held assumption, scientists are subject to the same weaknesses as the rest of humanity. I am a scientist. I would admit that as a scientist I tend to tell myself that I am immune to illogical, emotional arguments. The reality, however, is that I am subject to the same human biases as everyone else. There is much evidence in the history of science to support the claim that the scientific community has always been resistant to changing long-held beliefs. The tendency of scientists toward group behavior and their resistance to new ideas was highlighted in the ground-breaking work of Thomas Kuhn, *The Structure of Scientific Revolutions*.[6] In this book and in subsequent work, Kuhn described the tendency of scientists to think as a group and to resist new, fundamental ways of thinking about natural laws. He coined the word "paradigm" to describe the underlying model or assumption scientists use to organize the information they observe. The point of his work is that scientists tend to almost unconsciously force their interpretation of observations of the natural world according to preconceived underlying models.

The reason Kuhn's idea was accepted by philosophers of science is that it so readily explains the major features of the history of science. More than a generation before Kuhn published his idea, Max Planck, one of the pioneers of modern quantum theory, said, "A new scientific truth does not triumph by convincing its opponents and making them see the light, but rather because its opponents eventually die, and a new generation grows up that is familiar with it." What is interesting is that scientists are aware of this tendency, and yet seem to succumb to it anyway because scientist are people, too. In view of this tendency, we should bear in mind the words of Thoreau, "No way of thinking, no matter how ancient, should be accepted without proof."[7]

There are many scientists who had the nerve to propose a new theory, only to be initially rejected by an establishment unprepared to have their underlying assumptions challenged. In some cases, scientists were persecuted for propounding theories which are now universally accepted. The story of Dutch scientist Jacobus van't Hoff comes to mind. Organic chemists of his day believed that when a carbon atom had four atoms bonded to it, the resulting molecule (had a flat shape or "lay flat, in a plane), with the four attached atoms at right angles to one another. While still a graduate student in 1874, van't Hoff proposed that carbon, with four substituent atoms attached, had a three-dimensional, tetrahedral shape (a three-sided pyramid with carbon at the center of the pyramid). Notable scientists of his day opposed his view, despite the fact that it explained facts known to be inconsistent with the current theory. He was temporarily blacklisted from academic positions as a chemist. Eventually the old guard was forced to give in as the huge weight of evidence supported the tetrahedral theory.

This story is by no means an isolated case. In fact, for large shifts in scientific model, it has been the rule rather than the exception as pointed out by Kuhn. A certain amount of skepticism to new and untried ideas is a necessary aspect of scientific inquiry. However, scientific methodology requires an open mind in order to function.

Why were the scientists of van't Hoff's day so closed-minded? Perhaps their intellectual pride was offended. It is always easier to continue thinking the way one was trained to think. This is no less true for scientists than for others.

Let's look at another case of resistance to a new paradigm. When Isaac Newton first published the Law of Gravity, Gottfried Leibniz (philosopher and mathematician who is given credit, along with Newton, for inventing calculus) vilified him. Leibniz accused Newton of heresy, because his belief in the attraction of objects to one another by "gravity" was "subversive of natural and inferential revealed religion." In other words, Leibniz was claiming that the theory of gravity not only contradicted the evidence; it also contradicted the Bible. Did the theory of gravity disagree with the data or with the Bible? Neither! It disagreed with the commonly held view of the day. Leibniz' opposition to Newton's theory of gravity is particularly significant to us because it is one of many in the history of science in which religious preconceptions were a factor in the opposition to a new scientific theory.

Galileo Galilei was familiar with the tendency for dubious Bible interpretation to engender resistance to new scientific ideas. He published overwhelming evidence that the earth and planets move around the sun (heliocentrism), rather than the sun and planets around the earth (geocentrism) in his book *The Starry Messenger*.[8] Soon after, the Roman Curia accused him of heresy for "holding to the false doctrine that the earth moves."[9] Galileo was forced to recant and to stop "teaching, writing or even discussing the false and heretical view that the earth moves."

Again, we see believers allowing a particular interpretation of the Bible to control how they interpret empirical evidence discovered by scientists. In this case, theologians took statements in the Bible such as "from the rising of the sun to the place where it sets" (Psalm 50:1) to imply that the sun literally moves around the earth. Galileo vigorously defended the right of scientists to let empirical evidence determine what theories should be accepted. In a letter to the Duchess Christina, he said, "The Bible was written to tell us how to go to heaven, not how the heavens go."[10]

I find myself agreeing with Galileo. With hindsight we can easily see the mistake theologians made in the past when they accused Galileo of opposing the Bible. Even today, we say that the sun sets. In fact, the sun does not literally set; rather, it is the earth that spins. This tendency to allow a particular literal reading of the Bible to affect the interpretation of empirical evidence will be a familiar pattern as we proceed.

PRECONCEIVED NOTIONS

These events in the history of science cast light on the debate that continues to rage between atheists and creationists. Before launching into discussing this debate, it would be helpful first to define both the atheistic and the creationist view of the natural world. At the risk of stereotyping and oversimplifying, the atheist view of nature can be summarized as follows:

> *Every event which has ever occurred or ever will occur in the universe can be explained by the laws of nature (whether they are known or as of yet unknown).*

For the atheist, supernatural explanations (i.e. those which invoke the work of God) are rejected out of hand. According to this view, the scientist's job is to discover these laws of nature and use them to explain such difficult questions as the origin of the universe, the rise of life, the origin of species, and the geology and structure of the earth. A quote from John Desmond Bernal's book *The Origins of Life* serves to represent this view:

> *Now with both of these alternatives-self-ordering or transcendent design—it is always open to the skeptic to refuse to choose between them. However, in practice, the skeptic can only concentrate*

on the materialist alternative because this is the only one which gives
anything to argue about or experiment with. [11]

In other words, in choosing to look at the evidence nature offers us, a scientist can choose to consider possible transcendent explanations (allowing for the existence of God and his work in creation) or one can assume that these things can only be explained by the laws of nature. Scientist like Bernal, and atheists in general, choose at the outset to assume that the origin of the universe, of life, and so forth all have a natural explanation. They do not allow for the possibility of a supernatural explanation. This, the standard position of atheists, is clearly an unproven assumption. Bernal is more honest about his way of thinking than most other atheists are! Let it be said again: The basic assumption made by many if not most scientists-that there are not now, nor have there ever been supernatural events-is just that, an assumption. Their conclusions can be no better than their assumptions. Either way, whether right or wrong, when atheist scientists conclude that God does not exist, it is worth noting that they analyze scientific evidence having assumed there is no God before they examine the evidence. With this line of reasoning, their final conclusion is foreordained.

This fundamental presupposition of many scientists, is exemplified in the statement of the humanists Norman and Lucia Hall: [12]

> *Science, on the other hand, assumes that there are no transcen-*
> *dent, immaterial forces and that all forces which do exist within the*
> *universe behave in an ultimately objective and random fashion...*
> *[A] non-mysterious understandable universe is a basic assumption*
> *behind all science.*

I would agree with these authors that the assumption of an under-standable universe is part of how scientists approach their work, and that this working assumption has been useful. However, to state a *priori* that transcendent forces have never affected the universe-that all causes and ef-fects are random-is not justified. This author does not speak for all scien-tists. I am a scientist and I do not make unfounded assumptions against the possibility of transcendent forces operating in the universe.

The application of this presupposition to a specific issue—the origin of man—is illustrated by a quote from Julian Huxley, twentieth century biologist (and brother of Aldous Huxley, author of *Brave New World*). In discussing to how man came to be, Huxley said,[13]

> *We are as much a product of blind forces as is the falling of*
> *a stone to earth, or the ebb and flow of the tides. We have just*
> *happened, and man was made flesh by a long series of singularly*
> *beneficial accidents.*

This amounts to a religious statement of faith. We will see that acceptance of this precept requires a much greater leap of faith than belief in the God of the Bible.

Another statement that illustrates the religion-like preconceptions of many atheists comes from perhaps the most famous evolutionist of modern times, Richard Dawkins:[14]

> *In the universe of blind physical forces and genetic replication, some people are going to get hurt and other people are going to get lucky: and you won't find any rhyme or reason to it, nor any justice. The universe we observe has precisely the properties we should expect if there is at the bottom, no design, no purpose, no evil and no good. Nothing but blind, pitiless indifference. DNA neither knows nor cares. DNA just is, and we dance to its music."*

CREATIONISM

What is creationism? Creation scientists do not fit easily into a single definition. Broadly, a creationist is a person who believes that scientific knowledge is consistent with belief in a creator. Creationists include in their number deists, theists, intelligent design believers and young earth creationists.

Deists believe the universe and the laws which govern it were created. They believe that the creator put the universe in motion but does not influence the creation. This view does not allow for supernatural, miraculous forces to operate. This view is incompatible with biblical teaching. The increasing influence of deists in the scientific community due to evidence for design in nature will be described in chapter ten.

Theists believe in a creator who takes an active role in the world. To the theist, miraculous, supernatural intervention in the course of nature is a possibility. Some theists believe that evolution is part of God's plan to create the life forms found on the earth. Broadly, theism is consistent with biblical teaching. Those who associated themselves with the intelligent design movement are theists. They attempt to use empirical evidence to prove that one must invoke the existence of God to explain what is observed in nature, specifically in the complexity of living beings. Most advocates of intelligent design believe that scientific knowledge and biblical interpretation allow for an old earth.

Young-earth creationists are also theists. Arguably, they are supporters of intelligent design as well. What distinguishes this group is that they are committed to a literal interpretation of the scientifically relevant content in the Bible, especially the first few chapters of Genesis. The young earth creationists are particularly influential in the United States. They dominate

many Christian groups which are described as "fundamentalists." The political influence of this group has become sufficiently dominant that in the
eyes of the American public, the word "creationist" has come to be associated exclusively with this approach. Ronald Numbers has published an
excellent summary of the history of the creationist movement, especially
the young earth creationists.[15]

For the sake of simplicity, in this work I will use the word creationist to
refer to those who would properly be labeled young earth creationists. I do
this for simplicity but also because Americans generally apply the word creationist to the young earth creationists. My apologies go to those who are
creationists but do not agree that the Bible definitely implies a young earth.

With this proviso, the (young-earth) creationist perspective on the
relationship between science and the Bible can be summarized in a fairly
simple statement:

> *The universe is a few thousand years old. The preponderance of
> empirical scientific evidence is in agreement with this claim.*

Many creationists feel that all faithful Christians ought to agree with
this viewpoint and that their theory should be taught on at least an equal
footing with the atheistic view in public schools. This has led to considerable
controversy across the United States. As a statement which could represent
the typical view of creationists, examine this quote from the book *Scientific
Creationism* by Henry Morris, a leader in the creationist movement.

In the preceding chapters it has been shown that the basic facts of
science today fit the special creation model much better than they do the
evolution model. Although there are certain problems that still need solu-
tions, none are of sufficient gravity to disturb the basic creation framework,
whereas the many problems in the evolution model are serious.[16]

> *In using the phrase the "special creation model," Morris means
> that the earth was created no earlier than "about 5500 BC at most."
> In his books, Morris does point out some interesting problems with
> modern evolutionary theory, but the claim that the preponderance
> of evidence supports belief in an earth which is only a few thousand
> years old is patently false. This point will be discussed in some detail
> in the second chapter.[17]*

We will see that the claims of both atheists and creationists do not
stand up to scientific scrutiny, but that the Bible, understood correctly, does
in fact agree with accepted scientific facts. In other words, the debate between the atheists and the creationists are often off the mark because of
incorrect assumptions and biases.

Both the atheists and the creationists err because their approach has a deep and fundamental flaw: they assume the answer before they ask the question. One crucial question in the study of science and religion is whether supernatural events have occurred. Atheists begin by assuming that supernatural events do not happen. As a result, their final conclusion is predictable. Another crucial question in the study of science and religion is the age of the universe. Many creationists (e.g. you are a creationist, as am I, though we are not "scientific creationists") approach their investigation of this question by assuming that the earth is only a few thousand years old. Their final conclusion is also predictable. A study of history and everyday human experience will show convincingly that if a person or group makes a firm choice to believe something, they will be able to bend, alter, misinterpret, or selectively read the evidence until they have "proved" their point. We will see in chapters three and four that atheists are forced to play these same intellectual games in order to conclude what they already believe by faith-namely, that God does not exist.

A classic case of a group who reached an unfounded "scientific" conclusion due to deciding the answer before looking at the data is those who did the so-called scientific research under the influence of the Nazi regime. This "research" had as its aim to prove that the Germans/Aryans are the superior race of humanity. Hitler had researchers with PhDs cull questionable data from eugenics experiments and skull size measurements to back up their perverted theories. Naturally there were no blacks, Latinos, or Asians on the research committee which concluded the Teutonic people were the superior race. The Nazi scientists are an extreme case, but they illustrate the problem agenda-driven scientific research.

Speaking of making the mistake of assuming the answer before studying the evidence, what about those who profess belief in the Bible? Might they make the same mistake? Have they ever allowed a presumed religious bias to influence what theories they accept? The answer is absolutely yes. The experiences of Newton and Galileo, described above, prove this to be true. Unfortunately, it is tempting to be intellectually lazy. We do not want to ask ourselves the hard questions. Christians are at times challenged by their friends to defend their belief in the Bible and the gospel message based on evidence. It is intellectually dishonest to investigate the evidence supporting Christianity while maintaining a mindset that it certainly is true. If one does not examine evidence for alternative theories, then one's conclusions might be suspect.

As a college professor I teach a class on the history and philosophy of science. I ask my students to write an essay on the evidence in support of the creation of life by natural processes and an essay in support of design as evidence for a creator. A wise person has said that if you cannot write a good thesis in support of your opponent's viewpoint, you do not understand your own argument very well. Why should a non-believer accept that the Bible is of divine origin? Why should a truth-seeker reject the Koran (the scripture of Islam) or the Vedas (part of the scripture of Hinduism) in favor of the Bible? Why should he or she believe Jesus Christ was raised from the dead? In Acts 17:10-12, the Bereans are commended both for their enthusiastic reception of Paul's teaching and for having enough healthy skepticism to check what he claimed about the Old Testament to see if what Paul said was true. If the Bible is truly from God, then it will stand up to any level of honest and sincere criticism. This also applies to statements in the Bible related to the laws of nature.

If, when asking questions about the Bible and science, one is unwilling to accept the possibility that the Bible is wrong, then it is easy to predict one's conclusion. But a conclusion which is really a foregone conclusion has nothing to do with evidence or reason. Maintaining Christian convictions requires an ever-increasing faith. This requires a willingness to take an un-biased look at the evidence. Those who claim to follow Jesus Christ need to exhibit integrity to the world through right thinking and in intellectual honesty, not just right living.

The way the defenders of religious orthodoxy in Galileo's time treated the question of heliocentrism versus geocentrism is a historical example of letting a religious bias determine what theories will be accepted. To quote the Catholic curia, "An opinion can in no wise be probable which has been declared and defined to be contrary to Divine Scripture."[18] In other words, "No matter how much empirical evidence exists to the contrary, you need to believe our own private interpretation of the Bible." A more reasonable view would be that if something is obviously not true, people should stop believing it. If the Bible is the inspired creation of God, then its truth should hold up to careful inspection. To quote Galileo's defense of the Copernican theory of the sun-centered solar system:

> ...to bar Copernicus now, would seem in my judgment to be a contravention of truth, and an attempt to hide and suppress her the more as she revealed herself more clearly and plainly.[19]

FAITH OR FACT?

Another common error that many religious believers make is to con-fuse what they know by faith with what they know by fact. Perhaps a few personal examples will make the point. Based on my own careful investiga-tion, I believe by fact that Jesus Christ was resurrected from the dead. For me, the historical evidence, the accounts of the biblical witnesses and the inability of the alternative theories to explain this evidence is conclusive.[20] On the other hand, I believe by faith that heaven exists. There is no concrete empirical evidence to support the idea that heaven is real. In fact, according to the Bible, for human beings, heaven is a thing of the future, not the present. Nevertheless, I believe in heaven because the Bible describes it. Fact supports belief in the inspiration of the Bible. However, I have no evidence to support my belief in heaven. This belief is entirely by faith, not fact.

As a second illustration, because of a careful study of historical evidence, I believe by fact that the Bible is an accurate historical document. Being an amateur historian, I have invested a lot of time into examining the historical evidence surrounding the claims of the Bible. I take pains to look at the available information in an open-minded way. I have read many books by believers and critics. I have read books which make the claim that King David was not a real person, but was the invention of pious Jews in the fourth or fifth century BC. I have also studied the Tel Dan inscription, discovered in 1993 in the ruins of the biblical city of Dan. This inscription mentions "the house of David." Evidence tells me that the biblical writers did not make up the existence of King David. Similarly, the account in 2 Kings of Judah being conquered by the Babylonian king Nebuchadnezzar is confirmed by historical and archaeological evidence. The Babylonian Chronicle was discovered in Babylon. It records details in remarkable agreement with what can be read in Jeremiah and 2 Kings. The Hittites were a real people, not just part of a biblical fantasy as some in the nineteenth century claimed. The discovery by Hugo Winkler of the Hittite capital Hattusha in 1906 settled that question. Skeptics in the past have called all these Biblical claims into question, but now archaeological evidence supports these accounts.

On the other hand, I believe by faith that Jesus will "come again to judge the living and the dead." I believe this because the Bible says so. There exists a mountain of reasons, including some explained in this book, for us to believe the Bible is the inspired Word of God. Therefore I believe its claim that Jesus will come again. Of course, there is no direct evidence one can present to support the belief that Jesus will come again: no one can go out and dig up proof. The return of Christ can only be accepted by faith.

If a skeptic has difficulty believing Jesus will come back to the earth, it would be hard to blame him. A careful inspection of the world around us does not lead one to believe that Jesus will come back to the earth as taught in the Bible. However, one could point the non-believer to the Bible and the mass of evidence supporting its inspiration and reliability. However one must admit that belief in the second coming is by faith, not fact. It is a mistake to fail to separate what is believed because of the evidence from what is believed because of faith in the authority of the Bible.

This brings to mind another illustration of the difference between belief by fact and belief by faith which is more germane to science and religion. Personally, I believe Adam and Eve existed. Why? Quite simply, I believe in Adam and Eve because their story is recorded in the Bible. Is there any direct evidence to support this claim—any historical or archaeological data? No. No one has yet discovered a radiocarbon-dated grave inscription such as "Adam and Eve were buried here." It would be a mistake to be deceived on this point. Belief in the existence of the actual persons Adam and Eve can only be by faith. Those who claim it can be believed by fact are on dangerous ground.

Although there is no physical evidence that Adam and Eve existed, the Bible account is not in direct conflict with any known fact of science. Yes, it is true that the evidence from paleontology shows that *australopithecines* lived before *homo sapiens sapiens* (anthropologists designation of modern humans). Yes, it is true that apes and men have a very similar genome. Nevertheless, if the Bible is inspired by God, then two conclusions are strongly implied. First, Adam and Eve were created and second, their creation was a supernatural event. Supernatural events, if they do occur, by their very nature do not lend themselves well to scientific investigation. Whether the "creation" of Adam and Eve was an instantaneous ex *nihilo* (out of nothing) event or whether God miraculously breathed a soul and spirit into proto-humans is a question to be debated. However the overwhelming evidence to support belief in the inspiration of the Bible causes me to believe this supernatural event occurred. (The subject of creation versus evolution of man is discussed in chapter nine.)

For the sake of clarity, consider a definition of the term "miracle." A miracle is an event that defies the laws of nature. It is a "supernatural event." Some of the miracles described in the Bible can only be believed by faith in the power of God and the truthfulness of the writer. Other miracles described in the Bible can be believed because of the evidence. One of the strongest claims of this book—one which will be proven beyond a reasonable doubt—is that life was created. The first living thing was produced by an act of creation. If true, then that was surely a supernatural event! Here, then, is a miracle described by the Bible, which can be believed because of the evidence.

The mistake of not separating faith from fact is a major factor in the errors of the creationists. If God created the world, whether in six days or fifteen billion years, it is still a supernatural event, without scientific "explanation." So why misuse the data to force it to agree with your own private interpretation about how God did it? If God created the earth with an appearance of age, then it will appear old. Why try to claim it appears young, when even the simplest look at the evidence available to students at the junior high school level makes it clear that the world appears to be at the very least many millions of years old? The age of the earth will be reviewed in some detail in the next chapter.

FOR TODAY

1. *Can you think of any "theories" you have held to in the past which you had to give up later in light of new evidence or information? What did that feel like?*

2. *Do you agree with the young-earth creationist view of nature as described in this chapter?*

3. *Do you agree with the atheistic view as described in this chapter?*

4. *If the answer to the two previous questions is no, what do you believe, or are you simply not sure?*

5. *Can you identify any "preconceived notions" you bring into reading this book that relate to science and religion?*

6. *Where do you believe the concept of "healthy skepticism" fits in with faith?*

7. *Can you think of something you believe in "by faith," as opposed to something you believe in because of the evidence?*

6 Thomas Kuhn, *The Structure of Scientific Revolutions* (Chicago: University of Chicago Press, 1964).

7 Henry David Thoreau, *Walden*, first published 1854 (New York: Houghton Mifflin, 2004).

8 Galileo Galilei, *The Starry Messenger*, first published 1610.

9 An excerpt from the Roman Curia's statement to Galileo at his second trial, 1632.

10 Galileo Galilei, *Letter to the Duchess* Christina, 1614.

11 John Desmond Bernal, *The Origin of Life* (London: Weidendorf and Nicolson, 1967), 140.

12 Norman F. Hall, Lucia K. B. Hall, "Is the War Between Science and Religion Over?" *The Humanist*, May/June, 1982.

13 Quote taken from Anthony Smith, *The Human Degree* (Philadelphia, Pennsylvania: J. P. Lippincott, 1976).

14 Richard Dawkins, *River Out of Eden*, (San Francisco, California: Harper Collins, 1996) 133.

15 Ronald Numbers, *The Creationists*, (Berkeley: The University of California Press, 1992)

16 Henry M. Morris, *Scientific Creationism* (El Cajon, California: Master Books, 1974), 203.

17 Another illustration of the tendency toward preconceived notions among creationists is found in the comment of Frank Lewis Marsh,, (Ph.D. biologist, and member of the creationist-oriented Geoscience Research Institute): "In my opinion, we cannot use our senses in the manner of uniformitarians in interpreting what we see in the earth.... This is an extremely important point. Special Revelation takes precedence over natural revelation because natural science can be correct only when in harmony with special Revelation." This is an excerpt of a letter by Marsh to flood geologist George McCready Price, from the Marsh Papers. In other words, if scientific evidence and the Bible appear to disagree, we will assume the Bible is right, and ignore the scientific evidence.

18 From the Roman Curia's sentence statement to Galileo, 1632.

19 From Galileo's letter to the Grand Duchess Christina, 1614.

20 Useful resources presenting the evidence include, John Oakes, *Reasons for Belief: A Handbook of Christian Evidence*, (Spring, Texas:, Illumination Publishers, 2005), ch. 3. and Frank Morison, *Who Moved the Stone?* (Grand Rapids: Zondervan, 2002).

PART I

Is There a God?
Science and Religion

CHAPTER 2

TRUE ASSUMPTIONS MUST SAVE THE APPEARANCES.

—*NIKOLAI COPERNICUS*

HOW OLD IS THE EARTH?

"How old is the earth?" Although I could provide my best estimate based on the scientific evidence, I can honestly say I do not know. One thing that can be said with confidence (as will be shown in this chapter) is that the earth *appears* to be very old. How old? Well, one's estimate will depend on what evidence one chooses to look at: uranium/lead dating, the core temperature of the earth, the amount of salt in the oceans, the distance from the earth to the moon, Martian meteors, studies of comets, or any of a number of other means which have been applied to estimate the age of the planet we live on.

Actually there are two separate but related questions to be asked: "How old is the earth?" and "How old is the universe?" In order to investigate the evidence related to the age of the universe, one can consider the distance to the farthest known celestial objects. Other arguments relevant to the age of the universe include theories about the origin and life cycle of stars and galaxies, as well as measurements of the apparent temperature of the cosmic background radiation. After collecting all the available evidence, whether one concludes that the earth appears to be one hundred million years old or ten billion years old does not seem to be crucial to issues relating to science and the Bible. If in fact the earth appears to be extremely old, then the assumption of a recent special creation as defined by many creationists is in big trouble, because an age of seven thousand or even fifty thousand years is completely out of range.

One other possibility to entertain is that the earth was created "with an appearance of age." In other words, perhaps the universe was created by an all-powerful God in a well-evolved state so that it already appeared to be extremely old at the first instant of creation. This intriguing possibility is more theological speculation than testable scientific theory. It complicates discussion of the scientific facts. However, in an open-minded search for the truth about origins it must be considered.

At this point it might be helpful to ask oneself what would be implications for scientific observations if it were true that the earth was created "with an appearance of age."

Does it really matter how old the earth is? It would be fair to admit that it is not a factor most people take into account in choosing their career, or their friends, or for that matter what brand of toothpaste to buy. Nevertheless, as stated in the introduction, there are several reasons to spend some time thinking about these issues. How does the claim that the earth appears to be very old make you feel as a Christian? Does it challenge some long-held beliefs? Some believers become angry when they hear other believers make this claim. The truth seeker's task is to take what he already knows through both fact and faith and to be willing to take an honest, open-minded look at this question.

There exist a great number of empirical scientific facts in support of the view that the universe is very old. The same could be said for the age of the earth. In this chapter evidence will be given which supports the claim that the earth and the universe it is part of are billions of years old.

DISTANCE OF CELESTIAL OBJECTS

A prime way of judging the age of the universe is the distance of celestial objects. For relatively close (by cosmological standards) objects such as stars in our own galaxy, scientists use the method of parallax viewing to determine the distance to these objects. Basically, this method requires looking at both a relatively nearer and a farther object in the sky from two distant points. For example, one can look at the planet Jupiter and at the star Alpha Centauri from two different points on the earth. Alternatively, one could look at a relatively close star and a more distant star from the earth at opposite sides of its orbit around the sun (in the spring and again in the fall). The nearer object will appear to move just slightly with respect to the farther object. The angle of displacement determines the distance to the farther object or the nearer object, whichever was not previously known. The calculation is a simple matter of geometry. To try this method, you can hold up a finger at arm's length and line the finger up with an object hundreds of feet away. Moving your head just a couple of inches will make your finger move with respect to the distant object. If you know the distance to your finger, the distance you moved your head and the angle of displacement, you can calculate the distance to the other object.

USING PARALLAX TO DETERMINE THE DISTANCE OF A STAR.

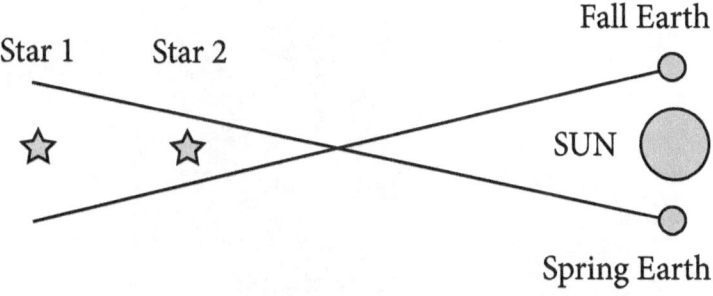

(FIGURE 2.1) IN THE FALL, STAR 2 APPEARS TO BE TO THE RIGHT OF STAR 1, WHILE IN THE SPRING, STAR 2 APPEARS TO BE TO THE LEFT OF STAR 1.

A second method used to estimate the distance to objects in our galaxy and in neighboring galaxies involves using the apparent brightness of a special class of stars known as Cepheid variables. Such stars have a brightness which varies with a period which is dependent on the absolute brightness of the stars. Comparing the apparent brightness of a Cepheid star to its period allows one to calculate the absolute distance to the star. The publication of this method in 1912 by Henrietta Swan Leavitt was the key to Hubble's discovery in the 1920's that the universe is expanding.

A third method used to estimate the distance to extremely remote objects, such as galaxies and quasars, involves looking at the magnitude of the "red shift" of light from those objects. (The red shift will be discussed in some detail in a later chapter.) The greater the red shift, the more distant the celestial object. There are other methods of estimating the distance to extremely remote objects, including measuring the relative brightness and size of very distant galaxies and estimating the distance by assuming the absolute sizes of the galaxies are at least similar to those of ones closer to us. Even if those who argue the universe is young choose to dismiss some of these distance-measuring techniques, they are faced with the inescapable fact that there are billions of galaxies in the universe, each containing billions of stars. The known universe is clearly very, very big!

The distance of objects in the universe affects a discussion of the age of those objects. Take the spiral galaxy M31 in Andromeda. It is approximately 2.25 million light years from our solar system.

(FIGURE 2.2) M31, A SPIRAL GALAXY

How long ago did the light hitting an astronomer's telescope leave the M31 galaxy? Since light travels a distance of one light year per year (the definition of a light year), evidently the galaxy being viewed is at least 2.25 million years old, because the light entering a telescope on earth left the galaxy about 2.25 million years ago. (Actually, according to the theory of stellar evolution, to be discussed later, cosmologists interpret many of the stars in the M31 to be billions of years old). In fact, looking at extremely distant objects is one way scientists can literally look into the past. The most distant known objects are quasars, which, according to red shift data, are several billions of light years from us. Presumably, when astronomers observe these quasars, they are viewing light which was emitted from the objects billions of years ago. The conclusion from this evidence is that the universe *appears* to be several billion years old.

Does this evidence prove absolutely that the universe is billions of years old? The answer is no, it does not, but it is very strong evidence in support of that conclusion. An all-knowing, all-powerful God such as the one described in the Bible could certainly create stars out of nothing anywhere and at any time he wanted. However, logically speaking, if a star were created *ex nihilo* (out of nothing) seven thousand years ago at a distance of seven thousand and one light years from us, it should suddenly become visible to us some time in the next year. We do not see stars suddenly popping into view, so we naturally conclude most or all of them are extremely old. An object such as the spiral galaxy M31 which is 2.25 million light years away is at least that old.

One can argue it is conceivable that a God who is able to create a galaxy *ex nihilo* could also simultaneously create light to be in transit from that distant galaxy toward the earth at the point of creation. This would make it appear that the star is millions of years old, when it is in reality its age is only several thousand years. This argument may not sound convincing, but the fact is we are not in a position to ultimately "prove" the age of an extremely distant object. The point is by the scientific evidence, the universe appears ancient. The young earth view does not agree with the evidence in this case. The actual age is another question. Theological speculation may allow for a younger age. However, what one can say with certainty is that the universe appears very much older than seven thousand years based on this evidence. Young earth creationists should not claim otherwise.

How do the creationists resolve this problem? They have attempted to preserve the young universe hypothesis by calling into question the use of Euclidean geometry.[21] Einstein's theory of special relativity implies that space is curved, requiring the use of Riemannian geometry to describe the universe. That is all well and good. However, whether one uses Euclidean or Riemannian geometry, it would be safe to say that there is not a physicist alive today (except perhaps a young-earth creationist) who would agree that Riemannian geometry supports the idea that light could travel ten billion light years in just a few thousand years. This is an obvious case of bias influencing the interpretation of empirical evidence.

Another creationist attempt to defend the young earth view in light of the apparent size of the universe is to claim that the speed of light has changed over time.[22] This is a remarkable claim! The constant value of the speed of light is the underpinning assumption of the theory of relativity. However, there is no credible support for the proposition that the speed of light has changed over time. A thorough treatment of this claim can be found in a book by Alan Hayward.[23] Let us be honest about the evidence: The universe appears old. Whether it is one hundred million or one hundred billion is beside the point.

GEOLOGICAL DEPOSITS

Let us shift from calculating the age of the universe to evidence for the age of the earth. One piece of evidence for an ancient earth is found in the clearly defined layers within the sedimentary rocks in the earth's crust. Sedimentary layers were the bedrock on which James Hutton, the "father of geology," laid his argument that the earth is very old in the late eighteenth century. Anyone who goes to the Grand Canyon will immediately notice that the Colorado River has cut through millions of nearly horizontal layers of rock, to a depth of over five thousand feet. These are sedimentary rocks, which reason would seem to require must have been laid down over great periods of time through deposition of sand, dirt, dust and organic matter.

In fact, the column of sedimentary rock on the earth's surface is as much as sixteen miles (80,000 feet) deep in places. It averages over one mile in depth over the entire land surface of the earth.

How were these thousands, and in some cases many millions of layers of rock created? In order to prove the great the time over which they were created, let us look at the Green River shale deposits in Colorado and Utah. These valuable deposits contain up to several million pairs of alternating light and dark layers of sediment found right on top of one another. By looking at fossilized pollen remnants, it can be shown that the dark layers represent the spring and summer seasons, while lighter, pollen-free layers represent sediment laid down in the fall and winter. The analogy of the Green River shale deposits to the rings on a tree is obvious. The layers in these shale deposits represent years—millions of years—over which they were laid down by sedimentation. Here we see what seems to be clear evidence that this area of Colorado and Utah was for at least several million years a fairly shallow "inland sea." What was once continental shelf is now several thousand feet above sea level.

Consider as well the Bahamas Banks—the geological formation on top of which sit the islands of the Bahamas, off the coast of Florida. Drilling into the surface has shown that underlying the Bahamas area is a deposit of almost pure limestone, approximately 18,000 feet thick. The most reasonable conclusion is that this limestone deposit was laid down over a great period of time by living coral reefs. The process of growth is still visible today. The rate at which limestone is created by the corals and other creatures living in a reef has been estimated[24] at about one inch in one hundred years. Using this number and the thickness of the limestone, one can estimate an age of the lowest layers of limestone underlying the Bahamas to be about twenty-two million years. The estimate of one hundred years per inch is debatable. Besides, it can be assumed that the rate would not be constant as variations in climate would affect the rate of growth of the deposits. Nevertheless, one is left with clear and seemingly incontrovertible evidence that the reefs have existed for many millions of years.

Returning to the Grand Canyon, one could attempt to actually count the successive layers, making a depth-per-year estimate in an attempt to calculate the age of the lowest layers of the canyon. Whether the sediments were deposited at an average rate of one millimeter per year or one centimeter per year, the numbers calculated for the age of the lowest layers would be many millions of years.

The concept underlying the kind of calculation mentioned above is called uniformitarianism. This idea was first put forth by Scottish scientist James Hutton. Uniformitarianism is one of the two main paradigms of geology, along with plate tectonics. It can be defined as the idea that the geologic features of the earth were created gradually over vast periods of time through processes which are observable today.

(Young-earth) creationists claim that the sedimentary layers found at the Grand Canyon—all five thousand feet of them—were laid down in the seven thousand years or so during which the earth has existed. Not only that, but they claim the millions of paired layers in the Green River shale formation, as well as the Bahamas Banks, and indeed all the sedimentary deposits over the entire earth were laid down within the few thousand year history of the earth. Simple inspection of the data seems to indicate that this explanation cannot be supported.

How do the creationists explain the sedimentary layers—up to eighty thousand feet deep in places? They claim that most or all of these layers were laid down in one great flood—the flood recorded in Genesis chapter seven and eight. According to flood geologist Henry Morris, possibly the foremost leader in the creationist movement:

The question is simply whether the model of a single global cataclysm, primarily hydraulic in nature, can explain the data of geology better than the uniformitarian/multiple local catastrophe model.[25]

By the phrase "single global cataclysm, primarily hydraulic in nature," the author means the flood recorded in Genesis. Morris and most creationist authors claim that a single flood is the most reasonable explanation for the up to 80,000 feet of sedimentary rock at the surface of the earth. (Please remember that I am using the word creationist in a very limited way. Not all believers in creation would say this!) One should ask at this point, is this a reasonable explanation? Several facts inconsistent with this conclusion become obvious immediately. First, sediment does not normally form into rock in just a couple of thousand years.[26] Second, a single flood could only distribute an amount of sediment equal to the soil and other loose material already at the surface of the earth when the flood occurred-at most a few dozen feet at any one location. Third, in many locations, different portions of the sedimentary layers have a radically different chemical content from those immediately above or below. Perhaps most significantly, the fossilized remains found at different points in the sedimentary record represent almost completely different plants and animals. Trilobites are always found below dinosaurs which are found below modern mammals in the fossil record, without exception.[27] None of these facts are consistent with the one-flood idea.

Can anyone believe this explanation? The answer is yes, someone who has already made up his or her mind to reach this conclusion before even beginning to look at the evidence might accept the flood geology theory. Without the influence of an extreme bias, the answer is no, no one could believe this theory. The creationists have to perform great feats of illogic to explain how the "older" fossils always seem to be below the "younger" fossils. It cannot be coincidence that trilobites are never found above dinosaurs in the fossil record. The creationist's explanation: trilobites are smaller than dinosaurs, so sorting puts them below! Does the person who gives this explanation believe that the dinosaurs which are always found below "modern" mammals in the fossil record are smaller than the mammals? Creationists believe all these species lived at the same time and somehow during the flood the trilobites got sorted out from the dinosaurs, which got sorted out from the mammals and so forth by various sorting mechanisms.[28]

We can see that the creationist attempt to explain the fossil record and the alluvial deposits requires making illogical use of the evidence. It requires us to not see what we see. One way to call attention away from this fact which they employ is to introduce one or two pieces of evidence which might legitimately call into question the theory that the earth is very old. In other words, although they cannot provide evidence the earth is young, at least they can find one piece of evidence inconsistent with the theories of orthodox geology. Upon doing so, they hope that people will accept the idea that their theory deserves equal time, despite the lack of supporting evidence.

To illustrate this approach, many creationists have claimed the supposed discovery of human and dinosaur footprints in the same rock formation. They have argued for years that human beings and dinosaurs lived at the same time. This would certainly throw a wrench into orthodox geology/paleontology. The most well known and publicized evidence that humans and dinosaurs co-inhabited the earth is known as the Paluxy Riverbed man tracks, found near Glen Rose, Texas. Films such as *Footprints in Stone* have been produced which purport to show "scientifically" that dinosaurs and people lived at the same time. If this claim were true, it would certainly turn the current system of chronology used by paleontologists on its head.

Upon careful study of the evidence,[29] the dinosaur footprints in the Paluxy Riverbed appear to be genuine, but the "human" prints have been shown to be either random deformations in the rock, misinterpreted dinosaur prints, or recent carvings. Even some of the original creationist investigators have since backed down on their claims that these tracks are legitimate evidence that dinosaurs and people once lived together. Interestingly, young-earth believers have at times referred to this claim as proven.[30] The problem is that once word gets out that there is scientific "proof" that man and dinosaurs lived at the same time, it is hard to "put the genie back in the bottle." It can be predicted that for years to come, misinformed people will continue to quote this supposed evidence as proof that geologists have it all wrong.[31]

The conclusion from the evidence of sedimentary deposits is that the earth is hundreds of millions of years old or more. Does this prove (in the strictest sense of the word) that the earth is at least hundreds of millions of years old? This is an important question to be asked at this point. The answer is no. God certainly could have created the earth out of nothing with an appearance of age. When Jesus fed five thousand people, as recorded in John 6:1-15, he created fish which not only had an appearance of age, but which was ready to be eaten. Bear in mind, however, that if this were true, it would amount to a belief, not a scientific theory. Science, by its very nature, cannot predict or explain a supernatural event.

Did God create the earth with an appearance or age? Did he do it in a way analogous to the fish created out of nothing recorded in the sixth chapter of John? If one is to answer yes, then he or she should be aware that this conclusion is not a "scientific" one. This is a theological statement, not a conclusion which can be drawn from scientific evidence. It is based on faith rather than fact. Creationists who claim otherwise are simply wrong. If God did indeed create the earth with an appearance of age, there would be scientific evidence of age, not youth.

If someone believes that God created the earth with an appearance of age, just a few thousand years ago, then there are implications which should be examined based on scientific evidence. In that case the fossils buried deep within the earth must have been created right along with the earth. A six thousand year old earth does not leave time for deep sedimentary deposits to be created. It would imply that dinosaurs, trilobites and a host of other species which appear in the deeper fossil layers, never actually lived at all. This being true, it would make it seem as though God were tricking us by putting the fossils of animals and plants which never lived into the ground.

DATING TECHNIQUES

Since the creationists claim the mass of scientific evidence supports the belief that the earth appears young, one might think that they have a large body of evidence to underpin this view. The fact is that they have almost no positive evidence for an age of only a few thousand years. Their primary approach is to poke holes in the evidence for an old earth. They have virtually no empirical evidence they can point to which can be used to say, "Look, here is hard evidence that the earth is just a few thousand years old." Rather than presenting data that supports their view, they will draw into question the accuracy of uranium/lead or potassium/argon isotope dating, which is used for estimating the age of some of the oldest rocks in the earth. The oldest earth rocks recovered and studied by scientists so far have been estimated to be about 3.8 billion years old, while moon rocks and meteors produce an age of 4.5 billion years.

Perhaps the creationists have a good point in their criticisms. The fact is that due to issues such as sample contamination and leeching, the ages of rocks determined by radioisotope methods can have a fairly large uncertainty. Scientists now claim precision for some uranium/lead-determined ages as good as one per cent. Let us assume a rather generous uncertainty of 50%. To illustrate, if the 238U/207Pb uranium/lead isotope ratio in a particular rock implied an age of 3.0 billion years, due to uncertainty, the rock could be as young as 1.5 billion years. That is still much older than seven thousand years! The question remains, what scientific evidence exists for a young earth?

The fact is that creationists have little evidence for a young earth and what they do have is questionable. None of their supposed evidence holds up under the scrutiny of non-believers, or even of believers who do not have an extreme young-earth bias.

To illustrate the generally poor quality of evidence used to support the young earth theory, let us look at one creationist claim to have data which supports a young age for the earth. This argument involves using measurements of the amount of certain ions in sea water. Scientists can use the average concentration of sodium (a component of salt) and an estimate of the total volume of the oceans to approximate the total mass of sodium in the oceans. This number, along with an estimate of the amount of sodium entering the ocean from rivers in a year, allows one to estimate the time it would take for the total amount of sodium now there to have accumulated. Under a couple of assumptions, this allows one to estimate the age of the oceans. There are a few issues with the precision of the numbers used as well as the requirement to assume zero initial salt in the oceans, as well as a constant rate of inflow. However, if one will take the accuracy of the numbers with a grain of salt, it is possible to reach some sort of useful conclusion. Quoting from a table in one of the young-earth publications:[32]

Ocean Ion	Implied Age of the Earth
Sodium	260,000,000 yrs
Chloride	164,000,000 yrs
Lead	2,000 yrs
Nickel	9,000 yrs

This data is excerpted from a much longer table. The lead and nickel numbers seem to the untrained to be evidence that the earth is young. In fact, this is simply not the case. As any student of introductory chemistry learns, lead and nickel carbonates are only very slightly soluble. It just so happens that there is a considerable concentration of carbonate in the ocean due primarily to absorption of carbon dioxide from the air. The small amount of lead and nickel in the ocean is not due to a young earth, rather it is due to precipitation of the relatively insoluble compounds lead and nickel carbonate (precipitation of other insoluble lead and nickel compounds may also be a factor). On the other hand (see the list above), sodium and chloride are quite soluble ions which can build up to a much higher level in the oceans. The fact is that based on solubility data from chemistry, one can conclude that the numbers in the table represent a possible *minimum* age for the oceans. Therefore, the data used by creationists to supposedly support a young earth implies that the earth is at least 260 million of years old, not several thousand years.

Again, does this absolutely prove that the oceans are hundreds of millions of years old? No it does not. God could have created the oceans with salt in them. Did he? The readers should decide for themselves. However the one thing which can be said with confidence is that from this date the oceans *appear* to be very old.

It would be fair to ask why a creationist would use evidence such as the ocean ion data above to support the contention that the earth appears to be young. This is not a matter of a simple mistake. The author of the work referred to above is a PhD geologist. He has to be aware that this data supports the old earth theory. Why would someone publish data which unambiguously supports the old-earth theory, while claiming to untrained readers that it can support the young earth theory? This is further support for the thesis that when we set out to study a question with our minds already made up about the answer, we will inevitably fall victim to our bias. We will end up sifting and manipulating the evidence in order to reach our preconceived conclusion.

There are a number of methods available to scientists that can be used to estimate the age of the earth and of the solar system. These include the amount of volcanic rock on the surface of the earth, meteoric dust on the moon, the age of moon rocks, the age of meteors from Mars, the amount of craterization of the moon, the earth/moon distance, racemization of chiral biomolecules and so forth.[33] From the salinity of the oceans, the earth has been estimated at between one and seven billion years old. From radioactive decay of unstable isotopes in earth rocks, it has been estimated to be between four and four and one-half billion years old. From theories about the origin of the moon and loss of kinetic energy of the moon due to tides, it has been estimated to be three to four billion years old. Meteoric and moon rocks give a consistent age of about 4.55 billion years. When taken together and analyzed carefully, the evidence points to an age for the earth of about four and one-half billion years.

It would be appropriate to point out that scientists have a tendency to be overconfident in trying to give precise numbers for the age of the earth. Nevertheless, although these methods do not give identical answers, all current techniques imply an age of billions of years for the earth and the solar system. There is no credible scientific evidence that the earth is only a few thousand years old. One is left with two possible explanations of this fact. Either the earth is ancient—probably about 4.5 billion years old, or it was created more recently, by supernatural means, with an appearance of great age.

The claim that the earth is 4.5 billion years old is supported by scientific evidence. The claim, despite this evidence, that the earth was created recently with an appearance of age is not scientifically supported. However, it is perhaps possible from a theological perspective. It cannot be absolutely disproved by science, because supernatural events are outside the realm of science. The claim which cannot be supported and which should not be made is that scientific evidence supports belief that the earth is a few thousand years old. There is no reliable scientific evidence to support this conclusion. Period. Dinosaurs did not live at the same time as people! That is a fact. If the reader finds it difficult to accept what is admittedly a rather strong conclusion, then he or she should make the effort to read some of the references in this chapter.[34]

This argument can be taken one step further. Creationism as taught by some can be dangerous to the faith of those who believe in the Bible. Think about the situation of a young student in a high school or college science class. This student was raised being told that creationism is legitimate science, and that it strongly supports belief in the reliability of the Bible. In fact, this student was raised under the assumption that belief in the young earth theory is an essential aspect of being a faithful Christian. This student will surely have their faith sorely tested when they carefully research what they are learning in their geology, chemistry or biology classes. This student will be questioning the Bible, not because their teacher is an atheist, hell-bent on subverting belief in God (although there are some professors who could be described way). In such a scenario, the believer will be questioning the Bible because a deception has a way of being shown for what it is in the clear light of the truth. This is true even when the deception comes from a sincere religious person.

The fifth century theologian Augustine put it very nicely. Concerning those who let their personal interpretation of the scripture control their understanding of how nature works, he made the following comment:[35]

> *Now it is a disgraceful and dangerous thing for an infidel to hear a Christian, presumably giving the meaning of Holy Scripture, talking nonsense on these topics, and we should take all means to prevent such an embarrassing situation, in which people show up vast ignorance in a Christian and laugh it to scorn. The shame is not so much that an ignorant individual is derided, but that people outside the household of faith think our sacred writers held such opinions, and, to the great loss of those for whose salvation we toil, the writers of our Scripture are criticized and rejected as unlearned men. If they find a Christian mistaken in a field which they themselves know well and hear him maintaining foolish opinions about our books, how are they going to believe those books in matters concerning the resurrection of the dead, the hope of eternal life, and*

the kingdom of heaven, when they think that their pages are full of falsehoods on facts which they themselves have learnt from experience and the light of reason?

Those who espouse belief that scientific evidence proves the earth to be only a few thousand years old ought to ponder these words carefully.

If young-earth creationism does not work as a scientific theory, what will that do to assumptions about the infallibility of the Bible? What about the ideas which have been produced by creationists who do not assume a young age,? What about the biblical accounts of creation in Genesis chapter one and two? How will that fit in? We will discuss the Genesis creation account in chapter five.

Now that we have considered young-earth creationism as a theory, we will now move on to discuss the atheist/agnostic approach to the same data. This will be accomplished in chapters three and four. We will see that the methodology required to reach the atheist conclusion has much in common with that of the creationists. It will be shown that although the bias may be more subtle, the atheistic conclusion can only be reached by ignoring major aspects of physics and chemistry, and by choosing to ignore some very interesting coincidences. In the end, the atheist conclusion will show itself for what it is: a faith which borders on religion. Remember that if a person approaches a question with a preconceived answer in mind, they will inevitably manage to accommodate the data to their answer.

FOR TODAY

1. *How old do you think the earth is? ("I am not sure" is a legitimate answer.)*

2. *Does it matter how old the earth is?*

3. *What does the claim that the earth was created with an appearance of age mean?*

4. *How would you explain the "sedimentary rock" layers that are thousands of feet deep at many locations around the earth?*

RECOMMENDATION

Decide to read a book written by a creationist as well as one written by an atheist on the subject of origins.

Suggested books from the young-earth creationist perspective:

John C. Whitcomb and Henry M. Morris, *The Genesis Flood* (Phillipsburg, New Jersey: Presbyterian and Reformed Publishing, 1961)

Henry M. Morris and Gary E. Parker, *What is Creation Science?* (El Cajon, California: Master Books, 1987)

Walt Brown, *In the Beginning* (Phoenix: Center for Scientific Creation, 1995)

Alan Hayward, *Creation and Evolution* (Minneapolis: Bethany House Publishers, 1995)

Suggested books by creationists who accept the earth is ancient.

Michael J. Denton, *Nature's Destiny* (New York: The Free Press, 1998)

Gerald L. Schroeder, *The Science of God* (New York: Broadway Books, 1997).

Michael J. Behe, *Darwin's Black Box* (New York: The Free Press, 1996)

William A. Dembski and Michael J. Behe, *Intelligent Design: The Bridge Between Science and Theology* (Downer's Grove: Intervarsity Press, 1999)

Hugh Ross, *The Fingerprint of God* (New Kensington, Pennsylvania: Whitaker House, 2000)

Kenneth R. Miller, *Finding Darwin's God* (New York: HarperCollins Publishers, 1999)

SUGGESTED BOOKS FROM AN ATHEIST OR AGNOSTIC PERSPECTIVE

Richard Dawkins, *The Selfish Gene* (Oxford: Oxford University Press, 1989)

Richard Dawkins, *River Out of Eden* (City: Harper Collins, 1996)

Niles Eldridge, *The Triumph of Evolution, and the Failure of Creationism* (New York: W. H. Freeman and Company, 2000)

Stephen J. Gould, *Rocks of Ages* (New York: Ballantine Publishing, 1999)

21 For (example), H. S. Slusher, *Age of the Cosmos*, (San Diego: Institute for Creation Research, 1980), 33-37.

22 For (example), Walt Brown, *In the Beginning* (Phoenix: Center for Scientific Creation, 1995), 158-161.

23 Alan Hayward, *Creation and Evolution* (Minneapolis: Bethany House Publishers, 1995), 99-102.

24 D. E. Wonderly, *Time-Records in Ancient Sediments* (Interdisciplinary Biblical Research Institute, 2013), 113-126.

25 Henry M. Morris and Gary E. Parker, *What is Creation Science?* (El Cajon, California: Master Books, 1987), p. 248.

26 Special cases have been noted in which sediments can form into rocks fairly quickly. For example, under exceptional circumstances, a kind of limestone known as "beachrock" can form on tropical beaches within just a few years. Nevertheless, for the more typical categories of sedimentary rocks, such as shale formed from mud or sandstone, the sedimentary rocks mentioned in this section form only after very long time, and usually under great pressure.

27 Except in the case of overthrust faults, to be discussed below.

28 It is beyond the scope of this book to describe the proposed mechanisms creationists use in an attempt to explain how this could have happened. For a well-written and thorough account of how this could be explained according to creationists, a good source is Walt Brown, *In the Beginning* (Phoenix: Center for Scientific Creation, 1995). In this book, Brown does a better than average job, compared to most creationist writers, of quoting other authors fairly and honestly. The entire book is online at www.creationscience.com.

29 For example, Ronnie J. Hastings, *The Rise and Fall of the Paluxy Mantracks*, "Perspectives on Science and Christian Faith," Vol. 40, 1988, 144-154, and other references alluded to in this article.

30 Henry M. Morris, *Scientific Creationism* (El Cajon, California: Creation Life Publishers, 1974), 122.

31 A concise summary of "mantrack" claims and a reasonable refutation is contained in Alan Hayward, Creation and Evolution (Minnesota: Bethany House Publishers, 1995), 149-151.

32 Henry M. Morris and Gary E. Parker, *What is Creation Science?* (El Cajon, California: Master Books, 1987), 288-291.

33 The amino acids in proteins can exist in both right handed and left handed structures. However, in naturally occurring biomolecules, only the left handed amino acids are found. The rate at which the amino acids randomize (racemize) to a 50:50 mixture of right-and left-handed molecules can be used to calculate the age of remnant protein molecules found in very old samples.

34 Again, I would refer the reader to the book by Walt Brown mentioned above for several reasons. It is well written and relatively objective. Brown tends to avoid sarcasm and unreasonable, out-of-context quotations. Also, it is a fairly recent publication with a great number of references, providing access to the literature for those so inclined. The entire manuscript of this book can be found at *www.creationscience.com*.

35 Augustine, *The Literal Meaning of Genesis*: Eng. trans. in Ancient Christian Writers, no. 41 (New York: Newman Press, 1982), bk. 1, ch. 19.

CHAPTER 3

[WE SHOULD] REJECT ALL FIXED PRESUPPOSITIONS ABOUT NATURE-
TO APPROACH NATURAL PHENOMENON WITH A FREE AND UNCON-
DITIONAL MIND.

—*FRANCIS BACON*

DID THE UNIVERSE
JUST HAPPEN?

Does God exist? Does science have anything to say on this matter? Some would insist that the existence of God is a question for theologians to discuss-that it is an irrelevant question for the practitioners of science. To quote from Niles Eldredge:

> *The nineteenth century scientists who were true creationists took both their faith and their interpretation of nature from the Bible, and there never has been any other source of inspiration or support for the "creation model."*[36]

Eldredge asserts that there is no evidence whatsoever to support the supernatural creation of life. What makes his conclusion suspect is that Eldredge assumes, out of hand, that the supernatural does not exist. We have already seen the inevitable result of such presuppositions. He believes one can choose to accept the Bible with all its "myths and fables," but there is no basis in fact or reason to believe it was produced by divine revelation, especially from a scientific perspective.

There are two possibilities: God exists, or he does not. Simply assuming that God does not exist or saying his existence is irrelevant would be a very ineffective way of making him go away if God were real. An open-minded person, even if they were coming from an atheist background, ought to accept at least the possibility that God exists. To do otherwise is to beg the question. If in fact God exists, there will be evidence of that fact in the nature of the universe he created. For Eldredge and other atheists to assert that there is no evidence for God and leave it at that is intellectually dishonest. In this chapter, some of the evidence for a creator will be presented.

Some atheists try to create the impression that belief in God is for the unintelligent or the superstitious. Some use intellectual intimidation to quiet those who think differently. A brief study of the history of science will produce a different conclusion. Notably, all the great men in the early history of science were believers in God. The scientific revolution was brought about by men who believed that there was one God; a God of order who does not change. Logically, these early philosophers of science concluded from a belief in monotheism that the universe should work according to invariant laws which work according to mathematical precision.

The fact that Christianity is the historical root of science was pointed out by the Nobel Prize winner Melvin Calvin. Calvin is a noted atheist and supporter of the idea that life came about by random forces. Nevertheless, Calvin said about the historical foundation of science:[37]

> *"The fundamental conviction that the universe is ordered is the first and strongest tenet [of scientists]. As I try to discern the origin of that conviction, I seem to find it in a basic notion discovered 2000 or 3000 years ago, and enunciated first in the Western world by the ancient Hebrews: namely that the universe is governed by a single God, and is not the product of the whims of many gods, each governing his own province, according to his own laws. This monotheistic view seems to be the historical foundation of modern science."*

In other words, science is the historical and philosophical child of monotheism. If one thinks about this, it only makes sense that belief in a single, unchanging God led to a search for a single, unchanging set of laws which govern the universe. Almost all ancient cultures held to animist or polytheistic beliefs. Such beliefs led to an understanding that nature is chaotic and unpredictable-subject to the whims of the gods. It required visionaries such as Roger Bacon (1214-1292), a monk and natural philosopher, to put the monotheistic perspective to practical use in studying nature. Bacon believed that in studying nature and uncovering its laws, we would come to appreciate God more fully. In order to study nature, he advised, we should use,[38] "External experience, aided by instruments, made precise by mathematics." Bacon was the first to propose that God created natural laws which should be describable by mathematical equations.

William of Ockham (1285-1349) was another of the founding fathers of science. He taught that the religious hierarchy should not have authority over matters of science, but that the source of truth about nature should be empirical study. According to Ockham, "Nothing is assumed as evident unless it is know per se, or is evident by experience, or is proved by authority of scripture." As applied to natural philosophy (the medieval term for science), Ockham believed that natural laws will be true if they can be derived from other true laws, or are observed empirically. He also held that the Bible has ultimate authority to determine theological truth.

Nikolai Copernicus (1473-1543), the first modern experimental scientist, followed the lead of Bacon and Ockham. He was a canon of the Catholic Church. He resurrected the Greek idea of heliocentrism, which puts the sun at the center of the planets. Copernicus believed that God set the celestial bodies in orderly motion. Galileo, despite his run-ins with the Catholic hierarchy, believed that order in the universe demonstrated the existence of God. To quote from him:

> *The phenomenon of nature proceeds... from the divine Word.*

> *The glory and greatness of Almighty God are marvelously discerned in all His works and divinely read in the open book of heaven.*

> *I think in the first place, that it is very pious to say and prudent to confirm that the Holy Bible can never speak untruth-whenever its true meaning is understood.*[39]

Johannes Kepler was the scientist who proved empirically that the planets move in elliptical rather than circular orbits around the sun. He wrote an interesting book entitled *The Music of the Spheres*, in which he described his view that the harmonious motions of the planets describe a musical symphony created by God for his glory. Robert Boyle, the first modern chemist and the first to do careful scientific measurements on gases, was also a theologian who wrote Bible commentaries and religious novels. William Harvey, Isaac Newton, Carl Linnaeus, Joseph Priestly, Michael Faraday and Albert Einstein were all believers in God. In fact the belief that science and atheism are compatible is a relatively recent phenomenon, only becoming common about the middle of the nineteenth century.

These scientists saw the hand of God at work in creating the laws of nature. The next step, then, is to look at what is known about the universe to see if this view holds up. The fact that all the great men of science were believers—that their science was motivated by their faith—does not prove the existence of God. However it does prove that making such a connection is not intellectually suspect!

Let us move to the question at hand. What does our fundamental knowledge about the laws of nature reveal with respect to the existence of God?

The following argument for the existence of God begins with one assumption.[40] With any argument, one must look carefully at the assumptions being made. In this case, the underlying assumption which will be made is that the universe exists. That is not a hard assumption to accept. Philosophers may argue about whether a tree makes a sound when it falls to the ground without a hearer. From a philosophical perspective this argument may not be as trivial as it sounds. It is an argument over the empirical nature of truth. Nevertheless, for the more practically minded, we know that trees make sounds when they fall. In fact, we could record the sound on tape. Similarly, we know from empirical evidence that the universe exists.

Given that the universe exists, there are two possibilities which follow from this assumption. Either the universe has always existed or it has not always existed. If it has always existed, then it was not created. If it has not always existed, then the universe was created. A thing cannot create itself. Physicists and philosophers call this the law of causality. The best we can tell, everything which happens in our reality has a cause. Since the universe could not create itself (cause itself to exist), that would imply some sort of creator. The argument can be outlined as follows:

Assumption: The Universe Exists.

This leaves us with two possibilities:
1. The universe has always existed (which implies no creator).
2. The universe has not always existed (and therefore it was created).

If the universe was created, then there is a creator. The outline of this argument is very simple. If one can show logically from the evidence that the universe was created, a creator is implied. The skeptic could protest use of the words "created" and "creator" in the argument above as too suggestive, but any synonym would still imply that the universe has a creator.

Has the universe always existed? What is the history of the universe? For simplicity, we will discuss three possible descriptions of the history of the universe.

1. The Steady State Theory.

2. The Big Bang Theory.

3. Creation with an appearance of age.

THE STEADY STATE THEORY

We will examine the steady state theory first. Actually, it would be more accurate to refer to the steady state theories, as various versions of this idea have been proposed over the years. If one distills it down, the steady state theory implies that the universe has always existed. According to this theory, the laws of nature which scientists study have been in effect infinitely far into the past. Presumably, they will continue infinitely far into the future.

The earliest steady state theorists held to the idea that all the matter and energy which are in existence now have existed forever. The natural processes observable to us at the present time have always been occurring. By this model, all that can happen is that the matter and energy of the universe can be redistributed. This theory does not require the existence of a creator. It was therefore a natural product of the budding atheistic/materialistic philosophy of the nineteenth century. Materialist philosophers and scientists such as David Hume (1711-1776) and Pierre-Simon La Place (1749-1827) sought a non-supernatural explanation for the existence of the universe.

(FIGURE 3) A HUBBLE PHOTOGRAPH OF A NUMBER OF GALAXIES.

The philosophical materialism of the eighteenth century was not the only cause which motivated scientists to ask new questions about the history of the universe. Copernicus and Galileo had already proved that the earth is not at the center of the universe. This was the first cosmological shock of many (cosmology is the name given to the study of the history of the universe). Suddenly humans and the planet they live on seemed less significant. Later, Sir William Herschel (1738-1822) provided evidence that the sun we revolve around is also moving. This further eroded the human sense of stability.

These discoveries were inconsistent with the world-view of many believers. They caused some to question their concept (perhaps a better word would be misconception) of God as well. The biggest shock of all was produced by Edwin Hubble (1889-1953). In 1923 he showed[41] that some of the "nebulae" observable in the sky are actually other galaxies besides our own

Milky Way. Using the Hubble telescope, we have now proved that there are somewhere around one hundred billion galaxies. In about three hundred and fifty years of thinking and research the earth went from the center of the universe to a small planet on a larger sun, to a small planet on an average star in a typical galaxy of one hundred billion stars, in a universe of one hundred billion galaxies. It should surprise no one that this radical change in world view caused some to question their view of God. Our job is to look at the evidence and the theories proposed to explain that evidence and to ask whether or not they are consistent with belief in a creator.

Remember, either the universe was created or it was not. The earliest steady state theorists did not actually attempt to explain how the universe came to be. They held to the idea that the universe has always existed. In other words, it was not created. We will see that the problem with this theory is that it is inconsistent with the laws of nature. In fact, even among steady state theorists this form of the theory is out of favor because it does not hold up to the laws of thermodynamics.

Thermodynamics is the branch of chemistry and physics which deals with the relationships between matter and various forms of energy on a macroscopic scale. It is often summarized in two or three simple "Laws of Thermodynamics." It is in its conflict with these laws that the steady state theories run into trouble. For this reason, the first two laws of thermodynamics will be stated in a simple form to help convey how they relate to the origin of the universe. The first law of thermodynamics can be stated as follows:

In a closed system, the sum of mass and energy is conserved.

A closed system is one in which matter and energy do not enter or leave. In other words, assuming the universe is in fact a closed system, the amount of mass and energy in it does not change. Types of energy may be interconverted. For example the energy stored in gasoline may be converted to heat and mechanical energy, but the total amount of energy is constant. Einstein, with his famous equation $E=mc2$, proposed that matter and energy can be interconverted, leading to the development of nuclear energy but also requiring the first law to include both mass and energy in its statement.

How does this relate to the steady state or any other theory of origins? The noted atheist mathematical physicist Pierre-Simon La Place claimed that the laws of nature can be used to explain all past present and future events. This materialist assumption may or may not be true, but if it is applied to the first law of thermodynamics, then it would require that all the matter in the universe has existed forever. This is what early steady state theorists claimed. According to this view, any supernatural event, such as the creation of the universe is ruled out.

How does one resolve whether or not the matter and energy of the universe have existed forever? Are the observable facts about the universe consistent with this theory? In order to answer this question, consider a statement of the second law of thermodynamics.

For any spontaneous process in a closed system, entropy increases.

Unfortunately, the concept of entropy is a bit more abstract than that of energy, but a few illustrations will help. Entropy can be defined as a measure of randomness or disorder. A messy room has a lot of entropy. Applying the second law to a room in a house (a questionable application for a scientist, but it may help understand the second law), the natural tendency for a room is to go from order to disorder. The second law allows an outside force such as the person who lives in the room to put in energy and lower the entropy locally, but only at the expense of increasing entropy globally. Hopefully your children have done this recently.

Consider a second scenario. A house built out of cards has a lot of order by comparison to a random pile of playing cards. A pile of cards (with relatively high entropy) would never spontaneously pick itself up and be built into a house of cards (with relatively low entropy). The slightest gust of wind will naturally turn a house of cards into a pile of cards, increasing the entropy. The second law of thermodynamics defines the natural direction of events in the universe.

Entropy has been called "time's arrow" because it can be used to decide the forward direction of any process. If we were to view a film in which a huge cloud of dust and rubble suddenly came together to form a building, we would know immediately, beyond a doubt, that we were seeing the film in reverse. The second law does not allow for a pile of rubble to turn into a building under any circumstances. Another illustration of this principle can be taken from chemistry. Smoke, ash, carbon dioxide and water will never come together spontaneously to create a piece of paper, whereas the reverse process is spontaneous. The second law of thermodynamics will be discussed in greater detail in the Appendix.

How does this law apply to the origin and current state of the universe? Stated simply, the second law of thermodynamics implies that given sufficient time, in the absence of "supernatural" intervention, the universe will run down completely. Entropy will reach a maximum. Eventually, all the fuel in each of the stars will be used up. The universe will become extremely cold. Ultimately, given enough time, no life could be supported anywhere in the universe.

This fact has dire consequences for the earliest forms of steady state theory. If the universe, including all its matter and energy, has always existed, then it should already have reached the logical conclusion of the second law. It should be completely cold and dark. There is no way around this deathblow to the older form of the steady state theory.

Either the universe has always existed, or it has not. If the universe is a closed system, then according to the laws of nature, it cannot have always existed. If it has not always existed, then it was created. The conclusion one is left with, then, is that the universe was created.

Actually, disproving the steady state theory is not quite as simple as that. In 1948 three physicists, Hermann Bondi, Thomas Gold and Fred Hoyle, devised a new version of the steady state theory. Their proposal was startling in its time. They proposed that the universe is not a closed system. In other words they theorized that matter is continuously and spontaneously being created everywhere in the universe out of nothing! This theory is sometimes called the theory of continuous creation. It would seem to eliminate the problem of applying the second law of thermodynamics to the steady state theory.

According to the theory of continuous creation, the stuff out of which stars form is created spontaneously, at a continuous although very slow rate, out of nothing. This would explain why there are still stars around, giving off light and continuously increasing the entropy of the universe. In other words, Hoyle, Gold, Bondi and others proposed that the first law of thermodynamics is not strictly true. Matter and energy are not conserved because they are continuously being created everywhere in the universe. They claimed that the universe has always existed: that this matter has been in the process of being created forever. As could be imagined, this created quite a stir in the scientific community, which was used to taking the first law as being proven. If matter has been created out of nothing forever, shouldn't there be an infinite amount of matter? Doesn't this mean the universe should be a lot more crowded?

This question requires the introduction of one of the greatest discoveries of astronomy in the twentieth century. In 1929 Edwin Hubble published his empirical finding that the universe is expanding very rapidly. The evidence Hubble used to support his conclusion was called the "red shift." The term red shift describes what happens to light as it approaches us from very distant celestial objects.

This effect can be explained using an analogous everyday occurrence. Think about the sound you hear when a speeding race car passes by. When the car is approaching, the sound of the engine has a relatively higher pitch. After the car passes, the pitch of the sound becomes lower. Using physics terminology, the sound has higher frequency for an approaching object and a lower frequency for a receding object. The reason for this effect is that when a vibrating object is moving toward an observer, it is moving into its own sound waves, making the waves in front of the object closer together. The shorter wavelength results in a higher frequency for the sound than for a standing sound source. Behind a moving source of sound, the sound waves are farther apart than those produced by a non-moving source, resulting in a lower frequency. This shift in frequency for a moving source of waves is known as the Doppler effect.

The Doppler effect also applies to light waves approaching the earth from distant celestial objects. The colors of the visible light spectrum go from red to orange, yellow, green, blue and violet. Of the visible colors, red light has the lowest frequency and the longest wavelength, while violet light has the highest frequency and the shortest wavelength. By the Doppler effect, light approaching the earth from a very rapidly receding object is shifted toward a lower frequency like the race car in the analogy above. It shifts "toward the red." This is why the great discovery of Hubble is known as the "red shift." If a light source were moving toward the earth at high speeds, the light it produces would be shifted to higher frequency. It would experience a "blue shift." Figure 3.1 provides an explanation of this effect.

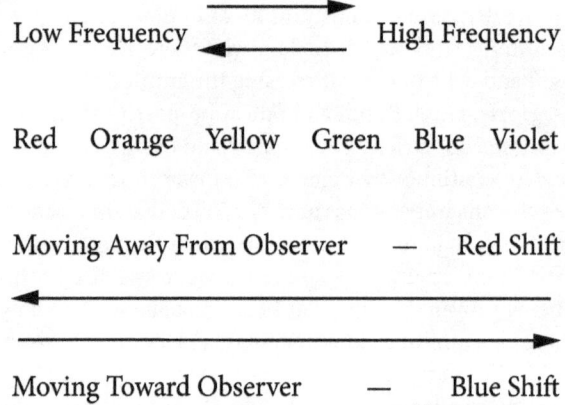

(FIGURE 3.1) THE ÎRED SHIFTÎ IMPLIES A LIGHT-PRODUCING OBJECT IS MOVING AWAY FROM AN OBSERVER

In 1868, Sir William Huggins was the first to apply the Doppler principle to measure the speed of a star. He determined that the star Sirius is moving away from the sun at 29 miles per second. Some of the stars in the Milky Way galaxy are approaching us (blue shifted), while others are receding (red shifted).

It was when Hubble observed the light approaching us from other galaxies that the discovery which revolutionized cosmology was made. What he discovered, quite surprisingly, was that almost all galaxies produce light which is red shifted. Even more remarkable, the farther away a galaxy or quasar other extremely distant light source is from us, the greater the red shift. A graph of the size of the red shift versus the distance to a galaxy produces a straight line. This fact eventually led to Hubble's law of universal expansion. The bottom line is that the universe appears to be expanding very rapidly. This will have important consequences when the Big Bang theory is discussed.

We will get to the Big Bang soon, but first, let us ask what is the affect of universal expansion on the steady state theory. If the universe is expanding at a constant rate, then this could explain why the universe is not totally packed with matter, even though new matter has been created forever. As unlikely as this theory seems on the face of it, it is logically consistent.

This is true. However, the steady state/continuous creation theory (the one which does not require a creator) has come to be dismissed by nearly all physicists because the theory makes certain predictions which are simply not reproduced by experiment. If this theory were correct, then the stars at great distances should be, on average, the same age as those near us. This is not the case. Stars in galaxies ten billion light years from us appear to be about ten billion years younger on average than in our own region of the universe. Presumably, this is because the light left those stars ten billion years ago, and that when the light left those extremely distant galaxies they were literally ten billion years younger than they are now. When astronomers look deep into space they are looking back in time.

Second, if the continuous creation theory were correct, then the distribution of galaxies should be roughly even throughout the universe. This prediction of the theory is also in disagreement with astronomical observations. Galaxies are not even close to being distributed evenly throughout space. The universe contains great clusters of galaxies and even "superclusters" of galaxies. Therefore, the distribution of galaxies is not even, as would be predicted by the steady state theory.

The continuous creation model runs into another problem for its proponents. How does this matter come into existence out of nothing? Hoyle and others have postulated a "creation field," a sort of creative force in the universe. It sounds an awful lot like they are resorting to a creator to explain the universe! The problem is that there is no evidence to support the existence of this force.

The history of science includes many theories, which have proposed the existence of previously unknown forces or unobserved substances to explain mysterious phenomenon. Early scientists proposed that living beings contain a substance called "anima" to explain how they differed from inanimate objects. This substance was never isolated, and eventually the anima theory died. Flammable substances were theorized to contain "phlogiston." Phlogiston had never been isolated or even detected. Later, when it was discovered that flammable substances react with oxygen, the phlogiston theory was dropped. When scientists could not explain how light waves can pass through the vacuum of space, they proposed that empty space is actually filled with "ether." The ether theory suffered the same fate that the continuous creation model is suffering: it ended up in the theory trash-heap, not because the scientists who proposed them were bad scientists, but because the models were unsupported by scientific measurements.

What was the motivation of Bondi, Gold and Hoyle in creating the continuous creation theory? These cosmologists devised this theory, not so much because any evidence supports it, but rather because they find the idea of creation unacceptable philosophically. It is generally considered bad form for a scientist to allow their philosophical/religious presuppositions to determine what theories they support, but apparently this is what motivated the formation of the continuous creation theory. According to a cosmologist who has no particular reason to oppose the steady state theory:

> *The basis for acceptance or rejection of the evolutionary [Big Bang] and steady-state theories can be divided into two categories: observational [experimental] proof and philosophical reasoning. The evolutionary theory rests heavily on the former, while the greatest appeal of the steady-state theory, at least at the present time, lies not so much in its mathematical formulation and predictions as it does in its broad philosophical implications.*[42]

If science works as most of its practitioners claim that it does, philosophically appealing theories are rejected in favor of the ones which are supported by empirical evidence. Therefore the theory of continuous creation is now rejected almost unanimously, even by those who are philosophically predisposed against supernatural creation.

The lack of evidence to support the idea of the universe existing forever explains why most cosmologists now believe in the sudden creation theory commonly known as the big bang theory. Let it be stated clearly. The Big Bang is a theory of sudden and spontaneous creation of the universe out of nothing (*ex nihilo*). From a very informal and unscientific survey done by the author, I have found that a majority of physicists have at least some sort of belief in God. Christianity may not dominate physicists' ranks, but most are at least deists. The influence of the Big Bang theory and the data which supports it may be part of the reason many physicists have come to find atheism inconsistent with their world view.

THE BIG BANG THEORY

The Big Bang theory was first proposed in 1927 by the Belgian priest Georges Lemaitre. On principally theoretical grounds, he proposed that the universe may have begun as a "primeval atom." This speculation came before Hubble's discovery of the expanding universe. In the 1940s Russian-born George Gamow, along with Ralph Alpher, refined Lemaitre's ideas to produce the beginnings of the modern Big Bang theory. A simple statement defining the theory is as follows:

> *All the matter and energy in the universe were created in an instant of time and at a point in space at incredibly high temperatures. Since that time, the universe has been expanding at the speed of light and cooling to its present background temperature of about four degrees Kelvin.*

STANDARD TIMELINE FOR THE BIG BANG

TIME	TEMPERATURE	DESCRIPTION
10^{-32} seconds	10^{25} Kelvin	Singularity has occurred. The universe is almost entirely composed of light.
10^{-6} seconds	10^{13} Kelvin	The universe is still mostly light. Quarks and electrons begin to form.
1 second	10^{10} Kelvin	Quarks begin to condense. Neutrons and protons form.
3 minutes	10^{9} Kelvin	Deuterium nuclei (a proton and a neutron combined) begin to form.
380,000 years	3000 Kelvin consistency? 3×10^{3}	Atoms, with electrons captured by nuclei, begin to form. The universe becomes transparent to light.
100,000,000 years	100 Kelvin or 10^{2}	Matter has cooled sufficiently for gravity to begin to cause hydrogen and helium to condense into galaxies and stars.

The initial creation was unimaginably dense and hot. The temperature was so high that most of the "stuff" in the first moments was in the form of photons (particles of light). If current Big Bang models are correct, not only were matter and energy created in the initial event, but time and space were created as well. Time itself began with the initial "bang." There was literally no universe before the initial singularity. The universe expanded super rapidly in the first moments by a process known as inflation. As the substance of the universe cooled in the first fractions of a second, fundamental particles such as electrons and quarks formed. Within a few minutes, the universe cooled from trillions to billions of degrees. Quarks condensed to form neutrons and protons. Within hours and days, the universe cooled to millions of degrees. It was now cool enough for protons and neutrons to combine to produce some helium nuclei. Within an estimated three hundred and eighty thousand years, the universe cooled sufficiently for electrons to adhere to the hydrogen and helium nuclei and form atoms. As matter and light separated, the universe became transparent to light photons. The matter in the universe had very slight variations in density. Because of this, further expansion over the next few million years yielded huge conglomerates of matter-mainly hydrogen and helium, which eventually coalesced into galaxies and discrete stars within those galaxies. See the chart on the previous page.

It is impossible to prove that the scenario described above actually happened. Scientists cannot do experiments in a laboratory to reproduce the entire chain of events. They also cannot go back in time to the initial expansion to prove it happened. What we can say is that the data we observe is consistent with this model. This evidence is summarized below.

How long ago did this universe-creating event occur? There are two main avenues used to estimate the age of the universe. Very large instruments such as the Hubble telescope have been used to look at the oldest and most distant objects in the observable universe. The size of the red shift of light from these objects yields an estimate of the distance to and the age of quasars and galaxies. In addition, cosmologists use the best models of the big bang and the subsequent expansion along with current conditions in our part of the galaxy to estimate the amount of time since the big bang. Both methods now yield an age of the universe of about thirteen billion years.

The first body of evidence which supports the Big Bang theory is the "red shift" which can be observed in light reaching us from very distant celestial sources of light. If the universe did in fact begin at a single point in space, followed by a very rapid expansion, then all the matter in the universe should be moving outward from the point of singularity with great speed. In this case, all galaxies other than our own should be moving away from us (galaxies in our immediate neighborhood could be an exception).

Logically, the farther a galaxy or cluster of galaxies is from the earth, the faster it should be moving away from our own. This must be true because objects near us are moving from the point of beginning at about the same speed as we are, but distant objects must be moving at different speeds and/or in a different directions. If this is true, then light reaching the earth from the most distant galaxies, should be shifted to lower frequency (a bigger red shift) than light from a relatively closer galaxy. In fact, this prediction from the Big Bang theory is in very good agreement with the evidence as mentioned above. The principle reason the Big Bang theory was initially accepted was that it can explain the rapidly expanding universe.

Since the Big Bang theory was formulated, cosmologists have developed a model using more recent knowledge of the behavior of fundamental particles to predict the precise nature and history of the evolution of the universe. In doing so, the models predicted as early as the 1960s that there should be a weak microwave "background radiation" still echoing throughout the universe. A theoretical prediction of both the intensity and frequency of this radiation was made in 1964.[43] In a stroke of serendipity, two radio astronomers, Penzias and Wilson,[44] happened to be doing an experiment involving observation of microwave radiation from space in the same year. These two scientists were not even aware of the prediction that there should be a weak and almost homogeneous background of microwave light. They observed microwave "noise" in the sky at a frequency equivalent to a source at about three degrees Kelvin. This annoyance in their data turned out to be the second line of support for the Big Bang model. The intensity, distribution and frequency of the radiation were in close agreement with the predictions of theoretical cosmologists. This discovery is the reason the big bang model was accepted by almost all physicists by the late 1960s.

In 1989, a satellite called the Cosmic Background Explorer (COBE) measured the background microwave radiation with great precision, finding the data to fit the big bang model. It showed that the background radiation is almost exactly homogeneous. The very slight fluctuations represent regions of slightly higher and lower matter density in the universe. This slight clumpiness of the original material in the universe explains the observed formation of clusters of galaxies. This data are also in agreement with theory.

When a theory is used to predict the existence of a then unknown phenomenon, after which scientists go out and discover the prediction to be true, this is the strongest kind of support a theory can have. This background radiation provides further supportive evidence that the big bang is the correct model for the beginning of the universe.

There is a third category of evidence to support the big bang theory. Theoretical models of the Big Bang predict that the original expansion occurred so rapidly that significant amounts of only the lightest elements were produced. To be specific, the best models predict about five percent of the atoms created in the Big Bang should be helium, and ninety-five percent should be hydrogen. All other elements should be present in very low proportional amounts in the initial material in the universe. Heavier elements such as carbon, nitrogen, iron and so forth would only have been created later inside of stars. Again, astronomical observation produces data in striking agreement with the theoretical prediction. No other model has been able to predict the observed data.

If the Big Bang model is correct, this would mean that at the moment of the creation of the universe an inconceivable amount of light suddenly appeared out of nothing. This is reminiscent of Genesis 1:3: "And God said 'Let there be light,' and there was light." If this theory of origins is true, and the evidence available supports the theory, then the universe was created by something or someone outside the universe itself. The universe could not have created itself. It was caused by a creator. When thinking people ponder the Big Bang theory, they must ask themselves what caused it all to happen. What force created all this light? The name that has been given to this "force," this creator, is God. In his book *Kinematic Relativity*, E. A. Milne,[45] who never referred to divinity in the entire volume, concludes: "The first cause of the universe is left for the reader to insert, but our picture is incomplete without Him."

It is worth reiterating that this does not prove that the universe was created with a Big Bang. In fact, in the case of theories about events of the distant past, scientists will remain unable to provide absolute proof. Scientifically derived conclusions must always remain tentative, pending the possible discovery of new evidence. This is especially true when trying to explain events which occurred eons ago, and which therefore are not subject to direct experiment. In conclusion, in the light of scientific evidence and the laws of science, the idea that the universe has always existed-that there was no creator-has been shown to be false. Although one cannot say with certainty that the Big Bang happened, the evidence scientists have thus far collected is in dramatic agreement with this theory, a theory that implies the universe was created out of nothing.

CREATION WITH AN APPEARANCE OF AGE

This leads to the last theory of the origin of the universe to be discussed. This is the theory that God created the universe with an appearance of age. The God one discovers in the Bible certainly could have created planets, stars, galaxies, and super-clusters of galaxies in place out of nothing. In fact, he could have done it only a few thousand years ago. It should be noted that this would be an unfalsifiable theory, which means that it cannot be proven untrue by any conceivable experiment. To scientist, an unfalsifiable theory does not qualify as scientific. If the universe was created with an appearance of age, then there would not necessarily be any direct scientific evidence to either support or disprove the youth of the universe. This theory would be consistent with a simple and literal interpretation of the first chapter of Genesis, but by its very nature, no one could ever prove or disprove creation with an appearance of age using science. It is essentially a non-scientific theory. Those who hold to this idea should be aware of this fact.

Certainly atheists will be uncomfortable with this theory. They assume, before even looking at the evidence, that the origin of the universe has a "natural" explanation. However, we already have shown that the universe was created. Whether this creation was brought about by the Big Bang or with an appearance of age, either way it was a supernatural event.

Which of the three proposed theories is true: steady state, Big Bang or appearance of age? It has been shown that the steady state theory, the one consistent with atheism, is insupportable. Between the other two, it will be left to the reader to decide. As a scientist, I confess that I am pulled toward the "scientific" conclusion. As a science teacher, when I lecture on astronomy, I usually only spend significant time on the Big Bang theory because it is the only "scientific" theory in agreement with the evidence. I do mention very briefly the theological possibility of creation with an appearance of age. As I tell my *Intro to Scientific Thought* students, that something is not "scientific" does not prove that it is not true. By faith, I believe God could have created an expanding universe with the background radiation already echoing through it, but this would be a belief based on faith, not measurable fact. Since neither theory can be proven, it would be a mistake to be dogmatic in condemning the Big Bang theory or the theory of creation with an appearance of age.

To conclude, the very existence of the universe as we know it shows that there is a creator. The nature of the universe does not tell us a lot about this creator except that he/it is certainly very powerful. In fact, the logical conclusion of the argument from cosmology is deism. At the risk of over-simplifying, deism is a theology which defines God as the creator of the universe. Whether this creator is a personal god or not is not made obvious by the mere existence of the universe and the laws which govern it. In the next chapter, by looking at the nature of life, we will learn a bit more about the qualities of the creator.

FOR TODAY

1. *How do you believe the universe came to be? Do you believe the big bang occurred?*

2. *Do you believe that faith in God is a form of superstition? Why or why not?*

3. *According to the chapter, why can we be confident that the universe has not always existed?*

4. *What does the existence of the universe—of stars, galaxies, planets and so forth—say about the nature of its creator?*

36 Niles Eldredge, *The Monkey Business* (New York: Washington Square Press, 1982), 142.

37 Melvin Calvin, *Chemical Evolution* (Eugene: Oregon State System of Higher Education, 1961), 258.

38 A translation from his work, *Opus Majus*, 1267.

39 Excerpts from Galileo's letter to the Grand Duchess Christina,1614.

40 Although the details of the argument in chapter three are mine, I must acknowledge that the outline of the argument was inspired by the work of John Clayton, a lecturer and the author of a number of articles on the subject. Clayton's website is *www.doesgodexist.org*.

41 With some credit also going to Henrietta Leavitt and Harlow Shapley.

42 James Coleman, *Modern Theories of the Universe* (New York: Signet, 1963). Although this is a rather old source for the quote, it would be even truer today with so much more evidence in support of the Big Bang.

43 R. H. Dicke, P. J. E. Peebles, P. G. Roll and D. T. Wilkinson, "Cosmic Black-Body Radiation," *Astrophysics Journal*, **142**, 414 (1965).

44 Arno A. Penzias and Robert W. Wilson, "A Measurement of Excess Antenna Temperature at 4080 Mc/srd," *Astrophysics Journal*, **142**, 419 (1965).

45 E. A. Milne, *Kinematic Relativity* (Oxford: Clarendon Press, 1948).

CHAPTER 4

No way of thinking, no matter how ancient,
should be accepted without proof.

THOREAU

Did Life Just Happen?

What about the life that exists on the earth? How can one explain the origin of millions of species of plants, insects, reptiles, birds, mammals, and most complex of all, humans? How can we explain the origin of the very first living cell from inorganic matter? For many Christians the explanation of all this beauty and wonder in nature is no problem. As Jesus said in Matthew 3:9, "I tell you that out of these stones God can raise up children for Abraham." The Bible believer accepts this claim of Jesus without difficulty. They believe that God could take the matter in rocks and make living, breathing adult humans out of them. He could do it even though the elemental composition of the material in the rocks is not of the right proportion to create organic matter. God could do that. In fact, Christians believe that Jesus could have made children for Abraham out of nothing at all.

In the Bible it is recorded that Jesus turned water into wine at a wedding feast (John 2:1-11). He created fish and bread, from nothing, in order to feed several thousand people (John 6:1-15). When a person who believes these biblical accounts looks at the astounding variety and beauty of nature, the source of it all is obvious. It was created by God. However, this argument will not be convincing to the non-believer. Besides, this explanation is too vague. How exactly did the creation occur? In what order and how did it progress?

To the atheist or agnostic, the existence and diversity of life is equally a thing of beauty and wonder. The explanation of its source is more problematic. He or she believes that every observable phenomenon has a reasonable explanation based on the laws of nature. The supernatural is ruled out before the question of the origin of life is even raised. How such an incredible phenomenon as a living organism could just happen by pure chance is a notion awesome to contemplate. However, the committed materialist is sure there is a natural explanation. For those philosophically inclined to reject belief in God, it is simply a matter of searching high and low until the scientific explanation for the origin of life can be found. The question to be asked in this chapter is whether or not this "natural" explanation is real or just an illusion.

This, our second argument for the existence of God, begins with a simple assumption. It will be assumed that life exists. We already know that life has not always existed because the universe has not always existed. The question, then, is how did life originate from non-life? Two possible explanations present themselves, either life was created by someone or something, or it occurred by some natural process (to quote from Julian Huxley again, it "just happened"). The first explanation requires the existence of some supernatural power—what we call God. The second explanation would not automatically imply there is no God. It is not inconceivable that the creator could have produced a reality in which life could originate spontaneously. Nevertheless, this second explanation is consistent with the materialist/atheist view. To outline this argument:

ASSUMPTION: LIFE EXISTS.

This leaves us with two possibilities:
1. The first life was created supernaturally (which implies an intelligent creator)
2. The first life came about by random, natural processes (which is consistent with, but does not require atheism)

It is important to note that the theory of evolution is not part of this line of reasoning. The evolutionary model is an explanation of how life which already exists can change over time. It is not a theory of the origin of life from inorganic matter. Evolution will be discussed in chapter nine.

THE THEORY OF SPONTANEOUS GENERATION: CREATION OF LIFE BY RANDOM PROCESSES

We will first explore the proposition that the origin of life may have been by natural processes. Is this possibility reasonable from what we know of the requirements for life and natural laws? The technical term for creation of life out of inorganic matter by natural chemical processes is spontaneous generation or abiogenesis. Evolution of life after it is created is principally a question of biology, but the creation of life by spontaneous means is principally a question of chemistry. Before the first life, by definition, there was no biology.

There exists a sub-branch of chemistry dealing with theories about the chemical processes which might have produced the first life. The most famous experiment mentioned by scientists in this field is that of Urey and Miller, performed in 1953 and published in *Science*.[46] In this experiment, Urey and Miller prepared a mixture of methane (CH_4), water (H_2O), ammonia (NH_3) and hydrogen (H_2) in a glass vessel. They then applied an electric spark to the gaseous mixture above the solution. After some time, they analyzed the liquid which precipitated out of the mixture.

Upon analyzing the reaction mixture, Urey and Miller discovered that it contained a number of amino acids. Their discovery was significant because amino acids are the building block molecules out of which proteins are synthesized. Proteins are very important component molecules which make up all living things. The amino acids produced by Urey and Miller's experiment were small molecules, containing about ten to twenty atoms, but they were more complex than the methane, water, ammonia and hydrogen which were put in the reaction vessel.

Urey and Miller proposed that the early atmosphere of the earth may have contained principally water, methane, ammonia and hydrogen. Geologists now dispute this claim. Putting aside such disputes, many have staked the claim that the Urey/Miller experiment is the first step toward explaining how the protein molecules in the first spontaneously generated life came to be. This experiment has been cited as the first great discovery on the path toward explaining how life was created. In an article in the *Parade* magazine, Carl Sagan referred to this experiment.

> *From the standpoint of a 19th-century biologist, the achievement of experiments like Urey and Miller's is stunning.*[47]

Sagan proceeds to quote from Darwin:

> *"It is mere rubbish thinking at present of the origin of life,"* wrote Charles Darwin. *"One might as well think of the origin of matter."*

Sagan's dramatic conclusion follows:

> *How amazed he (Darwin) would be today! There is still much to do. No one has performed such an experiment and, at the end, discovered a creature, however simple, crawling out of the test tube. Many mysteries remain. We don't know how early nucleic acids "instructed" the formation of early proteins (a problem called the origin of the genetic code). We don't understand the origin of the first cell... There are scientists who are dazzled by*

our deep ignorance of many phases of this subject, who despair of
our ever understanding its more complex aspects and who look
longingly toward extraterrestrial or even divine intervention.

But such ideas do not solve the problem of the origin of life;
they merely postpone having to deal with it. While by no means
underestimating the depth of our ignorance, I am amazed by how
much we've learned. Understanding the origin of life no longer seems
intractable. The progress begun by Urey and Miller stands as a
landmark of modern science and our understanding of the universe
and ourselves.

This statement is a good representation of the mind set and line of argument of those who believe in spontaneous generation. Notice from Sagan's quote that Darwin believed the creation of life as well as of the universe was beyond the realm of science in his time. In fact, Darwin made a rather interesting statement in his original 1859 edition of *Origin of Species*. To quote:

Therefore I should infer from analogy that probably all the or-
ganic beings which have ever lived upon this earth have descended
from one primordial form into which life was first breathed by the
Creator.

Was the discovery of Urey and Miller a "landmark in our understanding of the universe" as claimed by Sagan? The answer is an emphatic no. From common knowledge, an experienced organic chemist could have predicted before doing such an experiment that an electrolyzed mixture of methane, ammonia and water with a little hydrogen would produce a very low concentration of amino acids (Even I could have, except for the fact that I was not born until the year after the work was published). Amino acids are relatively stable molecules. As a chemist I can also predict that if Urey and Miller continued to add the spark and heat to the mixture, the amino acids concentration would have eventually peaked and fallen back to lower levels, leaving a dark polymerized mixture that organic chemists affectionately call "tar" at the bottom of the flask. Although this was an interesting experiment, it was not a great discovery because it led to results that any organic chemist could have predicted beforehand. The question is not whether amino acids could have been produced in some model early atmosphere. The fundamental question is whether this is a significant step toward explaining how life came to exist in the universe.[48]

What are Carl Sagan and others like him really claiming? They are claiming that the chemical environment on the earth about three billion years ago allowed the right combination of molecules to spontaneously come together and produce a living thing. In order to explore this subject further, let us look at what is required on a chemical level for a collection of molecules to be alive.

All living things are composed principally of four classes of molecules: proteins, nucleic acids, carbohydrates and lipids, along with a smaller number of molecules which do not fit in these categories. Those who study the chemical origin of life assume that the first living thing was composed of molecules in the same categories. Proteins are very large molecules made up of many amino acid molecules bonded together. Proteins molecules are responsible for digestion, nutrient transport, energy production, immune system function, blood clotting, and an innumerable number of other functions in any living thing. Enzymes, the chemical factories which do most of the work in cells, are a type of protein molecule.

Nucleic acids are huge polymeric molecules which include nitrogen containing bases called purines and pyrimidines, connected to one another through a backbone of sugar and phosphate units. DNA (deoxyribonucleic acid) is responsible for heredity in all living things. The discovery of its spiral staircase-like double alpha helical structure by Watson and Crick is one of the greatest stories in the history of science. Another important type of nucleic acid is RNA (ribonucleic acid) which is needed to interpret the information stored in the DNA and turn this information into protein molecules. It is important to note that any primordial soup recipe which could conceivably produce proteins spontaneously would almost certainly not have the proper mix of starting materials to simultaneously produce nucleic acids in useful amount. The spontaneous creation of the building blocks of these molecules is quite sensitive to the reducing or oxidizing strength of the chemical environment.

Carbohydrates are a third category of biological molecules. They are commonly known as sugars. They are mostly smaller molecules whose principal function is as a source of energy. Their synthesis is also required for a number of other essential biological functions. In fact, sugars are one of the components of nucleic acids as mentioned above. Cellulose is the biomolecule which forms plant cell walls. It is a sugar polymer.

Lipids are a broad class of non-water-soluble molecules. They would include fats, a primary source of energy, and steroids such as cholesterol. Many steroids are hormones, regulating numerous biological functions including reproduction. Life cannot exist without lipid molecules. This is because the solvent both in a cell and outside a cell is water. It is absolutely required that some sort of barrier or membrane separate the contents of the living material from its environment. The only way for this to happen is to enclose the contents of the cell in non-water soluble lipid molecules.

The theory of spontaneous generation requires the conditions for production of all four types of compounds to have existed on the primeval earth at the same time. In fact, purines and pyrimidines, the building blocks of nucleic acids have been created in a separate experiment somewhat like that of Urey and Miller. However, the proposed primitive atmosphere required for this experiment contained different molecules from those required to produce amino acids. Carbohydrates have also been created in a different "primitive atmosphere." The conditions under which carbohydrates can be spontaneously generated require a strongly oxidizing (oxygen-containing) atmosphere, while the conditions required for the production of amino acids require a reducing (hydrogen-containing) atmosphere. The problem is that these two types of primitive atmospheric conditions are logical opposites. Scientists to this day debate whether the early atmosphere of the earth was reducing or oxidizing. More likely, it was higher in hydrogen. One thing they would presumably be unanimous on is that it was not both reducing and oxidizing at the same time.

Which is the right atmosphere? Which one actually existed? The one which would allow amino acids would not allow carbohydrates or nucleic acids to be created spontaneously. To date, no primitive atmospheric conditions have been proposed under which lipid molecules such as fats or steroids have been shown to be produced spontaneously in significant concentrations. Perhaps they could be produced somewhere else. Even if a spontaneous lipid-producing natural environment were discovered, this would not change the problem for the materialist. No conceivable chemical environment could spontaneously produce the range of building block molecules required for spontaneous generation of life.

Modes other than atmospheric deposition of organic molecules have been proposed. Scientists have posited that proteins might be formed on clays. They have explored the possibility that certain organic components could be produced spontaneously at deep-ocean hydrothermal vents, or that they could be synthesized in interstellar media, and deposited on the earth by meteorites. None of these proposals solves the problem of simultaneous production of lipids, carbohydrates, amino acids and nucleic acids.

Let it be granted that the earth could have four different sets of local atmospheric conditions or at least four chemically distinct environments in four separate locations (as unlikely as that seems). For the sake of argument, let it be conceded that amino acids could be produced at the surface of the ocean, nucleic acids could be produced in terrestrial clays, and carbohydrates could be produced spontaneously at hydrothermal vents. Where lipids could be spontaneously created it would be hard to say, but for now let it just be granted that lipid molecules could be spontaneously produced somewhere on the earth. Once produced in four chemically and physically isolated locations, all four of the basic types of building block chemicals would have to be transported to a single location without being changed. At this meeting point, all these molecules would have to exist in sufficient concentrations and the right proportions to allow the formation of a living thing, despite the fragility of even some of these building block molecules.

Let's examine this theory in greater detail. Even if a "soup" containing all four types of molecules were miraculously produced in the correct proportions for life to form, such a soup would be far from being able to advance life—very far. In fact, our knowledge of chemistry demands that it could never happen. What would be required in order for the first living thing to be viable? The simplest first living thing would have to be able to:

1. Recognize, ingest and digest food.

2. Turn that food into usable energy.

3. Grow.

4. Reproduce.

It would probably have to be able to move as well. Bacteria are the simplest known form of life which passes this test. It is debatable if viruses are alive. They are far too small and simple in their structure to be self-sustaining and are dependant on other more complicated life forms to survive. We will therefore use bacteria as our model for the simplest conceivable first life form. Since *E. coli* is one of the simplest types of bacteria, let's consider it as a model for the simplest possible original life form. *E. coli* are about one micrometer by three micrometers (0.001 by 0.003 mm) in size. They contain approximately 7×10^{11} atoms (that is about seven hundred billion atoms!)

The single cell of an *E. coli* contains about three thousand different protein molecules, fifty different carbohydrate molecules, forty different lipid molecules and 1000 different nucleic acid molecules, as well as about five hundred other simple organic molecules which do not fit into any of the above categories. One can debate if this is the best possible model for the first spontaneously generated life. Perhaps the first life form could have been somewhat simpler than an *E. coli*, containing only one hundred billion atoms, two thousand different protein molecules and so forth. This would not change any of the arguments or conclusions below.

The point of this model is to help us come to grips with fantastic level of complexity of this simple life form, which supposedly was created by a natural chemical process. Although we do not know the exact chemical makeup of the first life, one thing all biologists would assume is that it contained a great variety of protein molecules Proteins are large, complex chemical species. A model of a relatively simple protein molecule is given in Figure 4.2 below in order to give a feel for the complexity of these essential components of all life.

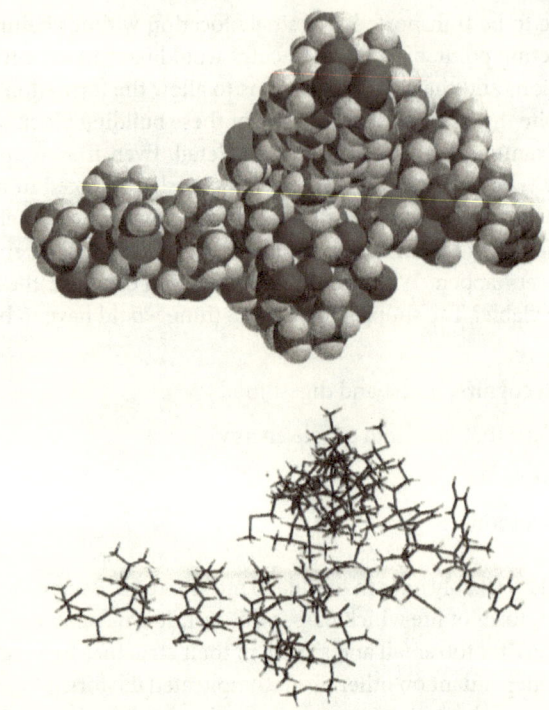

(FIGURE 4.2) A MODEL OF A VERY SIMPLE PROTEIN MOLECULE, REPRE-
SENTING BOTH THE SIZE AND THE GEOMETRIC COMPLEXITY OF ONE COM-
PONENT OF THE ORIGINAL LIVING THING.

Proteins in even the simplest life are composed of thousands or even tens of thousands of hydrogen, carbon, oxygen, nitrogen and sulfur atoms, each connected in a precise way which, if changed even slightly, causes the molecule to not function. We can get a feeling for the size of a protein molecule by looking at one of the heme subunits of the hemoglobin molecule. Heme is not a particularly large protein, even for simple living things such as bacteria. The formula of heme is $C_{738}H_{1166}O_{208}N_{203}S_2Fe$. Each of the over two thousand three hundred atoms must be connected in exactly the right order for the heme molecule to perform its function. The Heme molecule contains one hundred and forty-three amino acids linked together. Naturally occurring proteins are made of twenty different amino acids. In order for the Heme molecule to work properly, each of the amino acids in the chain must be the correct one of the twenty possibilities. Sickle cell anemia is caused by changing one of the one hundred and forty three amino acids.

Urey and Miller may have shown that some of the twenty naturally occurring amino acids in proteins could be synthesized in a model atmosphere. This is a big leap from producing all twenty of the required naturally occurring amino acids under the same conditions. It is an even bigger leap from there to the exclusion of all other amino acids (i.e. ones not from the list of twenty out of which proteins form) from the mixture out of which the first life arose by accident. Probability arguments preclude the formation of even a single functioning protein molecule with biological activity out of any conceivable randomly produced soup of amino acids. Remember that any protein molecule has to be composed of a specific list of twenty different amino acids. It is extremely unlikely—one might claim it would be impossible—for any environment to spontaneously produce all twenty amino acids in a proportion and at a concentration which would allow even a single protein molecule to be produced. The second law of thermodynamics makes this scenario impossible.

To summarize what we have seen so far, there are several requirements for life to have formed by a chemical accident, all of which present themselves as chemical impossibilities. There is the requirement for separate formation and later coming together of all four categories of building-block molecules out of which the simplest life could form. In addition, random processes would have to produce all twenty amino acids in correct proportion and at sufficient concentration. Besides, all other amino acids other than the twenty would have to be excluded from the mixture. A fourth apparent impossibility is for the soup of accidentally assembled amino acids to self-assemble into a biologically active protein molecule. Let us consider another chemical requirement for random assembly of a living cell. What about nucleic acids?

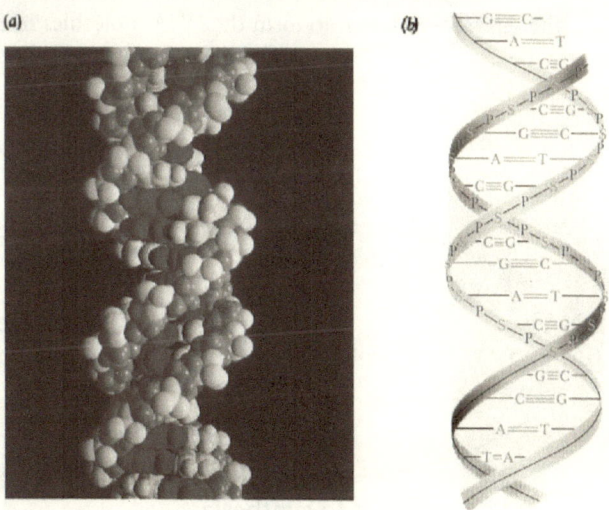

(FIGURE 4.3) FIGURE (A) ON THE LEFT SHOWS ALL OF THE ATOMS IN A SMALL PORTION OF THE DOUBLE-HELICAL STRUCTURE OF DNA. FIGURE (B) ON THE RIGHT SHOWS THE SAME PORTION OF THE MOLECULE SCHEMATICALLY. S=RIBOSE SUGAR MOLECULE, P=PHOSPHATE GROUP, AND C, A, G AND T REPRESENT PURINE AND PYRIMIDINE MOLECULES.

Nucleic acids are the molecules of which genes are composed. There are two important categories of nucleic acids, DNA and RNA. Like proteins, DNA and RNA are extremely complex molecules. A picture of one small proportion of a single strand of DNA is given in Figure 4.3.

In 1953, James Watson, Francis Crick and Rosalind Franklin discovered the beautiful "double-helical" structure of DNA. A DNA molecule is a coded template which cells use to store information and to manufacture proteins. The process by which protein synthesis occurs includes the involvement of RNA as well as a number of protein molecules. This process is very complex-beyond the scope of this book. In order for life to have begun spontaneously, a large number of different nucleic acid molecules, all with the correct double helical structure would have had to form simultaneously in the same place. Not only that, but each of these DNA molecules would have needed to be able to successfully manufacture protein molecules which were in turn able to ingest and metabolize food, to regulate nutrient levels, and to perform thousands of different tasks in the cell.

The formation of all these DNA molecules by random association of the accidentally formed soup of chemicals would involve a lot of coincidence. In fact, the probability of even one useful DNA molecule forming spontaneously out of even a carefully prepared organic soup is essentially zero. Not only this, but there is a logical impossibility built into this supposed formation of the first cell by accident. In living things, the formation of DNA molecules requires protein molecules called enzymes, while the synthesis of the enzymes required to form the DNA molecules in the first place requires the existence of DNA molecules (See Figure 4.4). There is no exception to this rule in nature.[49]

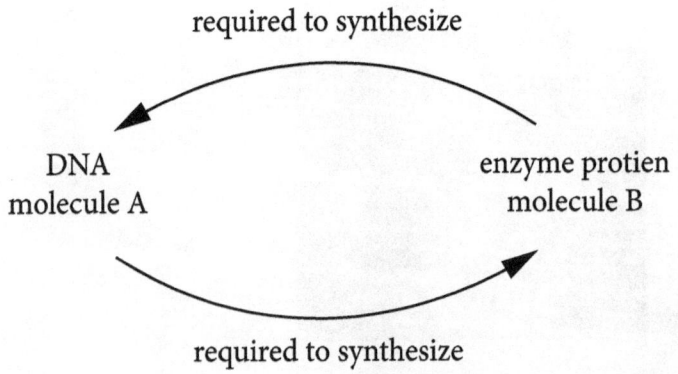

required to synthesize

DNA   enzyme protien
molecule A   molecule B

required to synthesize

(FIGURE 4.4) AN ILLOGICAL PAIR OF SIMULTANEOUSLYCREATED MOLE-CULES. TWO CLASSES OF MOLECULES, BOTH OF WHICH REQUIRE THE OTHER IN ORDER TO BE SYNTHESIZED. WHICH CAME FIRST, DNA OR ENZYMES?

Which came first, the chicken or the egg? The agnostic, of course, will answer that they both were formed at the same time. Now that is amazing! The claim is that DNA molecule A, required to synthesize enzyme B, was spontaneously formed by a chemical accident. The problem with this is that enzyme molecule B might be one of the proteins required for DNA molecule A to be synthesized. This creates an apparent logical impossibility, represented by the Figure 4.4.

Both of the uniquely paired molecules would have to be created simultaneously by accident, even though both are required to synthesize their partner. That would be an unbelievable coincidence.

There is another important aspect of the relationship between nucleic acids and proteins that needs to be pointed out. The sequence of DNA which is used to synthesize an individual protein molecule is called a gene. The gene is a series of hundreds of nucleotides. There are four different nucleotides which make up DNA. These four are analogous to the twenty amino acids which form proteins. A series of three of these nucleotides forms a codon. They are called codons because they form part of a code which is applied when DNA information is used to synthesize specific proteins. There are sixty-four different codons. Each codon is specific for a particular amino acid in a protein. Very complex molecules known as transfer RNA are required to read the code. A good question naturally arises. Where did the code come from? How could a code system to turn DNA information into protein structure be created without someone to design the code? Could this have happened by random accident?

Let us return to our model *e-coli*. The theory that life was created spontaneously requires that all three thousand of these complex biologically active protein molecules required for the first living cell to function and reproduce itself just happened to be created in the same place at the same time. Not only that, but one thousand different nucleic acid molecules would also have had to be spontaneously produced in exactly the same place—and not just any nucleic acids—ones which contain the code capable of synthesizing the correct proteins to produce an active cell which can eat, grow, and reproduce.

Let us add to all this the problem of lipids and carbohydrates. No biologist could propose a model for a living cell which did not include these vital molecules. In fact, without a bilayer of lipids, there is no conceivable way for the contents of a cell to be excluded from the water solvent in which the bacteria lives. Carbohydrate molecules are required for a wide variety of chemical reactions in all life forms. Admittedly, the lipid and carbohydrate molecules in cells are not anywhere near as complex as the proteins and nucleic acids. However, any chemical system which could accidentally produce a living cell must also be able to spontaneously generate sugars and fats. It has already been stated that any conceivable chemical soup which allows spontaneous formation of amino acids would be unable to synthesize carbohydrates and lipids. Remember also that our model simplest life form also has about five hundred other molecules, without which the *E.-coli* cannot live. Where will these molecules come from?

One would think that scientists who believe life "just happened" would have a theory to explain how all these incredibly complex molecules came to exist and managed to coalesce into a living thing. This leap in the theory from production of the simple amino acids, purines, pyrimidines and carbohydrates to supermolecules such as proteins, DNA and RNA is one place where the scientists are really grasping at straws. A statement from the book, *Evolution and Christian Thought Today*, by Hearn and Hendry, can give a feel for some of the arguments put forth on how large, information-containing biomolecules were created by random processes.

> *It now seems reasonable to believe that the earth's early atmosphere and the constitution of its crust favored the formation of organic compounds, at least locally, and that over the long periods of pre-biological time very large amounts of chemical energy were accumulated in this way.*

> *It seems highly possible, although still not clearly demonstrated, that natural forces existed which would have favored the formation of highly complex molecules and aggregates of such molecules, and that the chemical structures of such complexes could have had some ability to catalyze certain types of chemical reactions. If any of the reactions catalyzed were more favorable to the synthesis of the catalyst than others, a mechanism such as **natural selection** could begin operating, even at this pre-biological level. Gradually, this process could conceivably lead to increased catalytic efficiency, given the randomness characteristic of molecular interactions and **sufficient time.** It also seems likely that many of the metabolic reactions of modern living things could have arisen separately in these pre-living complexes, and that a complete metabolic machine may have appeared only after long periods of **chemical evolution** of such systems[50] (emphasis added).*

This quote is from one of the earlier books on the subject. Nevertheless it is a good representation of all arguments which have been advanced up to the present time. It is at the heart of every theory of how the first life form "just happened." This quote points out three elements necessary in any "scientific" explanation of the origin of life.

1. Natural selection of molecules.
2. Chemical evolution.
3. Sufficient time.

Is it reasonable for scientists to believe that molecules can undergo natural selection? Can non-living chemicals evolve over time into more and more complex molecules? Have these processes been observed in the laboratory? Do they agree with the laws of thermodynamics? Is there any theoretical basis for the idea of chemical evolution? The answer in each case is an emphatic no! The phrase chemical evolution is an oxymoron. Believers in spontaneous generation present the impression that "sufficient time" is a magic ingredient which can allow anything to be produced. The fact is that time does not make all things happen. Things with a low probability will happen if one waits long enough. Impossible events (i.e. ones which violate the second law of thermodynamics) do not. Given sufficient time and the right wind conditions, a scattered deck of cards thrown into a room might all end up in one corner of a room. However, no set of conditions will create a house of cards. Sufficient time will not make the spontaneous creation of a house of cards possible. At the risk of pushing the analogy too far, the theory of spontaneous generation is a house of cards.

In order to carefully address the questions raised in the previous paragraph, let us apply the second law of thermodynamics. This law governs what types of processes can and cannot happen. Processes which result in a net decrease in entropy of a system and its environment do not happen. Natural processes proceed from order to disorder. Proteins and nucleic acids are molecules with an extreme amount of order. They have very low entropy. The probability of a single active strand of DNA—of a gene—being produced by accident out of a solution, even if it contained some sort of favorable mixture of purines, pyrimidines, deoxyribose molecules and phosphate, is zero. The second law of thermodynamics does not allow for reactions which produce order and create information spontaneously. More detailed arguments about information and the second law of thermodynamics are found in the appendix.

The materialist/atheist will claim that given sufficient time, chemical evolution and natural selection of molecules can occur. Over a sufficiently long period of time, they claim, it is possible for larger and more complex molecules to form gradually. That is simply not true. Time will not increase the probability. Even the building block molecules needed to synthesize large biomolecules do not last very long in nature at all. Melvin Calvin, the Nobel Prize winner, comments on this in his book *Chemical Evolution*:

> *I should like to discuss the stabilities of these classes of molecular "fossils." There are two important classes of materials that I have not yet mentioned, namely amino acids coming from the peptides, and carbohydrates coming from various kinds of polysaccharides. I have not described the amino acids or carbohydrates of the mud because both of these compounds may be expected to, and do, disappear quite rapidly. They do not remain as stable compounds for very long periods of time in any large amounts.*[51]

In the article from which this is taken, Calvin is discussing studies of chemicals found in the decomposed mud below lakes. He notes that the building blocks required to produce life, in this case amino acids and poly-saccharides (sugars), are very short-lived. He could have said the same about the building blocks of nucleic acids as well. The fact is that even these much simpler building block molecules still have a fairly low entropy. Given sufficient time, they decompose to more stable molecules, thereby gaining entropy. Even under Urey and Miller type conditions, the molecular building blocks do not proceed to ever more complex molecules. Adding the magic ingredient of time makes the problem more insurmountable, not less.

To make this argument less abstract, let us return to the analogy of a large buildings which have been slated for demolition. Most of us have seen videos of a large building being blown up by carefully placed explosives. In such a film, the viewer sees entropy increasing very rapidly. Now, imagine watching the video of such a demolition backward. In such a film, entropy decreases rapidly. Our instinct tells us that the film is definitely being run backward. In other words, it is an impossible process. A random pile of twisted rubble made up of iron, concrete, pieces of broken glass, plastic, styrofoam, wood, and so forth would never spontaneously be turned into a building. Significantly, time would not increase the probability. In fact, it would actually decrease the likelihood of a building forming spontaneously, because the first wind storm would scatter the required building materials even more widely. By analogy, life could not have formed spontaneously. Any fortunate gathering of appropriate building block molecules would be dispersed long before these smaller molecules could evolve into larger ones. Time does not favor the building process under the influence of random forces.

To sum up this part of the argument, the laws of nature do not allow for life to "just happen." Covering up this fact with a lot of scientific jargon does not change the reality. The concept of "chemical evolution," with molecules gradually getting more and more complex over great periods of time is a non-starter. Natural selection of molecules and chemical evolution fly in the face of the what we know from thermodynamics. The large and complex molecules required for a living thing to function are not, never have been, and never will be produced spontaneously. If not even one of these molecules could be produced by chance, then surely a functioning combination of several thousand different biomolecules could never be produced simultaneously and in the same place. A more technical discussion of the relationship between the second law of thermodynamics and the origin of life can be found in the appendix.

Belief in the production of life by spontaneous generation requires a kind of faith in the ability for random forces to do almost anything. To use the concept developed earlier, it is a belief based on faith not fact. It requires a blind faith. Given the available evidence, I would argue that a greater amount of faith is needed to believe in spontaneous generation than to believe that Jesus Christ will come back to judge the world. Claims of the inspiration of the Bible and the resurrection of Christ should "not be accepted without proof" either, but at least both of these claims have a great deal of evidence to support them.[52] The level of faith required to believe in the spontaneous generation of life makes atheism in essence a religion. One might reasonably ask the scientist: "Do you really believe this happened?"

If the science behind the theory of the spontaneous generation of life is so weak, why do so many scientists accept the idea? The answer is that they assume that there is a natural explanation for everything. They "know" there is a scientific explanation for everything, including the origin of life. To quote Hearn and Hendry:

> *This does not mean that scientists will necessarily ever be able to create life, although this certainly seems within the range of scientific possibility; it does mean, however, that **reputable scientists do have faith that life arose from inanimate matter** through a series of physico-chemical processes no different from those we can observe today*[53] (emphasis added).

Here a scientist who believes in spontaneous generation is admitting that his belief relies on faith. We already know the inevitable result of an inquiry which begins with the answer already assumed. When a scientist begins investigating the question of the origin of life by assuming that it cannot be by supernatural means, we should not be surprised that he or she ends up concluding that it was the result of natural processes. It requires great faith to believe in atheism. I do not agree with Hearn and Hendry that all reputable scientists agree with the theory that life "came about by a long series of singularly beneficial accidents." I would like to think of myself as a reputable scientist, and I definitely do not agree that life came about by a "natural" process.

Why would anyone choose to put faith in the explanatory powers of science rather than in the God who created him or her? Let non-believers answer the question for themselves, but read this quote from Romans 1:18-20:

> *The wrath of God is being revealed from heaven against all the godlessness and wickedness of men who suppress the truth by their wickedness, since what may be known about God is plain to them, because God has made it plain to them. For, since the creation of the world God's invisible qualities—his eternal power and divine nature—have been clearly seen, being understood from what has been made, so that men are without excuse.*

According to the Bible, the observation of nature makes the existence of God obvious. This is certainly true. A scientist who examines the unimaginable complexity of the molecules and the intricacies of the biochemical processes which make up life has been provided with more than enough reason to believe in God. Given the evidence for the creation of the universe and for the supernatural creation of life, scientists have less excuse for rejecting belief in God than anyone else.

Paul continues in Romans:

> *They exchanged the truth of God for a lie, and worshipped and served created things, rather than the Creator—who is praised forever (Romans 1:25).*

God's admonition to his created beings is that they should worship him rather than created things. God created the laws of nature. Some people worship the laws of nature, rather than the God who created those laws. Nature and the laws by which it functions is a wonderful and beautiful thing to contemplate, but God is far more worthy of worship than the laws he created.

A question may arise at this point, "What about the evidence for evolution?" The creation of life and evolution of that life once it is created are separate scientific questions. As already stated, evolution is a theory of change, not of origin. The evidence for the theory of evolution and a discussion of how it relates to the Bible is discussed in chapter nine. Bear in mind for now that if God created one life form, it certainly seems reasonable to believe that he may have created a number of different species at different times. It will be shown that the evidence from the fossil record is consistent with this view.

We will now proceed to look at the evidence for design in nature.

FOR TODAY

1. *In your own words, what does the second law of thermodynamics say about the processes required for the creation of life?*

2. *What is the significance of the four classes of biological molecules to the argument against the spontaneous generation of life?*

3. *You were given a somewhat complicated argument for why protein creation requires nucleic acids and vice versa. Could you explain that argument to someone else?*

4. *How do you believe life came about? Why do you believe this?*

5. *What does the nature of living things say about the creator of life?*

---

46 S. L. Miller, "Production of Amino Acids Under Possible Primitive Earth Conditions," *Science*, 117, 528 (1953).

47 Carl Sagan, "How Life Began," *Parade*, December 2, 1984.

48 In this chapter we will discuss how life originated on the earth. One possibility which has been given serious attention by scientists is that life originated somewhere else. This theory proposes that life from elsewhere seeded the earth. It now seems likely that life existed at one time on Mars. The study of life outside the earth is called exobiology. None of the arguments in this chapter are affected by this issue, because the fundamental chemical questions of how life was created would be the same anywhere in the universe.

49 In 1982 Nobel-prize winning chemist Thomas Cech discovered that certain classes of RNA have catalytic properties, proving that not all biological catalysts have to be proteins. Some have proposed the existence of an "RNA world," in which RNA both carried information and catalyzed cell processes. There is no evidence that this sort of biochemical system ever existed. The catalytic properties of RNA are very limited, making it appear unlikely that this hypothesis is valid. Even if it were, the arguments in this chapter would still hold. It would only transfer the same general chemical evolution problems to a different set of molecules.

50 Walter Hearn and Richard Henry, *Evolution and Christian Thought Today* (London: Paternoster, 1959), 66.

51 Melvin Calvin, *Chemical Evolution* (Eugene: Oregon State System of Higher Education), 34.

52 See my book, *Reasons for Belief: A Handbook of Christian Evidence* (Spring, Texas: Illumination Publishers, 2005).

53 Walter Hearn and Richard Henry, *Evolution and Christian Thought Today* (Paternoster, London, 1959), p. 67.

CHAPTER 5

WHENCE IS IT THAT NATURE DOES NOTHING IN VAIN;
AND WHENCE ARISES ALL THAT ORDER AND BEAUTY
WHICH WE CAN SEE IN THE WORLD?

SIR ISAAC NEWTON

COULD THIS ALL BE JUST A COINCIDENCE?

For those willing to study the evidence, the physical universe and the wonders of life cry out that there is a creator. Truly, the words of Romans 1:20 are confirmed by virtually every aspect of the natural world. "For since the creation of the world God's invisible qualities—his eternal power and divine nature—have been clearly seen, being understood from what has been made, so that men are without excuse." Without excuse, that is, for not believing in the God who created all these things. On every level, from the submicroscopic particles of physics, to the workings of a living cell and the wonders of the visible world around us, to the mind-numbing expanse of the cosmos-one can see the hand of a careful designer. The Designer created a world both practical and beautiful. Full of wonders to behold, designed to support very complicated forms of life, one can see the Creator in every aspect of the world around us. Some aspects of design have already been discussed, especially in the chapter on the creation of life. This chapter will describe a number of other features in nature which point to the God who designed all these things.

What is the measure of a good scientific theory? One aspect that marks a successful theory is that with time and the accumulation of empirical evidence, it can be applied successfully to answer more and more questions. Also, with time, the remaining unanswered questions raised by the theory are answered. The atheist world view does not meet this criterion. In fact, the opposite has been the case. In this chapter we will see that as our knowledge of nature increases, logical problems with the anti-supernatural assumption have increased.

It seems that every year a number of new scientific discoveries provide further reason to believe in a creator. This growing tide of evidence for design is behind a recent trend among the scientific community. For the past hundred years or so the strident atheists have increasingly presented themselves as speaking for all scientists. Recently, this trend has begun to reverse as a greater number of scientists have publicly declared that scientific knowledge supports belief in a creator. Most notable of these "conversions" is that of Oxford don, Michael Flew in 2004. For decades Flew has been one of the most influential philosophers of science. He had argued vigorously that science supports atheism. *The Times* of London named Flew as "one of the most renowned atheists of the past half-century, whose papers and lectures have formed the bedrock of unbelief for many adherents." In a recent interview,[54] Flew said that he now agrees with Einstein, who believed in "an Intelligence that produced the integrative complexity of creation." He is not ready to convert to Christianity, but rather says he "has become a deist like Thomas Jefferson."

Vocal atheists have not gone away, but there is a definite trend for scientists to accept the overwhelming evidence for a creator. As physicists look at some of the facts to be described in this section, many have found themselves giving credence to what has become known as the *anthropic principle.* The anthropic principle is not a scientific theory per se. It is an organizing principle which can answer the big question, "Why?"

It is important for the reader to understand that, in general, scientists do not ask the ultimate questions of purpose. This is left to the realm of philosophers and religionists. However, the evidence for purpose in nature is so overwhelming that some have embraced the anthropic idea. Put simply, the anthropic principle is the idea that there is a unifying principle explaining the laws of nature. *The laws of nature are what they are and the fundamental constants which underlie them have the values that they have, so that advanced life forms, such as humans, can exist in the universe.* The prefix *anthropo* means human. The word was chosen because the anthropic principle posits that the universe is human centric. Many scientists find the universe to be so finely tuned to support life that it is easier to understand and predict the laws which govern nature by simply assuming the reason the gravity force is as strong as it is, or that the electronic force is as it is, or the forces which hold nuclei together are what they are because that is what they need to be in order to make life possible.

Atheists scoff at the anthropic principle, but the fact is, many who hold to this principle do so only reluctantly. Michael Flew, for one, tenaciously resisted accepting design as a scientific argument for God. Even those who do not agree that the universe was designed in order to support life often make statements which appear diametrically opposed to the atheistic assumption. In the end, design speaks for itself.

Resistance of scientists to design arguments is not without cause. A claim of design, no matter how convincing, cannot be proven by experiment in a laboratory. One person's design is another person's fortunate but inevitable accident. On a personal note, I came to believe in God, in part, due to studying science and finding inescapable evidence for a divine creator of the natural world. However, as a teacher of the philosophy of science, I acknowledge that the intelligent design argument is an irrefutable hypothesis. It cannot be disproved by any reproducible experiment. It is therefore, in the final analysis, not "scientific." Besides, in my experience, I have often found some of the evidence used as "proof" of supernatural design to be unconvincing. Having read a number of writers on the subject, I have occasionally found myself taking the devil's advocate position when hearing arguments for creation based on evidence of design.

Several years ago I attended a lecture on scientific evidence for God by a man for whom I have great respect. His favorite example of design was the arctic tern. This amazing bird flies in an annual migration from the Arctic to the Antarctic regions and back again-a total of 18,000 miles per year. The tern flies from the fringes of the Antarctic to the northernmost areas of North America in a single flight of about nine thousand miles. For the entire journey, the tern passes over an environment which contains nothing it is willing to eat. How, the speaker asked, did the tern learn to fly over these many thousands of miles? How did these birds know that there was another food source half a world away if God did not design it with this knowledge built in? The point of the speaker was that God created the arctic tern with both the ability and the knowledge required to make this amazing journey.

The majority of the audience was convinced that this is very strong evidence for design by God, but as a skeptical scientist (which is the only kind there is), and even as a believer in design, I was not convinced of this particular proof. An evolutionary biologist can provide a "natural" cause of this behavior readily. He or she might theorize the existence of a bird that at one time migrated a shorter distance; say from the central part of North America to the northern fringes of South America. This biologist might propose a set of environmental pressures, such as a gradual warming of the earth or the infringement of a competitor, causing the tern to gradually shift its range toward more polar regions. Perhaps over thousands of years, a particular subgroup of terns found itself eating principally foods found only in the summer in the permafrost regions of northern Canada and the southern tip of South America. Perhaps God programmed the arctic tern to fly from the Arctic to the Antarctic, or perhaps he did not. Science cannot answer this question. The point is that for the skeptic the arctic tern is not convincing proof for supernatural design.

A good argument for design is one for which there is no reasonable natural explanation for the cause of the observation. I have taken great pains in this chapter to choose only arguments which meet this criterion.

When I began my study of apologetics, I was initially skeptical of many of the design arguments I came across in Christian literature. Despite my initial resistance, I eventually concluded that there remains an overwhelming body of evidence that the universe we live in was designed with the specific goal in mind of creating a place in which advanced life forms can exist.

The design argument (also known as the teleological argument) is not new. Its most famous proponent in the eighteenth century was Sir William Paley (1743-1805). Paley is famous for his illustration of the blind watchmaker. He argued that if one were to stumble across a watch on a beach with its dials, gears, springs and so forth, one would have irrefutable proof of a designer. Without a designer there can be no watch. It is irrational to propose that a functioning watch could be produced by random, natural forces. Paley's point was that the universe shows even more convincing evidence of design, which implies the existence of a designer. The designer is God. In the nineteenth century, with the rise of scientific materialism and with the publication of Darwin's theory of evolution, many predicted the demise of the design argument. As we will see in this chapter, this is definitely did not happen. Research in the past two generations has brought to light one fact after another which shows the inescapable fingerprint of a creator. Let us proceed to examining the evidence and arguments for design.

CARBON, THE MIRACLE ELEMENT

An example of apparent design is found in the element carbon. We will see that there is a rather long list of properties unique to the element carbon which are absolute requirements for life to be sustained. Simply stated; if carbon did not have the properties it has, there would be no life. The molecule building ability of carbon show clear evidence of design, and therefore of a creator. Why is that? To evaluate this claim, we must first enumerate the unique properties of carbon, and then reflect on whether it is more reasonable to assume these properties were the result of chance or of a designer intent on creating life.

Living things are made up out of molecules. As has already been described, the molecules out of which living things are made are large and complex. Proteins, the molecules which control everything which occurs in cells, are made up of tens of thousands of atoms all joined together to form a complex, three-dimensional shape. The backbone of all these molecules is composed of carbon atoms. Why carbon? Of the ninety or so naturally occurring elements, carbon is the only one that has the properties which allow large, complex, three-dimensional molecules to be synthesized. The properties of carbon allow for strings of dozens and even hundreds of atoms to form. *No other element* has the property that long strings of the atoms *of that element* can form into stable molecules. The reason carbon can form the backbone for large and complex molecules is that it has the ability to form relatively strong bonds with itself. Carbon can form ringed structures. It can form three-dimensional structures as well. Also unique to carbon is that it can form single and double and triple bonds with itself and with a number of other atoms. This makes carbon-based molecules amazingly varied in the kinds of chemistry they can catalyze. All of these properties are unique to carbon, and all these properties are absolutely necessary for life to exist.

When teaching organic chemistry to my college students, I like to illustrate the list of unique properties of carbon by recalling one of the original episodes of the *Star Trek* television series. One episode of Star Trek had Captain Kirk and the gang coming upon a monster whose molecular structure was based on silicon, rather than carbon. Spock said that this was very logical. There is a chemical reason the writers of this episode had Spock identifying silicon as a "logical" alternative to carbon. Silicon is the only element, other than carbon, which has the correct number of valence electrons which allows it to form a stable tetrahedral molecule. The reason this ability is important is that a central atom capable of forming four bonds is required in order to build three-dimensional structures. Nevertheless, Spock's claim that a silicon monster is logical does not work. Silicon-silicon chemical bonds are very weak. Molecules with more than two silicon atoms bonded to one another are very reactive and unstable. It is impossible to build a large molecule joined together by silicon atoms. With apologies to Star Trek fans, based on the properties of silicon, one can safely conclude that there never has been, nor will there ever be a silicon-based life form.

Without carbon's unique ability to form large, stable molecules with ringed structures and long chains of atoms, there would be no life. Any biologist, biochemist or chemist will confirm this indisputable fact. There is exactly one element in the universe with the properties that are *necessary for building the kinds of molecules required* for life to exist. The fact that there is a single unique solution to the problem of molecule building is evidence that the properties of carbon were designed with molecule and life building in mind. If some intelligent being were designing the properties of electrons, protons and neutrons, and therefore the properties of the atoms to allow for there to be living things, this being would have to create at least one element capable of making large, complex, flexible molecules. Recognizing the problem, it would appear that God created carbon.

OTHER ELEMENTS WHOSE PROPERTIES REVEAL DESIGN

There is much more design hidden in the periodic chart of the elements. From the lightest element, hydrogen, to the heaviest naturally occurring one, uranium, the fingerprint of God can be found. Uranium is an unstable, radioactive element. It has a half-life of 4.5 billion years. It just so happens that this is also the approximate age of the earth, according to scientific evidence. This is important because it is the heat generated inside the earth due to the decay of uranium which keeps the center of the earth hot. It is this energy which is the engine for plate tectonic movement. This recycling is essential both to replenish the nutrients in the earth's soils and to maintaining the atmosphere of the earth. Without tectonic activity, the surface of the earth would long ago have ceased to be able to foster diverse and fruitful ecosystems. Without a source of heat inside the earth, there would be no advanced life forms on the earth.

Another byproduct of the heat generated by uranium is the magnetic field of the earth. The cause of the magnetic field of the earth in not completely understood, but almost certainly the flow of heat produced by uranium decay away from the center of the earth is part of the mechanism. The heat creates the convection currents which move the continental plates and which also produce the magnetic field of the earth. This is essential to life because the magnetic field of the earth is what protects us from bombardment by the intense solar wind. The lines of magnetic force creates what is know as the Van Allen Belts, which force the dangerous high-velocity particles from the sun away from the earth.

Uranium has other properties helpful to sustaining a variety of kinds of life. A lot of radioactivity is dangerous, but low levels actually help the process of evolution of species by causing mutations. Evolutionists tell us that the radioactive properties of uranium are helpful, in fact that they are required to sustain healthy ecosystems. The point of this is not to teach a biology or geology lesson. The point is that we will see dozens of parameters which are essential to creating a place where complex ecosystems can be maintained. The curious fact is that for each of these requirements, there is exactly one element available in the universe which meets this need. This is evidence for design.

In like manner, hydrogen has unique properties which are required for the universe to sustain life. Apart from its role in the molecule water, hydrogen is the only element which can be used to power the fusion reactions in stars, without which there would be no life on the earth. Hydrogen fusion in the sun is the source of energy for life on the earth. Most people are not aware that the mechanism by which the sun produces its tremendous energy was not fully understood until the 1930s. Atoms of hydrogen have relatively massive protons and neutrons. When these atoms fuse to form helium under conditions of very high pressure and temperature in the sun, they turn mass into energy (according to the famous equation of Einstein: $E = mc^2$). This process releases an almost unimaginable amount of energy. Without the energy source provided by fusion of helium, there would be no life in the universe. Hydrogen is the only element with the potential to lose sufficient mass upon fusion to create a star. Again, we have an example of an absolutely essential property which is possessed by only on of the elements.

Iron is another element with unique properties which are absolutely essential for advanced life forms to exist on the earth. Iron is the only element with significant permanent magnetic strength. By coincidence (or perhaps by design) it also just so happens to be the element with the lightest protons and neutrons, making it the most stable element in terms of nuclear energy. For this reason, supernova events produce a lot of iron. This explains why it is the most abundant element in the core of the earth. This coincidence is very fortuitous for us. The iron in its core is essential to the magnetic properties of the planet. It is the magnetism of the earth which protects the planet from the lethal effects of solar wind, cosmic radiation and other forms of ionizing radiation as mentioned above. One of the biggest problems for long term space travel is that astronauts will be outside of this shielding. Those who have seen the aurora borealis, or northern lights, have witnessed the protective power of iron. The light is produced when the dangerous particles from the solar wind which are deflected by the magnetic field strike the upper atmosphere where the magnetic lines of force dip toward the north magnetic pole. Without the special magnetic properties which only iron has, and without the fortunate fact of its nuclear stability, complex life forms would be unable to survive on the earth.

Next, let us consider the essential attributes of the element oxygen. There are several properties unique to oxygen without which higher-order forms of life could not be sustained. The element oxygen is very reactive. It is so reactive that in high enough levels in the atmosphere it is toxic. However, it is the high reactivity of oxygen which makes it essential to species with a high rate of metabolism. It is the oxidation of food which provides all the energy for animals to life. Without oxygen, there would be no animal life. Another absolutely essential property of oxygen is its ability to exist as ozone (O_3 rather than the more familiar O_2). Ozone is the only naturally occurring molecule which has sufficient ability to shield the earth from the destructive effects of hard ultraviolet radiation. If a significant fraction of the shorter-wavelength ultraviolet light from the sun were to penetrate to the earth's surface, virtually all life would disappear. Without the energy-producing properties of the reactive element oxygen, and without the UV protection of ozone, another form or oxygen, there would be no advanced forms of life on the earth. Evidence for design is seen when we consider that of all the elements, only oxygen has these life-sustaining properties.

It would be easy to extend this list of absolutely required attributes for life to exist which are met by only one of the elements. One could mention the properties and abundance of silicon. Silicon exists in the form of silicates. These silicates are the main component of the earth's continental plates. Silicates are relatively light rocks, which allowed the continents to form in the first place. They have several physical properties essential to creating rocks and soil which can support a diverse ecosystem. Evidence for design can be found in the essential properties of nitrogen, helium, sodium, potassium, phosphorus and others. In every case, only one of the naturally occurring elements meets the need. Perhaps the reader is beginning to get the idea. The designer's fingerprints are all over the periodic chart of the elements. Let us summarize with a quote from Michael Denton, author of *Nature's Destiny.*[55]

> *The maintenance of the approximately constant levels of each of the twenty-five or so elements essential to life in the hydrosphere over the past 4 billion years via a set of interlocking cycles—the water, carbon, iron, magnesium, tectonic cycle and so on—conjures up the image of a vast terrestrial clock with the size and configuration of all its component cogs superbly tailored to fit perfectly together to ensure that the whole turns harmoniously and fine tuned to ensure that the individual cycles turn at the appropriate rate to maintain the required level of each of the elements, essential to life, in the hydrosphere.*

WATER, THE MIRACLE SOLVENT

Life requires a solvent in order to move essential substances from one place to another within an organism. It requires a solvent with almost the exact properties that water happens to have. In fact, if it were not for the existence of water and its unique properties, there would be no life anywhere in the universe. This is a strong statement, but it will hold up to the strictest scrutiny. The existence of water is further evidence that there is an intelligence behind the scenes intent on creating life.

So, what is so special about water? I am trained as a chemist. When I teach introductory chemistry, I spend a great deal of time listing all the ways in which water is a unique substance. For this amazing molecule the list of properties essential to the sustenance of life is so long that even the skeptic is inevitably drawn to consider design.

One of the special properties of water is that its molecules are very sticky. Most small molecules are only very weakly attracted to one another. Of all the relatively small molecules that exist, water has by far the greatest intermolecular attraction. Water molecules consist of two hydrogen atoms bonded to a central oxygen atom. The molecule is bent at an angle of 105°. This bent shape (as opposed to linear, 180°) is essential to the unique properties of water. In fact, if water were a linear molecule, it would not have a strong intermolecular attraction and there would not be life anywhere in the universe. The reason water is "sticky" is that the hydrogen-oxygen bond is highly polarized. In other words, the electrons which are shared between the hydrogen and the oxygen atoms in the water molecule are not shared equally. Oxygen atoms attract electrons strongly, compared to hydrogen, lending a partial negative charge to the oxygen atom and a partial positive charge to the hydrogen atoms in the water molecule. See the picture below for an illustration of the polarized structure of water.

(FIGURE 10.1) THE STRUCTURE OF WATER MOLECULES AND WHY THEY ARE "STICKY".

Having a polarized bond is not sufficient to make water sticky. It is the combination of its bent shape and polarized bonds which causes water molecules to be so strongly attracted to one another and to other molecules. To illustrate this principle, the molecule carbon dioxide, although it has fairly polarized carbon-oxygen bonds, is linear and symmetric, and therefore not polar. This non-polar molecule is therefore not sticky. Even though carbon dioxide molecules have more than twice the mass of water molecules, CO_2 becomes a gas at almost one hundred below zero centigrade. Carbon dioxide is definitely not a molecule which could act as a solvent to support life.

When water molecules approach one another, the positively charged hydrogen atom on one molecule is attracted to the negatively charged oxygen atom on the other. The O-H bond in molecules is the most effective of all chemical bonds at creating this stickiness (chemists call this hydrogen bonding). This is because of the light hydrogen atom being able to exhibit what is known as quantum mechanical tunneling. The theoretical basis of quantum mechanical tunneling was discovered in the past fifty years, but it has been necessary for life to exist all along. Why is the strong attraction between water molecules so important? The hydrogen bonding in water is what causes its amazing properties as a life supporting solvent.

An appropriate solvent for living things to function obviously has to be liquid at temperatures amenable to life. Because water molecules are so strongly attracted to one another, it has an extremely high boiling point for such a small molecule. If it were not for the stickiness of its molecules, water would boil at around -150°C, way too low to support life. The chemical reactions of molecules are too slow to support life below about 0°C because the molecules do not have enough kinetic energy to react with one another. In addition, the stickiness of water allows it to be a liquid over an unusually large temperature range, an important factor in water's ability to control climate. Above about 50°C, molecules become too unstable to maintain the delicate structures needed to sustain life. Below about 0°C chemical reactions are too slow. Above about 50°C molecules are not stable. Water is a liquid across this range.[56]

Because water is so sticky, it has another unique property which is necessary for life. Water's polarity allows it to dissolve many minerals. There is no other molecular compound which is both liquid at the proper temperature range and able to dissolve ions essential to life such as sodium, calcium, chloride, magnesium, potassium, iron and so forth. The mobility of ions in water is key to nerve signals moving within the brain and to the extremities. Virtually every important chemical reaction in living things depends on the solubility of metal ions. Water is unique in that it can dissolve both a great variety of molecular compounds and many ions. Chemists know water as the "universal solvent." Actually, water does not dissolve all molecules. This is fortunate because if water dissolved all molecules, there could be no cell membranes and no distinct cells. Non-polarized molecules are insoluble in water, allowing for the formation of non-water-soluble cell membranes

The stickiness of water has an interesting effect on its solid phase (commonly known as ice) as well. Because of the strong intermolecular attraction between water molecules, the crystal structure of ice is unusually loosely packed with a lot of space between the atoms. For this reason, water is one of only a miniscule fraction of all substances which has the property that its solid floats in its liquid. For virtually all substances, the solid is more dense than the liquid, causing it to sink. This very unusual property of water is key to the survival of life on the earth. When water freezes in cold weather the ice floats on the liquid water. The ice acts to insulate the underlying liquid. No matter how cold it gets, lakes over a few feet deep do not freeze through. If ice sank, lakes would freeze right to the bottom in cold climates, killing most of the life in the lake. This in itself would not be so bad, but one function of water is to act as buffer to limit the swings of global temperature. If ice did not float on water, the temperature of the earth would swing wildly. Climatologists models predict that during past ice ages, the entire ocean would have frozen through, killing off all advanced forms of life.

Water has another temperature-related property. A general rule for all compounds is that in any phase (solid, liquid or gas), as the substance cools it gets more dense. The *only* exception to this rule for any compound is water. At most temperatures, as water cools it becomes more dense. However, at 4°C it begins to expand. Theoreticians still struggle to explain this amazing phenomenon. This causes water below 4°C to float on warmer water. Although scientists do not completely understand why this happens, it makes great sense if one applies the anthropic principle. The abnormal density/temperature behavior of water dramatically increases its ability to act as a temperature buffer for the earth. For large bodies of water, the colder water (below 4°C) floats on the warmer water, allowing the water at the surface to freeze, preventing the loss of heat in the body of water. This absolutely unique density property of water works in combination with ice floating on liquid water to keep the earth's temperate within a moderate range. Both properties are required for advanced life forms to be sustained on the earth.

Water is a great temperature buffer. Because it is a very small molecule and so sticky, water is very unusual in that it takes a large amount of heat to change its temperature and to vaporize it. Water has the highest heat capacity (the amount of heat required to change the temperature of a substance by one degree centigrade) of any substance known. It also has the highest heat of vaporization of any substance. Most people are aware that the weather is much milder near the ocean than farther inland. This is the case because water is a great climate/heat buffer. In fact, if there were no oceans of water to act as a heat buffer, there would be no complex life forms on earth at all, because the surface temperature would swing by hundreds of degrees annually.

There is no other compound in existence which comes even close to having the properties needed to be the solvent suited to support life. This is another example of nature showing evidence of design. Some scientists have propose the possibility of a world in which ammonia (NH_3) was sufficiently abundant to be a life-supporting solvent. Ammonia is probably the second best choice of all molecules to allow life, because, like water, it is a small molecule and exhibits hydrogen bonding. The problem for this proposal is that ammonia is a gas over the entire temperature range appropriate to supporting life. In addition, ammonia only creates an extremely low solubility for the ions needed for life. It also is a much poorer temperature buffer whose solid sinks in its liquid. Bottom line, in the universe we live in, there is only one candidate molecule for life.

In this sense, water is like carbon, hydrogen, iron and uranium, In each case, multiple absolutely necessary abilities for the sustenance of life in the universe is met by only one of the substances in existence. This is a very strong indication of design.

From the perspective of a person who does not accept the anthropic principle, it appears to be very fortunate indeed that water has all the required properties as life's solvent. Is it reasonable to believe that this is an accident? If an extremely intelligent being were trying to design the properties of matter in order to allow for life to exist, this creator would have to design a molecule with properties just like those of water.

By the way, we have not even mentioned a number of other uniquely appropriate properties of water, which include the viscosity of both ice and water, the surface tension of water, and other useful properties of this amazing molecule. Imagine the power and the intelligence of the being able not only to create all the matter in the universe out of nothing, but also to imbue that creation with the correct properties to form water; the solvent for life.

DESIGN AND THE BIG BANG

Startling evidence for design is found when one inspects in detail the evidence for the big bang model, as well. The outline of the big bang theory has already been described. According to cosmologists, the creation event started a cascade of processes which inevitably resulted in the creation of an environment in which complicated living creatures could find a place to live. In this section we will see that the details of the physics of the big bang reveal that the initial creation of the universe was fine-tuned to allow for life to thrive. To quote from Nobel Prize-winning physicist Steven Weinberg,[57] "Life as we know it would be impossible if any of several physical quantities had slightly different values." Weinberg goes on to relate that "One constant does seem to require incredible fine tuning." These are the words of an avowed non-believer in creation. Weinberg is not overstating when he calls the fine tuning incredible.

Weinberg is referring to the balance between two of the four fundamental forces of nature. There are a total of four fundamental forces which hold particles together; the gravitational force, the electromagnetic force, the nuclear weak and the nuclear strong force. It is not absolutely clear to physicists why or even how these forces exist, nor why they have their particular size. It becomes crystal clear when one adheres to the anthropic principle. The force of gravity is a relatively weak force which works over fantastic distances, pulling objects with mass toward one another. The nuclear weak force is thirty-six orders of magnitude stronger, but acts over very short distances. It is responsible for holding the neutrons and protons in atoms together.

What physicists have noticed when modeling the big bang is that at the earliest moments of creation, these two forces (gravity and the nuclear strong force) had to be balanced to one part in ten to the sixtieth power.[58] If the force of gravity had been smaller by one part in a million, billion, billion, billion, billion, billion, billion, billion, then the universe would have expanded indefinitely without ever forming galaxies and stars. *Clearly, life* would not exist in that case! If the size of the gravitational force had been bigger by about the same fraction, the universe would have collapsed within a few million years. In that case, galaxies, stars, planets and life would never have formed.

Another cosmological "coincidence" is found in the balance between the amount of energy in the big bang and the size of the gravitational force. According to radioastronomer Sir Bernard Lovell,[59]

> *If at any moment the rate of expansion had been reduced by only one part in a thousand billion, then the universe would have collapsed after a few million years... Conversely, if the rate had been marginally greater, then the expansion would have reached such magnitudes that no gravitationally bound system (that is galaxies and stars) could have formed.*

This is not just the word of one noted physicist. The most respected cosmologist of our generation, Stephen Hawking has described in detail the set of amazing coincidences which allowed the universe to produce galaxies, stars, planets, and eventually life.[60] As Hawking has described, if there was even infinitesimally more energy in the big bang, matter would have never condensed in a way which eventually allowed for the formation of galaxies, stars and so forth. On the other hand, if the energy of the big bang had been infinitesimally smaller than it was, the entire universe would have crashed in on itself in a relatively very short time, never expanding out to a sufficient size to allow for the formation of galaxies, stars, planets, and, of course, life. Another noted astrophysicist from the University of Chicago, Michael Turner, has used an analogy to describe the amazing accuracy of how well tuned the universe is to producing life. "The precision" of the creation of energy in the Big Bang "is as if one could throw a dart across the entire universe and hit a bulls-eye one millimeter in diameter on the other side."

This coincidence is so astounding that those who choose to hold to a naturalistic view have been forced to make an incredible proposal. Recently, physicists have proposed that there are an unlimited number of parallel universes. According to this model, each universe has slightly different laws. It is just a coincidence that the universe we happen to live in was formed with just the right properties to allow for life. The supporters of the multiple universe theory have no empirical evidence to support their belief. This is reminiscent of the physicists who proposed the theory of continuous creation in the 1940s, as mentioned earlier. With both continuous creation and multiple universe theory, it would appear that philosophical aversion to the idea of intelligent creation is the principal motivation of the theory rather than scientific evidence. The thought that our universe was carefully and intelligently designed is rejected for philosophical reasons. A better approach would be to look at the evidence and let it lead wherever it will. In this case, the evidence from the fundamental forces of nature leads inexorably to design and a designer.

The precise tuning of the amount of energy, the force of gravity and the nuclear strong force are not the only evidence from the basic laws of physics for design. As previously quoted, Steven Weinberg mentions that there are "several physical quantities" which had to have a very specific value to allow for a universe which includes life. These coincidental values are no secret to physicists. They are the motivation for some to believe in the anthropic principle, as mentioned above.

Among the physical quantities which are just right to support life, one can include the strong nuclear force which holds nuclei together. If it had been just slightly weaker, atoms larger than hydrogen would never have formed, and there would be no life. If it had been just very slightly larger, only larger atoms would have formed, and there would have been no hydrogen, no stars, no fusion in stars, and therefore no life.

Further evidence for design is found in the cosmic coincidence of the size of the electromagnetic force. This is the force which holds the electrons on atoms. If the electromagnetic force were just slightly larger, then only ionic compounds could form. There would be no molecules-the building blocks of life. If the electromagnetic force were just slightly smaller, no compounds would form at all.

A few other examples of cosmological constants which are precisely "tuned" to allow for life follow:

1. The ratio of the mass of the electron to the proton.
   a. If slightly larger, there would be no chemical bonding.
   b. If slightly smaller, there also would be no chemical bonding.

2. The homogeneity of the initial radiation in the Big Bang.
   a. If slightly smoother, no galaxies or stars would have formed.
   b. If slightly less smooth, virtually all matter would have already condensed into black holes.

3. The size of the fine structure constant (which depends on Planck's constant, the charge of the electron and the speed of light).
   a. If slightly larger, no stars big enough to support life could form.
   b. If slightly smaller, no stars small enough to support life could form.

4. The decay rate of the isotope ^{8}Be.
   a. If faster, no elements heaver than beryllium form in stars.
   b. If slower, fusion of heavier elements would cause catastrophic explosions in stars.

5. The decay rate of the proton.
   a. If faster, life in the universe would be impossible due to radiation levels.
   b. If slower, not enough mass in the universe to form galaxies, stars and planets.

Other evidence for fine tuning of the fundamental constants in the universe can be listed. Such cosmological precision is not the end of the story. Aspects of the physics of solar system formation as well of the particular environment where the planet Earth finds itself are also spectacularly tuned so that advanced life forms can exist. Scientists now know that for a solar system to contain rocky inner planets stable enough to support life over great periods, gas giants such as Jupiter and Saturn are required to provide gravitational shielding against asteroid and comet strikes. Scientists now believe that the last spectacular impact occurred about sixty-five million years ago, killing off dinosaurs, putting mammals on a path to dominate the earth.

The occurrence of supernovas (stars which collapse and explode with a spectacular release of energy) must also be fine tuned. Such cosmological fireworks are required for the formation of elements heavier than carbon, and therefore for life to exist. The stuff of which our solar system is composed contains material produced in a supernova event. So supernovas are required for life, but they are also extremely destructive. If a supernova were to occur within one thousand light years of us, all life on the earth would be destroyed by the intensity of the burst of radiation. If supernovas were less common, there would be no life. If they were more common, again, there would be no life.

Most star systems are binary or even tertiary (two or even three stars gravitationally bound to one another). Fortunately for us, we are on a single star, as rocky planets such as the earth cannot orbit multiple stars. The type of galaxy and the location within a galaxy are also essential to life. The sun is in an elliptical galaxy, toward the outer edge. In non-elliptical galaxies, radiation levels are either too severe, or heavy elements cannot form. If we were closer to the center of our galaxy, radiation levels would be too high, and supernovas would be too common. If we were further from the center, there would not be sufficient heavy elements to form a life-sustaining planet.

Certain aspects of our planet we take for granted, but they are required for the earth to support stable advanced life forms over many millions of years. The tilt of the axis on the earth is twenty-three degrees. This tilt creates the weather which distributes the solar energy making the environment stable. Either too great or too small a tilt creates unstable weather. Even having a relatively large moon is important. The presence of the moon creates far greater stability in the motion of the earth. Without the stabilizing presence of the moon, the climate of the earth would fluctuate wildly, not allowing for advanced life forms to exist. The earth is the only planet in our solar system with a moon anywhere near to the mass of the planet by proportion. Calculations show that the capture of a large enough moon to stabilize the motion of a planet is a very unlikely event.

Even such seemingly destructive processes as lightning are required. Lightning is required to turn elemental nitrogen, N_2 into biologically usable compounds such as NO_2 and NH_3. Earthquakes and volcanoes are the inevitable result of forces required to recycle the elements of life. Hurricanes and tornadoes can be unfortunate events if one is caught up in one, but without the forces which cause these catastrophic events to occur, an even greater catastrophe would result. There would be insufficient weather to distribute heat and water in such a way as to allow advanced life forms to exist.

How was the size of the gravity force set? Why does the fine structure constant have the value that it has? Why did the big bang happen in the first place? Why is matter distributed in an evolving solar system in such a way that inner planets are rocky and outer planets are gaseous? By its very nature, the scientific method does not lead to answers to questions of ultimate causes. This is not the purview of science. However, there is one unifying principle which can answer all of these questions. The anthropic principle; the idea that the laws of nature were created with a purpose in mind can address all of these questions of why. The laws and the fundamental constants of nature were created so that the universe could sustain life.

At the beginning of this chapter, we asked a question, Is this all just coincidence? If it is, then it is a mighty big coincidence. The only reasonable conclusion is that it is not a coincidence. The universe was created as it is because the creator wanted to make a place in which advanced life forms can be created and thrive. The more one looks at scientific knowledge, the more one finds evidence that virtually every aspect of how the universe, the solar system, the earth and life were formed shows the work of a careful, intelligent, powerful creator behind it all. These are the fingerprints of God.

FOR TODAY

1. *Can you explain to yourself why the author does not accept the migration of the arctic tern as convincing proof of design?*

2. *Can you think of any aspects of nature other than those listed in this chapter which show the fingerprint of God?*

3. *What does the Big Bang and it's design features infer, if anything, about the nature of the universe?*

54 From a published interview of Flew by James A. Beverley, *Christianity Today*, (Carol Stream, Illinois: April, 2005).

55 Michael J. Denton, *Nature's Destiny* (New York: The Free Press, 1998)

56 There are some one cell "extremophile" organisms which can live outside this temperature range. These are not likely to have been the original life forms. Complex life cannot live outside this temperature range.

57 Steven Weinberg, "Life in the Universe", *Scientific American*, October, 1994.

58 P. C. W. Davies, *God and the New Physics* (London: Dent, 1983), 179.

59 Sir Bernard Lovell, *In the Center of Immensities* (London: Hutchison, 1979), 122.

60 Stephen Hawking, *The Universe in a Nutshell* (New York: Bantam Books, 2001) and Stephen Hawking, *A Brief History of Time* (New York: Bantam Books, 1996).

PART II

Questions of
Science and The Bible

CHAPTER 6

BUT AVOID FOOLISH CONTROVERSIES AND GENEALOGIES AND
ARGUMENTS AND QUARRELS ABOUT THE LAW,
BECAUSE THESE ARE UNPROFITABLE AND USELESS.

TITUS 3:9

THE BIBLE WAS WRITTEN TO TELL US HOW TO GO TO HEAVEN,
NOT HOW THE HEAVENS GO.

GALILEO GALILEI FROM THE LETTER TO DUCHESS CHRISTINA

WHAT ABOUT GENESIS?

It is time to change gears dramatically. In chapters three through five it was shown that a materialistic presupposition about the universe—one which assumes that there is no God—is not consistent with the evidence. The evidence leads to the conclusion that universe was created. Scientific knowledge leaves virtually no doubt that life was created as well. There is a creator. The fingerprint of God's inscrutable intelligence and spectacular power are found everywhere we look. As the psalmist said, "I am fearfully and wonderfully made." (Psalm 139:14)

If we have seen sufficient evidence to conclude there was a creator, a reasonable question follows: What is the nature of the creator? Which "God" created life? Was it Allah (the Muslim God)? Was it Brahman (the chief of the Hindu gods)? Was it the God of the Bible? Maybe it was some still-unknown God who has chosen not to reveal himself to mankind. Maybe the deist is right. Perhaps there is a power and an intelligence behind creation, but this power is impersonal—not caring to be intervene in his creation. Can knowledge of science play some role in answering this all-important question about the creator?

Questions about the laws of nature do not play a significant part in the Bible. Its principle theme is God's desire to have a relationship with man. However, the Bible does contain information and claims with implications for science. Careful analysis of the parts of the Bible which shine light on the laws of nature provide dramatic evidence that the creator of the universe has revealed himself in this great book.

It is the author's opinion that questions of science and the Bible are not the primary proof of the inspiration of the Bible. In my book on general Christian apologetics,[61] it occupies only one chapter out of ten. We will see that biblical science provides strong support to faith in the divine nature of the Bible. However, even more convincing evidence for the inspiration of the Bible may be found in Messianic prophecies, in the internal consistency of the Bible, in its historical reliability and other topics. While other areas may give even more dramatic evidence for the Bible than that provided by science, a careful and thoughtful investigation of how science relates to the Bible will provide a leg of strong support for belief in its divine authorship.

Not all people will agree that science supports belief in the Bible. The statement of the well known atheist and Bible critic Delos B. McKown represents a very common line of thought about the Bible:[62]

> *Christianity is scientifically unsupported and probably insupportable, philosophically suspect at best and disreputable at worst, and historically fraudulent.*

This statement represents a typical attitude of a broad spectrum of intellectuals toward the Bible, especially as it relates to scientific knowledge. As early as the eighteenth century, Scottish philosopher David Hume was making claims that the Bible contains myths which are unsubstantiated by scientific discovery. It is easy to claim that the Old Testament is full of myths and scientific blunders. The question we will ask is, Does this claim of scientific error in the Bible stand up to an open-minded and reasoned analysis of the Scripture?

Those who would criticize the Bible often begin by confidently pointing out the Genesis "myth" as proof of the ignorance of the writers of the Bible. Let it be conceded that whoever wrote the account in the first chapter of Genesis was not a trained scientist. The questions remain: Which part of the Genesis creation account is mythical? Where are the scientific errors? We will see that the creation account in Genesis shows uncanny scientific insight. It is the very lack of scientific sophistication of the Jews who wrote Genesis which makes the evidence for inspiration all the more striking. Let us look carefully at the Genesis creation account.

Before going into detail, it will be helpful to review the first chapter of Genesis in order to get an overview of the creation story. As a starting point to understanding the account in Genesis, consider the following outline:

1. God existed before the creation of the universe.
2. God created the universe out of nothing.
3. After he created the universe, God created life.
4. Last of all, God created human beings.

Where is the scientific error in this outline? We have already seen that the scientific evidence strongly supports the belief that the universe was created "out of nothing." The evidence is also strong that life was created—that it was not the result of random natural processes. Scientists agree that the origin of homo sapiens is a very recent phenomenon on earth's time scale. Is there anything in the broad outline of Genesis chapter one in conflict with the established facts of science? Does Genesis get the order of things wrong? In fact, is it possible that Genesis offers a more reasonable explanation of how the universe got here "out of nothing" than the materialist/naturalistic alternative?

The atheist can describe the big bang, but cannot explain how or why it happened. The Bible's explanation is not "scientific," but it does not conflict with science. The big bang theory has the universe appearing out of nothing, in agreement with the Genesis account. The mystery of the Big Bang theory is that it cannot explain what caused the unfathomable burst of energy which initiated the universe. There is strong evidence that the Big Bang occurred, but what caused the creation event? Is there any scientific precedent for such massive amounts of energy suddenly appearing out of nothing? Conclusive proof that the Big Bang actually happened will prove elusive, but the biblical account can explain *how* and *why* it happened.

What about the creation of life? The Bible claims in Genesis that life in it many forms was created by God. Despite many bold statements to the contrary, the fact is that scientists cannot provide a believable naturalistic explanation of how life began. The supernatural creation of life may be unsettling to many scientists, but the laws of nature seem to demand it. Atheists may not be willing to admit it, but the existence of life on the earth seems to be the result of a miracle. God takes credit for this miracle in the Genesis creation account.

In addition, one finds in Genesis the claim that the final life form created by God, was man himself. Fossil evidence shows man, the most intelligent of all creatures, to be one of the most recent species to appear on the earth. Again, the outline of the Genesis creation account parallels scientific evidence.

Let it be pointed out that the biblical explanation of creation is not a scientific one. The creation of the universe and the creation of life have no "scientific" explanation. Why is that? Unless one excludes the supernatural from consideration before looking at the evidence, the best, the most reasonable conclusion, is that the origin of life is supernatural—a miracle. The supernatural is, by definition, not scientific. We have already seen that the closer one looks at the unimaginable complexity of even the simplest life forms, the stronger the case for miraculous creation becomes. In addition, the more physicists explore the possible origins of the universe, the more strongly the evidence requires a supernatural explanation for its origins. The important point is that the Bible just happens to get it right, despite the fact that the writers had little if any scientific training or knowledge to draw on as they wrote. First God, then the universe, then life, then man. The striking accuracy of the biblical creation account will be made even more obvious when we look at it in detail and when we compare it to the creation accounts of other cultures.

Now let us take a closer look at the details of Genesis chapter one. To quote a few phrases from the first five verses. "In the beginning, God created the heavens and the earth... And God said, 'Let there be light,' and there was light... And there was evening, and there was morning-the first day." Genesis describes six "days" of creation. A number of approaches to understand the Genesis creation account have been proposed and defended. To simplify the discussion somewhat, we will narrow the alternatives to four theories which span the main ideas which have been defended.[63]

1. *The Literal Theory.* This approach takes the entire Genesis account in its literal, face-value sense, including six twenty-four-hour days of creation. This would imply that the earth is very young.

2. *The Gap Theory.* This approach allows for a very old earth, but also six literal days of creation. It proposes that there is a huge "gap" of time between Genesis 1:1 and Genesis 1:2. At the end if the initial period, God caused a global cataclysm which wiped out most or all of the former creation. The proposal is that Genesis 1:2-31 is actually a re-creation of life by God which happened just a few thousand years ago.

3. *The Day/Age Theory.* This approach takes the account in Genesis one as a chronological outline from God of what he did in creating the earth. Supporters of the day/age theory assume that the six "days" are not literal, but represent geological ages over which creation occurred. The writer of the creation account in Genesis used a common literary device of the Jews in order to explain God's creation to scientifically unsophisticated readers.

4. *The Genesis Myth Theory.* Followers of this school of thought completely discount the Genesis creation story. It has no validity historically or scientifically. The biblical creation story is one of a number of similar creation "myths" which were a common feature of ancient cultures—a nice piece of poetry with theological but not scientific significance.

To the person who is not aware of the evidence for the inspiration of the Bible, the fourth approach makes perfect sense. In a secular/humanistic culture for which science has become a virtual alternative religion, why consider a book over two thousand years old as a source of truth, especially about the laws of nature? However, for the person who recognizes that science knowledge demands creation of the universe and implies creation of life, the idea of supernatural creation by God deserves attention. Scientific materialism is a strong force in our culture. Despite this, most people ask themselves the big questions of life. "How did I get here?" "Why am I here?" and "Where am I going?" Humans have an innate sense that there is a purpose to life. If science cannot explain the origin and purpose of man, perhaps the creator revealed himself in some other way. Many people asking such questions will inevitably end up reading the Bible. There, the open-minded person will find marks of inspiration in the Genesis account.

To the person who recognizes the Bible "...as it actually is, the word of God" (1 Thessalonians 2:13), the fourth choice does not work. The idea that the Bible contains fables is inconsistent with what he or she already knows to be true. Hopefully, this belief in inspiration is not an untested assumption, but rather a conclusion derived at least in part from the evidence. However, even for the believer, it is an honest and good intellectual exercise to at least consider the possibility that the Genesis creation account is a fable or a myth. We have already seen that intellectual honesty requires that we not assume the answer before asking the question.

THE "LITERAL" INTERPRETATION OF GENESIS CHAPTER ONE

Let us explore the first alternative described above: the literal, face-value interpretation of Genesis chapter one. There are two points we should mention about the literal interpretation with its six twenty-four hour days. First, for one familiar with Western culture and thought, this would be the most obvious interpretation of the chapter. If one were to simply read the first chapter of Genesis, without looking through the lens of modern-day scientific discovery, and without knowing the traditional modes of expression in Hebrew literature, the literal interpretation seems to be the most obvious. The Near Eastern literary norms of a Hebrew writer might imply something different, but to the Western mind, with its emphasis on analytical thinking it seems pretty obvious. "And there was evening, and there was morning the first day..." One cannot blame the literalist for concluding that this implies a twenty-four-hour period.

This leads to the second key point of consideration for the literal interpretation of Genesis. The fact is that the earth appears to be billions of years old. The empirical evidence is unanimous about this. Despite the attempts of the young earth creationists to fabricate an alternate view, the earth appears to be ancient. We will not review the scientific evidence already presented, but one can summarize as follows: there is an apparent conflict between the face-value, literal interpretation of Genesis chapter one and scientific evidence.

So how can the literal interpretation of the creation account be reconciled with the facts of science? If we take as given that the universe and life were both created, as was very strongly indicated in chapters three and four, the question which remains is the means and timing of their creation. This leaves us with a theological question. Could an all-knowing and all-powerful God create the world in six twenty-four-hour days? The answer is obviously, yes. To the person who is convinced that the Bible is inspired, and that the God of the Bible is all-powerful, the literal interpretation of the creation account in the first chapter of Genesis is quite reasonable.

When Jesus created enough bread and fish to feed five thousand people, the bread and fish were created with an "appearance of age" (John 6:1-13). In fact, the fish was cooked already. It would be difficult to determine how "hard" it is for God to do these sorts of things, but one thing we can be confident of is that the universe exists, and it was designed by a creator. Creation with an appearance of age is not necessarily bad theology.

It should be noted, however, that the literal interpretation of Genesis is not a scientific theory. By definition, a scientific theory concerns known or measurable physical facts, which are governed by predictable natural laws. A miraculous event, if it occurs, is clearly a violation of these natural laws. The law of conservation of mass was violated when Jesus made fish out of nothing that day by the Sea of Galilee! This "theory" that God created the world in six twenty-four hour periods, even if it is true, is not something to be taught in science classes. It could be mentioned as a theological alternative, but it is not verifiable by any scientific experiment. Although science can be used to support the concept of creation, it cannot prove a particular miracle occurred.

Some Christians are defensive about this point, but they should not be. Those committed to reviewing these issues carefully should not be intimidated by creationists into accepting the untenable position that scientific evidence supports an age of the earth of only a few thousand years. As discussed in earlier chapters science does not support a young earth. The literal understanding of Genesis chapter one is not scientific by any definition of science. Being based on belief in a miraculous event, it cannot be disproved by science, but it is not scientific. It is a belief based primarily on faith in the truthfulness of the Bible.

For those who take the Genesis creation account at face value, let the author play "devil's advocate" in order to challenge their thinking. First, if the earth is only a few thousand years old, how can the fossil record be explained? It includes such apparently ancient species as dinosaurs and trilobites buried under hundreds or even thousands of feet of younger-appearing sediment and fossils. One could turn to the flood theory, but the flood cannot explain the entire fossil record without abusing the empirical evidence and a common-sense application of natural laws. We must deal with this kind of hard evidence with integrity. The fact is that if the earth is only ten-thousand years old or less, then dinosaurs never lived and neither did trilobites. There were no ancient fern forests which created great beds of coal as most were taught in science classes. Bogus claims of dinosaur tracks appearing together with supposed human footprints not withstanding, if the earth is only a few thousand years old, then triceratops, pterodactyls and a host of other species found only as ancient fossils never lived. It seems impossible to reconcile the fossil and sedimentary evidence with both a few thousand year-old earth and the existence of some of these apparently ancient species.

Besides, what about distant galaxies, hundreds of millions or even billions of light years away from us? How has the light from a galaxy at a distance of one billion light years managed to reach us if the universe itself is only several thousand years old? Why are we not seeing new stars suddenly appear in the sky whose light has finally reached us after traveling through space since their creation?

There are many similar questions that could be asked, a few of which were raised in the second chapter. How will the person who takes Genesis chapter one at face value answer these questions? More to the point, how will they answer these questions without resorting to the false claims of young earth creation science?

These are good questions, but perhaps there is a reasonable answer which does not require abusing the scientific evidence. Those who are inclined to the literal interpretation of Genesis might reply by stating that when God created the world, he created it with an appearance of age. When the earth was formed, it included fossils already imbedded in the ground. Also, at the moment when God created the stars, he also created light on a path from the stars to the earth, just as if they had already been there for a very long time.

The one playing "devil's advocate" might come back with the question, "Why did God put fossils of animals in the ground if they never even lived? If the earth is in fact young, why did God make it appear old? Was God trying to test our faith?" If the earth really is young, some might even go so far as to say this would imply God is deceiving us. To be honest, this is the main reason I personally reject the literal interpretation. I reject it, not because it does not agree with the science, but because it raises troubling philosophical and theological questions about God. In the end, I will have to admit that what troubles me may not trouble God. I do not know the mind of God. As far as I am concerned, God can create the world any way he wants. He certainly did not consult my opinion.[64] Let the readers decide for themselves about this theory.

To summarize, is the literal interpretation of Genesis scientific—can it be reconciled with empirical evidence? The answer is no. On the other hand, could it nevertheless be true if we resort to supernatural explanation? The answer is yes. The literal interpretation relies on faith in the inerrancy of the Bible rather than scientific evidence. Faith in biblical inerrancy is not blind. Fulfilled prophecy, historical accuracy, the amazing words of Jesus, the internal consistency of the Bible and many other evidences support belief in the accuracy of the Bible. Creation with an appearance of age is a theological claim of a supernatural creation. For this reason, science will never be able to prove or disprove this theory. Although there are some reasonable philosophical criticisms of this theory, it seems that we should respect the intellectual and spiritual right of others to hold to the literal interpretation of Genesis chapter one.

THE GAP THEORY

There is a sense in which the gap theory is a compromise between the literal interpretation and the day/age theory of Genesis one. This explanation was not originated in response to modern science. Christian writers in the first centuries, as well as some in the Middle Ages proposed ideas similar to gap theology. Modern gap theorists surmise that Genesis 1:1 is a summary of all cosmological time, including the creation of the universe, of the earth and of life. "In the beginning God created the heavens and the earth." There is a massive "gap" of time from the initial creation to the events which begin in Genesis 1:2. This gap would include the expansion of the universe, the formation of the sun and the earth, the creation of life and so forth. Genesis 1:2 begins, "Now the earth was formless and empty,..." The Hebrew *hayetah*, which is translated "was" in most versions can also be translated as "became." Based on this relatively uncommon translation of the word, gap theorists propose that at a point several thousand years ago, God caused a world-wide cataclysm to erase the prior creation. The earth "became" (rather than "was") void.

Starting from this presupposition, those who hold to the gap theory propose that God recreated the natural world in six, twenty-four hour periods. According to the modern version of this view, animals such as dinosaurs, which had gone extinct long before Genesis 1:2, were not recreated. Rather, only plants and animals which were around at the great cataclysm were recreated on days three through six.

Gap theorists have sought theological justification for the earth's creation being swept clean before the first creation day. They have claimed that the cause was a rebellion of Satan and allied rebel angels. The wiping out of creation was God's way of repairing the damage done by Satan and his angels. This theory was popularized in the early twentieth century by the influential study Bible of C. I. Scofield.[65] Unfortunately for gap theorists, theological justification for this theory from the text in Genesis is completely absent. Scofield uses a weak argument based on belief that Isaiah

14:11-23 is a reference to Lucifer, or Satan. This argument is weak because from the context, Isaiah 14:11-23 is about God's judgment on Babylon, not about Satan's fall from heaven.

Although this theory predates the scientific revolution of the sixteenth century, it can be seen as a way to preserve both empirical science and literal twenty-four hour days of creation. Unfortunately, as with many compromises between logical opposites, it fails to accomplish its goal. One can argue that this theory cannot be disproved, but there is no biblical justification for imposing a global cataclysm onto Genesis 1:2. There does not seem to be any logical motivation for God to wipe out his creation at this point. In the absence of a clear theological imperative or any biblical hint of this cataclysm (other than a questionable interpretation of one Hebrew word), it seems best to put the theory aside. This attempt to combine science and the literal interpretation finds no scientific or biblical justification.

THE DAY/AGE THEORY
OF GENESIS CHAPTER ONE

Let us now analyze our third proposed explanation of the Genesis creation account: the day/age theory. Those who use this theory generally believe that the Genesis account is an accurate depiction of the sequence of events in God's creation. However, they propose that the phrase, "and there was evening and there was morning, the first day," was meant by the Genesis writer to be taken metaphorically. In other words, according to the day/age theorists, the "days" of creation are not to be taken literally, but as a literary device. Rather than six "days" of creation, they believe in six "ages" They propose that the Genesis creation account is God's way of explaining to his people how he created the world-that it is accurate in describing what happened, but metaphorical in describing the actual amount of time involved. Neither the level of scientific knowledge nor the vocabulary of the Hebrew language would allow God to reveal the concepts of genetics, geology, chemistry or physics necessary to fully explain what he did when he created the world.

Young earth creationists, atheists and even some liberal theologians argue that the genesis of this theory is not good Bible interpretation. They claim that the day/age theory was created in the twentieth century as an expedient way to sustain biblical inerrancy in the face of new scientific evidence from the eighteenth and nineteenth centuries. In other words, science, not good hermeneutics,[66] was the impulse for the day/age theory. Such critics may have a point, but it is worth noting that theologians proposed the non-literal interpretation of Genesis chapter one long before the scientific revolution. Philo, a Jewish theologian of the first century AD, proposed that the days of Genesis represent periods of time rather than literal days. Influential Christian writers such as Origen (3rd century), Augustine

(5th century) and Thomas Aquinas (13th century) allowed for non-literal days. These writers interpreted Genesis one metaphorically for philosophical or theological reasons, not because scientists were looking over their shoulders.

In defense of the non-literal day interpretation, we should remember that the Bible is not a science book. The Old Testament was not written to explain cosmology or geology, but to reveal the nature of God (to scientifically unsophisticated Hebrews necessary?). The day/age supporter makes the point that to expect a Near Eastern author in the second millennium BC to write a literal creation story would be a cultural anachronism. This was not the style of expression of the day. When we allow ancient Near Eastern ways of thinking to influence our reading of scientifically relevant statements in the Old Testament, we will find that there is a striking agreement between the Bible and empirical science.

To further illustrate this point, let us look at the creation account in more detail. Assume for the moment that the account is given from the point of view of an observer at the surface of the earth (Genesis 1:1). This "observer" would first note that the sun, as it was formed, began to produce light. When the earth took shape it was spinning, and there were already periods of light and darkness (Genesis 1:3). Later, as the earth "evolved" through volcanic action, a separate atmosphere and ocean formed (Genesis 1:6-8). Next, as the planet cooled, lighter rock such as quartz and granite rose above the heavier basalt. Tectonic plates of this lighter material rose high enough to appear above the surface of the oceans, creating the first continents (Genesis 1:9,10). God created the first life forms (Genesis 1:11-13), gymnosperms (non-fruit bearing) before angiosperms (fruit bearing). As photosynthetic life proliferated, it absorbed large amounts of carbon dioxide from the atmosphere, allowing the earth to cool succiciently that the thick clouds finally parted, allowing an observer on the surface of the earth to see the sun and the moon for the first time (Genesis 1:15-19). Next, God created many different species of the higher life forms such as birds, reptiles and mammals (Genesis 1:20-25). Last of all, God brought to fruition his highest creation:man, *homo sapiens* (Genesis 1:26-28).

It seems reasonable to ask at this point where all the supposed scientific blunders are to be found in this description. The Genesis "myth," as some call it, does not seem to reflect the lack of knowledge of its authors, but rather shows an uncanny insight into scientific truth. Allowing for the simplification in language God used in order to communicate with a people of no great sophistication, the first chapter of Genesis just happens to agree in outline with modern scientific knowledge. The Bible believer may not be surprised at this fact, but the skeptic should take note.

To put the account of creation in Genesis into context, it will be helpful to briefly review current scientific theories of the history of the solar system, the origin of the planets, and the effect of life on the chemistry of the earth. The evolutionary theory of stellar formation describes the history of a typical star and its planets. Due to gravitational attraction, at some point the density of a cloud of interstellar matter reaches a critical point. Gravity causes the "cloud," mostly hydrogen, along with helium and some heavier elements, to condense rapidly. According to the second law of thermodynamics, when gases contract they increase in temperature. Eventually, the material near the center of this cloud condenses and heats to a pressure and temperature sufficient to initiate fusion of hydrogen. The inward pressure created by gravity comes into equilibrium with the outward pressure created by fusion. A star is born.

As the disk-shaped cloud contracts, not all the material falls into the new star. Material with sufficient angular momentum to avoid falling into the star coalesces into individual planets. Initially, these planets have thick atmospheres composed mainly of hydrogen and helium, with smaller amounts of methane andwater, and lesser amounts of other molecules. Because of their smaller size, higher temperature and bombardment by the intense solar wind, the innermost planets lose most of their hydrogen and helium. These planets also lose much of their lighter elements in this manner, causing them to have a significantly higher proportion of the heavier elements than do the outer "gas giants." As these inner planets cool, an outer crust of solid rock forms. Volcanism and other geologic activity produce a new atmosphere of heavier molecules such as carbon dioxide, sulfur dioxide and nitrogen.

At this point, let us shift our focus to what scientists believe happened specifically on the earth. There, the proper temperature and sufficient quantity of water allowed the formation of a layer of water to cover the entire planet.[67] As the crust cooled, the lighter silicate rocks were pushed upward, forming the continents. As the proper conditions existed to support life, living forms appeared. First, very simple one-celled species were created. Eventually, simple organisms capable of photosynthesizing appeared. This led to the reduction of carbon dioxide in the atmosphere, but raised the amount of oxygen to significant levels, creating conditions suitable for respiration. Oxygen-breathing animals appeared. As time passed, ever more complex and adapted species were seen on the earth, first in the water, and later on land.

The account above is a fusion of theory and evidence. It just so happens that there is a striking correlation between the account in Genesis and this model. Supporters of the day/age theory believe that this agreement is not a coincidence. They claim that this striking correlation is evidence that the Genesis creation account is inspired by God.

The strong parallel between the biblical creation account and scientific models leads to another question. Is this agreement with the scientific record unique to the Bible? All ancient cultures had a creation "myth." Do any of these creation stories have remarkable parallels to scientific models, similar to the Bible? It will be helpful at this point to compare the biblical account of creation to those from cultures and religions of antiquity. For example, Greek mythology includes the claim that all the animals were originally formed by the gods Prometheus and Epimethius. They formed them from clay molds-analogous to the production of cast iron. Greek myth also includes the idea that Atlas holds the sky up above the earth on his shoulders,as well as the view that the sun rides across the sky each day in Apollo's chariot. It seems impossible to justify such myths scientifically. Living things being created from clay molds, the earth being held up by a powerful god, the sun orbiting the earth: these claims cannot be made to agree with the evidence.

Ancient Egyptian religion included a creation story as well. The common creation myth of the Egyptians was that at the beginning the universe was filled with a primordial ocean called the Nun. The waters of the Nun were stagnant. Out of the limitless flood rose the primeval hill. This primeval hill eventually became the landmass of the earth. The priests of each of the great cult centers of Egypt claimed that their city was the point where the landmass of the earth originated. Some believe the great pyramids at Giza represent the primeval hill.

The Babylonian creation myth involved gods emerging from a divine swamp which had existed forever. These gods came out of the swamp in male and female pairs. As the younger gods appeared, they did battle with the older gods. In one battle, Marduk, the son of Ea (the earth God) attacked and killed the first god of all, Tiamat. He caught her in a net and crushed her skull. As the divine blood of Tiamat spilled to earth, the Babylonian creation myth claims that the blood and mud mixed and formed the first humans.

The ancient and traditional religion of Japan is Shinto. Shinto scripture holds that two gods, Izanagi and Izanami, were given a gift of a spear adorned with jewels. At the time of this gift, the earth was a muddy chaos over which the gods had flung a bridge. Izanagi and Izanami went out on the celestial bridge and thrust their spear into the muddy chaos. They drew it back, all spattered with mud. Some of the mud fell from the spear to earth, and formed one of the Japanese islands. Then these two gods came and took up residence on this island. Out of their union the eight principal islands of Japan were created.

It is difficult to say with authority what the Hindu creation story is, as there are a great number of different and sometimes contradictory lists of gods and myths, depending on what period of Hinduism is being discussed. One myth has the first man, Manu, arriving on an earth devoid of animals. Out of a sacrifice Manu offered to the gods, the first woman was made. Manu lusted after the woman, so she changed into a cow. Manu changed himself into a bull, and their offspring were cattle. Next, the woman changed into a goat, and Manu changed himself into a he-goat-and so forth-until all the animals were created.

A creation myth of the Native American Indian Iroquois nation relates that in the beginning there were two brothers, Enigorio and Enigohahetgea. Onoe was good and one was evil. The former went about the world, furnishing it with gentle streams, fertile plains and good fruits. The latter followed him maliciously, creating rapids, thorns and deserts. Eventually Enigorio turned on his evil brother and crushed him into the earth, where he still lives, receiving the souls of the dead and existing as the author of evil.[68]

One could include creation accounts from the Popul Vuh (the ancient Mayan scripture), or from other Native American tales, or from the Buddhist scriptures. The accounts here are representative of the genre. These creation accounts make for an interesting study, but it is difficult to take them seriously from a scientific point of view. The Bible is a striking exception to this rule. Many scholars and theologians put the biblical creation account into the same basket as these manmade myths. It seems to be reasonable to ask whether or not this is good scholarship. Is the Genesis creation account a myth? Where does the evidence lead? Let the reader decide whether the day/age theory is the correct interpretation of Genesis chapter one. However, if the day/age model is correct, then the amazing agreement of Genesis with science becomes evidence that the Creator had a hand in producing the Genesis creation story.

ASIDE: OTHER CREATION STORIES

Genesis 1:1-2:3 is not the only account of creation in the Bible. For example, Psalm 74:13-17 is a description of how God created nature. More significantly for us, there is a second creation account in Genesis 2:4-25. It is common for Bible critics to attack belief in biblical inerrancy by pointing out what they see as problems with the second creation story in Genesis. The criticisms fall into two categories. First, some make the claim that the two creation stories are irreconcilable—that they are in contradiction with one another. Second, the critics claim that the second creation account is in contradiction with scientific evidence.

A number of scholars believe that the two creation stories in Genesis were written by different authors. They point out differences in writing style and different Hebrew words for the name of God. Some go so far as to claim that the two different creation stories represent opposing schools of Jewish thought. They say that the editors who put Genesis into its final form had a debate over which account to include, finally deciding to include both creation stories despite their "contradictions."

Christian tradition has long held that the book of Genesis had one author, and that its author was Moses. The problem with this tradition is that there is no reliable evidence from the text or from ancient sources to support this view (other than the fact that the tradition itself is ancient). There is no theological imperative for Moses being the author of Genesis. In fact the evidence, including the two creation accounts, argues against Moses being the single author of Genesis. Therefore, it is perfectly reasonable to propose that the two creation stories were in fact originally created by different authors.

It is well established that the Old Testament was written by many authors. If the two creation stories did in fact have separate authors, that in and of itself would not affect one's conclusions about the truth of the Bible. The question to be asked is whether the existence of two creation accounts is evidence of biblical error.

There are two possibilities. Either the differences between the stories are irreconcilable, proving biblical error, or they are providing different but complimentary information. If this is the case, the inspiration of the Bible remains intact. This question is not unlike one arising in the parallel gospel stories. Many have claimed that the differences among the details found in Matthew, Mark, Luke and John show that the New Testament is filled with errors. The reality is that the parallel gospel accounts are complimentary, not contradictory. They are independent but accurate records of the life and ministry of Jesus Christ.

In fact, Genesis chapter two (actually, the second creation story begins in Genesis 2:4, but for simplicity we will call the two accounts "Genesis one" and "Genesis two") is not an account of the creation of the world. It is an account of the creation of Adam and Eve. A study of the second chapter of Genesis will show that it is an account of the creation and fall of man. Genesis 2:4-6 is an extremely brief recounting of the first five "days" of creation. The rest of the chapter is about the first couple. "And God formed man from the dust of the ground" (Genesis 2:7). It represents a relatively small proportion of what is described in Genesis chapter one as having occurred on the sixth day..

Where is the contradiction between the general creation account in the first chapter and the specific description of part of the sixth day in the second chapter of Genesis? There is none. Both creation accounts have the earth, then life, then man being created. Although claims of literary differences are valid, theological disagreement between the two accounts is *more a matter of perception than reality*.

BACK TO THE DAY/AGE THEORY

There are other reasonable criticisms of the day/age theory which literalists or non-believers raise from time to time. It seems fair to ask supporters of the day/age idea, "Why do you choose not to take the text of Genesis chapter one at face value? God said 'there was evening, and there was morning-the first day'. What is your reason for assuming that God did not mean exactly what he said?"

This certainly is a reasonable question. The intellectually honest believer in the day/age theory will not duck this question. A basic rule of biblical hermeneutics is that the most obvious interpretation of a given biblical passage is usually the correct one. Any interpretation other than what would seem the obvious one must be justified . What is "obvious" is not always clear, but in this case, the twenty-four hour day literalist certainly has a case.

Let us bring in another reasonable question to challenge the non-literal view. It has already been stated that the metaphorical interpretation of the creation days preceded the scientific revolution. Having said that, the fact remains that if it were not for the existence of knowledge gleaned from science, very few believers would have been converted to the day/age interpretation. The bottom line in this case is that scientific knowledge has affected the interpretation of scripture. One does not find the following in any list of standard rules of biblical hermeneutics: "Before interpreting any passage, cross-check possible scientific implications with current empirical evidence." This criticism is the crux of the creationist argument. Philosophically, it was also the underpinning of the charges against Galileo by the Catholic Church in his famous trial over the motion of the earth in 1633. The conservative Catholic hierarchy charged Galileo with heresy for allowing physical observation to trump what was then accepted biblical interpretation (albeit seen through the lens of Aristotelian philosophy). Many are uncomfortable with allowing empirical knowledge of the physical world to influence biblical interpretation. Some believe it is not allowable at all. This is the view of many creationists. Let the reader decide.[69]

What is the response of the day/age supporter to these challenges? How are they to explain the appearance that they let scientific evidence influence their interpretation of the Bible? The first thing believers in the non-literal interpretation should do is admit that there is some truth to this charge. Despite the fact that this interpretation can be justified by legitimate hermeneutics (see below), scientific knowledge is indeed playing a role here. To claim otherwise is dishonest. Galileo defended his right to teach heliocentrism by saying, "The Bible was written, not to tell us how the heavens go, but how to go to heaven."[70] But does that make it acceptable to reinterpret scripture in light of science?

Speaking on the same subject, no less a theologian than Augustine (354-430 AD) said, "If it happens that the authority of Sacred Scripture is set in opposition to clear and certain reasoning (based on observation), this must mean that the person who interprets the Scripture does not understand it correctly. It is not the meaning of Scripture that is opposed to the truth, but the meaning that the interpreter has tried to give it."[71] The wisdom of Augustine's words seems inescapable, especially with the hindsight of history. I know of no one who uses the Bible to defend geocentrism today. This is not because the Bible has changed, but because the evidence that the earth spins on its axis is conclusive. However, the reader should be aware that even today many creationists vigorously oppose this hermeneutical approach.

Second, in order to defend the non-literal sense of Genesis one, it should be noted that the Hebrew language used in this chapter may support a metaphorical interpretation of the days of creation. The key Hebrew word [redundant] is the one translated as "day." This is the word *yom*. It is the same word contained in the most sacred of Jewish holidays, Y*om Kippur*, the day of atonement. In order to decide the meaning of *yom* in the context of Genesis one, let us consider how the word has been rendered in the Old Testament. The King James version of the Bible of 1611, the word *yom* is translated as follows:

- 1181 times as "day" (but with several different connotations of the word, some not being literal)
- 67 times as "time"
- 30 times as "today"
- 18 times as "forever"
- 10 times as "continuously"
- 6 times as "age"
- 4 times as "life"
- 2 times as "perpetually"

Clearly, this word has a number of possible meanings, depending on the context. Even when translators use the word day, the connotation is not always a twenty-four hour period. Consider a quote from Isaiah 4:2, "in that day the Branch of the Lord will be beautiful and glorious, and the fruit of the land will be the pride and glory of the survivors in Israel." Here, even though the translators used the word *day* in translating *yom*, the context does not imply a literal twenty-four hour period. Instead, it connotes an indefinite period of time. The "day" being referred to in this prophecy is the entire period of the Christian dispensation.

Translators of Genesis are unanimous in using day for *yom* (as opposed to time or age or another word) for good reason. The context does seem to demand the use of the word day because of its reference to evening and morning. In the end, whether the use of *yom* is literal or metaphorical is debatable, but the various uses of the word as shown above show that it does not have to be literal. In the end, it is unwise to be dogmatic on this issue.[72]

There is a third point to be raised in support of non-literal creation days in the Genesis account. If one attempts to take the information supplied by the Genesis author literally, the details provided about what happened on the sixth "day" appear to argue against a twenty-four hour period. It seems impossible that the number of things described as happening on that day could be compressed into twenty-four hours. This is especially striking if nearly all of Genesis 2:7-24 happened on this day as well.

Let us look at the sixth day of creation as described briefly in chapter one and in more detail in chapter two. On this day, God first created a number of kinds of animals. After this, he created Adam. On the same "day," Adam named all the creatures in the garden. Despite the novelty of all this, Adam had time to grow very lonely. He fell asleep, and while he was sleeping, Eve was created. It seems hard to believe all this could have happened in a literal, twenty-four hour day.

To summarize, one approach to understanding the Genesis creation account is to assume that each of the six "days" of creation metaphorically represents one of the ages which God used to create the world which we observe around us. It has been shown that, as an outline, the description in Genesis one is in agreement with scientific evidence and models. Yes, there are some legitimate-but not insurmountable-philosophical and hermeneutical questions with regard to this view of creation. However, on balance this is a reasonable view of the Genesis creation account.

THE GENESIS MYTH THEORY

Let us delve into one more approach to thinking about the creation account found in Genesis chapter one. We will now explore the possibility that it is a myth or a fable. According to this view, the biblical creation account is more or less the same as any of dozens of similar creation stories which almost all ancient cultures produced. It has value to the cultural anthropologist or to the historian of religion, but any attempt to find scientifically valid material is certain to fail, because it was produced by a people from a pre-scientific age. To understand the origin of the Genesis story of creation, the avenue most likely to succeed is to compare it to the even older creation myths of the Sumerians, the Babylonians or the Egyptians. This view is held by the majority of intellectuals in Western culture. It is a virtually unchallenged assumption of the academic elite. As has already been said, for the person who has not studied the mountain of evidence for biblical inspiration, this view appears to be the most logical and reasonable. Given that the Jews did in fact live in a pre-scientific culture, it is what common sense would predict.

First of all, note that the Genesis myth theory does not conflict with current scientific knowledge. It makes no scientific claims, so from a scientific perspective it is an irrefutable hypothesis. In this sense, it is not completely unlike the literal approach (creation with an appearance of age) mentioned above. However, the similarity ends there. Although this theory makes no positive scientific predictions, it does make a negative prediction. In other words, if Genesis one is a fable, then it must contain scientific nonsense. This is where the myth theory breaks down. How can the agreement of the Biblical account of creation with scientific knowledge be explained? This weight of this question is made more obvious when the creation story in Genesis is compared to creation myths created by other peoples as described above. The creation stories of the Egyptians, the Greeks, the Hindus and others certainly do not jibe with current scientific understanding!

Those who claim that the Genesis creation story is a myth support their conclusion by pointing out parallels with the creation stories of neighboring cultures, especially those of the Sumerians and the ancient Babylonians. The implication is that the Hebrew writers borrowed from the more dominant cultures in Mesopotamia.

To support this they point out that the Sumerian creation story starts with water, is followed by land, which is followed by life. It is possible that the parallel with the Hebrew story is not coincidence, but the Sumerian myth includes multiple gods. The mating of these gods lead to creation of other gods and the creation of life and of human beings. The Sumerian creation model is certainly not in accord with scientific models, nor is it consistent with the orderly nature of creation. Who borrowed from whom? It seems illogical that a creation story which has remarkable scientific accuracy and which implies cosmos rather than chaos cannot be borrowed from the Sumerian, the Babylonian or any other creation account.

Comparison of Genesis one with scientific knowledge implies a transcendent source for the creation story. Why do most intellectuals miss this strong implication? Perhaps this is partially explained by the fact that the vast majority assume before even asking the question that Genesis is the product of human, not divine wisdom. We have seen many times already that when people begin an investigation by assuming the answer, the final conclusion is a foregone one. Assuming that Genesis is mythical is a poor start for asking in an open-minded way whether there are signs of inspiration in the book.

The fact is that the overall evidence for inspiration of the Bible is very strong indeed. When one evaluates the weight of the evidence for the inspiration of the Bible, it seems wise to begin by giving the Genesis creation story the benefit of the doubt. Those who have not researched the evidence for biblical inspiration seriously would do well to study the evidence for the resurrection of Christ as well as biblical prophecies about the Messiah.

Speaking for myself, if I had never studied the Old Testament messianic prophecies which predict in amazing detail the birth, life, betrayal, death and resurrection of Jesus Christ, I might be less inclined to give the Genesis writer the benefit of the doubt. If I had never pondered the miraculous accuracy of the Bible as history, I might have reached a similar conclusion about the creation story in the Bible.[73] Obviously, most books are not inspired by God. One should not be surprised that those who have not looked at the totality of the evidence for divine revelation in the Bible reach an incorrect conclusion about Genesis. For them the assumption that Genesis is entirely of human origin seems reasonable. In view of the marks of inspiration which pervade the Bible, and which distinguish it from the writings of all other world religions, it becomes very difficult for a reasonable person to dismiss the book of Genesis as a myth. When the scientific accuracy of the Biblical account of creation is compared to the fabulous creation stories of ancient cultures, one cannot help but be impressed with the Bible—the Word of God. Genesis one is not a myth.

CONCLUSION

What is the conclusion of the matter? Four possible explanations of the Genesis creation account have been reviewed. Which is the "right" point of view? Was the earth created over six twenty-four hour periods just a few thousand years ago? Does the gap theory successfully save the evidence for an old earth and the literal interpretation of Genesis? Are the biblical creation days metaphorical representations of great ages? Is the whole thing a myth of human origin? The reader will make his or her own decision. "I do not know yet" is always an option.

In summary, evaluate these conclusions. The gap theory is inconsistent with scientific evidence and is not supported by biblical statements or by theological imperative. The Genesis myth theory cannot explain the scientific accuracy of the biblical creation account. Besides, it seems to fly in the face of great evidence for biblical inspiration. The literal creation-with-age view does not directly conflict with scientific evidence because it imposes a supernatural solution to the problem. However, it leaves some nagging theological questions. There may be some legitimate hermeneutical questions about the day/age theory, but it is consistent with biblical theology, with scientific models with empirical evidence, and with the great evidence overall for biblical inspiration. As I have analyzed and considered all the theories I'm convinced that day/age theory is correct. Perhaps my training as a scientist creates a bias. As you study you must come to your own conclusion.

Despite all the efforts of scientist and theologians alike, the fact is that one can never absolutely prove how or when the universe was created. It is impossible to go back into the past and do an experiment to determine what happened. The creation event is not reproducible. What we do know is that the universe was created (chapter three). Life exists because of supernatural creation, not random natural forces (chapter four). Scientific evidence supports the claim that these events occurred in the distant past. However, the possibility remains open that God could have created the universe with an appearance of age.

It seems reasonable to ask whether one's personal interpretation of the first chapter of Genesis is an issue of pivotal importance to Christian faith. Christian teaching can be divided into the essential, the important and the unimportant. Many creationists make strong claims that the acceptance of the literal interpretation of Genesis is an essential aspect of faith in Jesus Christ. One gets a sense from some young earth creationist writings that salvation may hang on whether one accepts the six twenty-four hour day creation doctrine. It is difficult to defend this contention biblically. In this context, the words of Jesus to the Pharisees are appropriate. To those who "majored in the minors," of the law, Jesus admonished that they had "neglected the more important matters of the law-justice, mercy and faith. (Matthew 23:23). It is reasonable to assert that any question which does not affect a person's salvation or his or her daily relationship with God can safely be categorized as an unimportant issue. To quote from Titus 3:9, "But avoid foolish controversies and genealogies and arguments and quarrels about the law, because these are unprofitable and useless." It seems that heated, drawn out debates about the "correct" interpretation of the Biblical creation account fall into the category of "unprofitable and useless" controversy.

Christians are well advised to think about the issue of creation from a scientific perspective. That is why this chapter was written. It certainly falls into the category of questions about which we should be "prepared to give an answer" (1 Peter 3:15). This is true, not so much because it is important to believers, but because of its importance to those who potentially may come to believe.

The Genesis creation account is not the only area of scientific knowledge dramatically supporting belief in the inspiration of the Bible. In the next two chapters we will look at a number of remarkable Bible statements and teachings which are in uncanny agreement with scientific evidence. This will provide further reason to believe in the divine authorship of the Bible.

FOR TODAY

1. In light of the discussion above, what do you believe is the most reasonable interpretation of Genesis chapter one and two?

2. This chapter leaves the final answer of how to interpret Genesis one to the reader. How do you feel about the fact that there is a significant question about the Bible for which you cannot determine the truth absolutely?

4. Do you believe it is a significant matter to the Christian faith whether Genesis chapter one was intended to be taken literally or not?

RECOMMENDATION

Read a book or do a careful study of material available on the internet about creation "myths" and think carefully about the claim in this book that the Genesis account stands alone among these stories.

61 John M. Oakes, *Reasons for Belief: A Handbook of Christian Evidence* (Spring, Texas: Illumination Publishers, 2005).

62 Delos B. McKown of Auburn University, an essay in *Science and Religion* (San Diego: Greenhaven Press, 1988), pp. 65-71.

63 A number of other approaches to explaining and interpreting the creation account in Genesis have been proposed. More thorough treatment of the alternative theories can be found in Douglas Jacoby, *Genesis, Science and History* (Billerica Massachusetts: DPI Books, 2004), 115-121, and in Alan Hayward, *Creation and Evolution* (Minneapolis Minnesota: Bethany House Publishers 1995), 161-168. Other theories include the Revelatory Day Theory, the Intermittent Days Theory and the Literary Theory.

64 See Job 38-41.

65 C. I. Scofield, *The Scofield Reference Bible* (New York: Oxford University Press, 1945), p 3-4.

66 Hermeneutics can be defined as the systematic methodology for interpreting literary passages.

67 The earth is not the only satellite in our solar system to be covered by a significant amount of water. Evidence increasingly supports the conclusion that Mars once had rivers and large bodies of water. Also, two of the moons of Jupiter, Callisto and Europa, are believed to be covered by oceans of water underneath kilometers-thick layers of ice.

68 The source used for these creation myths is Daniel G. Brinton, *The Myths of the New World*, reprint of the 3rd ed. (Baltimore, Maryland: Genealogical Publishing Company, 1974).

69 An excellent book which discusses the philosophical issues at the interphase between theology and science from an historical perspective is Wade Rowland, *Galileo's Mistake* (New York: Arcade Publishing, 2001).

70 Actually, Galileo probably did not originate this saying. It has been attributed to the Catholic church historian Caesar Baronius (1538-1607).

71 From Augustine, *Epistula* 143, n7 pl 33, col. 588. Translation taken from Wade Rowland, *Galileo's Mistake* (New York: Arcade Publishing, 2001), p 230.

72 A novel and interesting approach to thinking about the six days of creation can be found in a book by Gerald L. Schroeder, *The Science of God* (New York: Broadway Books, 1997). Schroeder uses the concept of relativistic time dilation to produce a mathematical model which contains the fifteen billion year history of the universe in six literal days of exponentially decreasing length. A Ph.D. physicist and a theologian, Schroeder combines mathematical rigor, careful theology and some speculation to produce a theory which the reader may find worthwhile wading through.

73 Evidence for inspiration of the Bible is found in the book, John M. Oakes, *Field Manual for Christian Apologetics* (Spring, Texas: Illumination Publishers, 2011).

CHAPTER 7

IF YOU LISTEN CAREFULLY TO THE VOICE OF THE LORD YOUR GOD
AND DO WHAT IS RIGHT IN HIS EYES, IF YOU PAY ATTENTION TO HIS
COMMANDS AND KEEP ALL HIS DECREES, I WILL NOT BRING ON YOU
ANY OF THE DISEASES I BROUGHT ON THE EGYPTIANS, FOR I AM
THE LORD WHO HEALS YOU.

EXODUS 15:26

RATTLESNAKE FAT, ANYONE?

It is a common belief that the Old Testament is a collection of myths and fables, created by various Jewish teachers to justify and explain their own concept of God. The truth of this claim is not all that difficult to test. If the Bible contains the musings and imaginings of a number of religious men separated in time by hundreds of years, then it can be expected to include inconsistencies of message and obvious historical exaggerations and mistakes. More relevant to the subject addressed in this book, if the Bible were the production of human intelligence, it would contain statements about scientifically related issues which would reflect the almost *complete lack of scientific knowledge of its writers*. It the Bible was of human origin, it would undoubtedly include many "old wives tales." Its concept of things such as the origin of the earth, medical knowledge, geology and world geography would be a reflection of the myths and folkloric beliefs of the Egyptian, Babylonian, and other cultures which surrounded the Israelite nation.

A look at extant writings from the ancient Near East at a time contemporary to the writers of the Old Testament reflects this observation. Consider the extant writings of the Greek historian, Herodotus. He lived from 484 to 425 BC. Along with Thucydides, he was the greatest of the ancient Greek historians) He is widely-regarded as the father of the study of history. Although he was a great thinker, innovator, and collector of historical information, his histories mix truth with legend, and are tainted by ethnic prejudice. His political bias was sufficient to earn him the epithet "the father of lies." Most of the histories left behind by ancient cultures were commissioned by a king or other government official as a record of their accomplishments. They were meant to impress both friend and enemy, not to record accurate history. These histories invariably show a blatant prejudice, extolling the virtues of the current regime, minimizing or ignoring its defeats and faults. If the histories of the ancient Near East are to believed, none of the kings who left behind records ever lost a war!

However, there is one historical record of the time which is in stark contrast to this pattern—the Bible. In the Bible, one finds a record uniformly consistent with archaeological and historical evidence about the rulers and cultures from the region where its characters lived at the time in which the accounts are set. Perhaps even more startling, the Bible records the defeats, mistakes, and sins of the leaders of the nations of Judah and Israel. It does so in lurid detail. The greatest king in the history of the Jews was David, the slayer of Goliath. He was the general who united the nation of Israel and defeated the Philistines, the Arameans and all the enemies of God's people. He is described as a man after God's own heart—the greatest poet and songwriter of the people of God. Yet in the Bible one also sees David's failure as a husband and as a father. David, the greatest king of Israel falls into lust, adultery and even murder. No book of its time comes close to the Bible in both accuracy and honesty as history.

But what about the science of the Bible? The Old Testament has a great deal of historical information which can be compared to external material for accuracy. On the other hand, statements with scientific relevance which can be used to ask about biblical inspiration are relatively scarce. We are talking about dozens rather than thousands of examples. Nevertheless, we will see that to the extent that the Bible does contain claims or prescriptions which are relevant to scientific discoveries, it provides further evidence of the inspiration of the Bible.

Of the different fields of science, it is the area of medical knowledge that the Bible touches on the most. There are a sufficient number of Biblical references to medical science issues that this entire chapter will deal exclusively with this topic. The next chapter will be devoted to areas of science other than medical knowledge which are mentioned in the Bible.

The first five books of the Old Testament were called "the Law" by the Jews. Jesus refers to the five books of the Law-the Pentateuch—when he says in Luke 24:44 "Everything must be fulfilled that is written about me in the Law of Moses, the Prophets and the Psalms." Here he is referring to the three divisions of the Hebrew Bible. These divisions are the Law (*Torah* in Hebrew, Genesis-Deuteronomy), the prophets (*Nevi'im* in Hebrew, Joshua-Esther except Chronicles as well as Jeremiah-Malachi) and the Psalms (or "Writings," *Kethubim* in Hebrew, Job-Song of Songs, Chronicles).

The third book of the Law is Leviticus. This book contains the greatest portion of the legal code in the Old Testament. A number of the regulations included in Leviticus cover health and diet issues. Many of the restrictions have implications which can be examined in the light of modern medical scientific knowledge. Before doing this, however, it will be helpful to mention the nature of medical knowledge in cultures bordering Israel in the time frame of the writing of Leviticus. It is reasonable to assume that if the Bible is a book written by man, reflecting human rather than divine wisdom, its allusions to medical questions will reflect the level of insight or ignorance of the dominant cultures in the Near East at the it was written. On the other hand, if the Bible is inspired by God, one would expect it to reveal medical wisdom which reflects that inspiration.

Of the ancient cultures surrounding Israel, the Egyptians are thought to have been the most advanced in medical knowledge. They performed dental operations and even brain surgeries. Because of a trial and error process, their books contain some helpful medical advice. However, some of the prescriptions in Egyptian writings will not stand up to modern scientific scrutiny, to put it mildly.

The best known collection of Egyptian medical practice is the Ebers Papyrus. This compendium of health advice was a sort of PDR (physician's desk reference) of its day. It was written about 1550 BC. This makes the Ebers Papyrus particularly relevant to our study, as it was recorded within a century or so of when the Levitical code was first received by Israel (assuming that it was given by God to Moses at Mt. Sinai).

For insight into the scientific reliability of the Ebers Papyrus consider one of its prescriptions: "To prevent the hair from turning gray, anoint it with the blood of a black calf which has been boiled in oil, or with the fat of a rattlesnake." Concerning hair-loss, the Ebers document advises, "When it falls out, one remedy is to apply a mixture of six fats, namely those of the horse, the hippopotamus, the crocodile, the cat, the snake, and the ibex."[74] Other prescriptions from the Ebers Papyrus include such drugs as dust-of-a-statue, shell-of-a-beetle, head-of-the-electric eel, guts-of-the-goose, tail-of-a-mouse, fat-of-the-hippopotamus, hair-of-a-cat, eyes-of-a-pig, toes-of-a-dog, and semen-of-a-man.[75]

These medicines may seem humorous to the modern reader, but the consequences of this medical and scientific ignorance was surely devastating to the people of that day. These medicinal concoctions are listed not so much to reveal the ignorance of the Egyptians at that time, but to provide a background against which one may compare the writings of the Old Testament-writings from approximately the same time period as those of the Ebers Papyrus. Here is the point. If the Bible was written without the influence of divine inspiration such unreliable and dangerous medical advice would certainly have crept into the health provisions in the Old Testament, especially in the book of Leviticus.[76]

Through most of its history, the Jewish nation as a whole has been noted for its medical knowledge. This fact can be partially explained by looking at the Bible passages we will review in this section. Through observing biblical commands regarding health practices, the Jewish people have been relatively advanced in medical science. To the extent that the Jews followed the "prescriptions" in the Old Testament, they were definitely ahead of their cultural counterparts.

Let us anticipate a response to the apparent medical wisdom in the Old Testament by a skeptic. Perhaps the Jews were somehow inherently more talented in discovering medical knowledge than their neighbors. Perhaps that can explain their medical skill and the unmistakable wisdom of the health advice in Leviticus. This explanation will be shown false if one looks at non-biblical Jewish medical writings. An excerpt from a Jewish book of medical knowledge from a time roughly contemporary to the writing of the New Testament will illustrate this point.[77]

> "*Whatever God created has value.*" *Even the animals and the insects that seem useless and noxious at first sight have a vocation to fulfill. The snail trailing a moist streak after it as it crawls, and so using up its vitality serves as a remedy for boils. The sting of a hornet is healed by the housefly, crushed and applied to the wound. The gnat, feeble creature, taking in food but never secreting it, is a specific against the poison of a viper, and this venomous reptile itself cures eruptions, while the lizard is the antidote to the scorpion.*

Would anyone like to try one of these prescriptions? Does it support the idea that the Jews were inherently better at discovering useful medical knowledge than other peoples? Also, note the scientific error regarding the digestive system of gnats. Actually, they do produce excrement. This may seem humorous, but the point is that if the Bible were of human origin, it would contain such obvious scientific mistakes. As we will discover, it does not. It seems reasonable to agree with the writer that "everything God created has value," but most people would presumably not be eager to try out these prescriptions. This passage is typical of the writings of the Jews of the age as well as those of the Egyptians and other cultures at that time. However, it is in remarkable contrast to what can be found in the Bible. Why? Because the Old Testament writers were lucky? Because the scribes were using the scientific method to carefully examine their medical practices? Or could it be a sign that the Bible is no ordinary book, but rather the inspired Word of God? As the following sections are presented, the readers will judge for themselves.

Please note that no one is claiming that all the medical knowledge of the ancients, be they Egyptian, Chinese, Indian, Greek, Native American, or any other culture is mere superstition. Through trial and error methods, ancient cultures evolved medical knowledge which is of some value. However, this folklore inevitably contains a large proportion of remedies which are about as effective as using rattlesnake fat to prevent premature grayness.

This study will focus primarily on Leviticus, a book of Law received by Moses from God at a time contemporary to the writing of the Embers Papyrus. According to the Bible, Moses was born in Egypt roughly one hundred years after the writing of the Embers Papyrus. Those who claim that the Bible is a collection of opinions of Hebrew writers from the first millennium BC ought to compare Leviticus to the Ebers Papyrus.

To begin, read this remarkable claim made by God through Moses to the nation of Israel while they were wandering in the wilderness, as recorded in Exodus 15:26:

> *If you listen carefully to the voice of the Lord your God and do what is right in his eyes, if you pay attention to his commands and keep all his decrees, I will not bring on you any of the diseases I brought on the Egyptians, for I am the Lord who heals you.*

Here Moses has God claiming that if the nation of Israel will obey his decrees, they will avoid all kinds of diseases common to their neighbors. History bears out the ramifications of this claim. The Jews have always been a relatively small nation, yet they have survived repeated invasions and even attempts at extermination. Time and again the Assyrians, the Babylonians, the Greeks, the Romans and others have attacked and scattered the Hebrew people. Although scattered, the Jews have somehow always managed to recover and to grow in number. There are undoubtedly cultural reasons for the Jewish resilience. There may even be divine reasons the Jews always bounced back from tragedy, but one factor in the remarkable stability of the Jews has been their health practices as recorded in the Old Testament.

Let us look at Leviticus chapter eleven. In this chapter, God tells his people that pigs, rodents, crustaceans, mollusks, lizards, and all carnivores are "unclean"-in other words not acceptable to be eaten. On the other hand, fish with scales, cows, sheep, goats, and certain non-carnivorous birds are "clean." Let us examine the two lists. It just so happens that all the animals on the unclean list are relatively dangerous to eat unless very thoroughly cooked. Pork is the type of meat which is most famous for being relegated to "unclean" status for the Jews. Pork is also famous for causing trichinosis and several other deadly diseases. Swine are also a breeding host for many viruses including influenza. Similarly, mollusks and crustaceans are now well known as carriers of disease. The eating of carnivores, because they are farther up the food chain, is also known to carry health risks. The same can be said for the eating of rodents. On the other hand, beef, fish and lamb are all relatively safe. Each of these types of meat, if handled properly, may be eaten safely even when uncooked (although certain safety precautions are highly recommended). Is this coincidence?

How did Moses know which types of meat were relatively safe? Was it cultural? Did he learn it from the Egyptians? Certainly not, for they often ate the meat of animals on the "unclean" list, most notably pork. Did he run some controlled scientific experiments? That seems very unlikely. The nation of Israel at the time was relatively ignorant scientifically, but the Law contained in Leviticus reflects a unique level of knowledge. It becomes reasonable to begin thinking that the ultimate author of the Law, God, was protecting his people from "the diseases I brought on the Egyptians." Further examination will make this conclusion even more reasonable.

Next, let us look at Leviticus chapters 13 and 14. Here one finds very specific laws regarding a number of different types of infectious skin diseases, including leprosy. Instructions are given to quarantine the subjects with certain skin diseases for a set period of time, to burn their clothing and even destroy the pottery implements off of which they had eaten. Without hindsight based on medical knowledge, some of these restrictions appear to be cruel treatment.

Throughout time, the spread of leprosy has been blamed on such causes as heredity, the eating of certain foods, or even on the alignment of the planets. These false ideas naturally led to an inability to stop the spread of the disease. Finally, after thousands of years of human suffering, leprosy was brought under control in parts of Europe in the Middle Ages.

> *Leadership was taken by the church, as the physicians had nothing to offer. The church took as its guiding principle the concept of contagion as embodied in the Old Testament... This idea and its practical consequences are defined with great clarity in the book of Leviticus...*

> *Once the condition of leprosy was established, the patient was to be segregated and excluded from the community. Following the precepts laid down in Leviticus the church undertook the task of combating leprosy... it accomplished the first great feat... in methodical eradication of disease.*[78]

The incredible devastation which was caused by leprosy (and a host of other communicable diseases) throughout Europe, Africa and Asia could have been largely avoided if medical practitioners had simply heeded the command in Leviticus 13:46. "As long as he has the infection he remains unclean. He must live alone; he must live outside the camp." In fact, once quarantine was initiated in Western Europe, leprosy was nearly eliminated. Can anyone believe Moses devised this law because he was a brilliant doctor, or because of the medical knowledge he had acquired in Egypt? Suppose for a moment that you are a skeptic who believes that the book of Leviticus was written by a group of Jewish priests around 500 BC rather than by Moses: How will you explain the discovery of quarantine by these priests over two thousand years before its general application in Europe? In 1873, Dr. Armauer Hansen identified the bacterium which causes leprosy, proving once and for all that it is indeed an infectious disease (medical science refers to leprosy as Hansen's disease). Today, if caught early, it is entirely curable.

> *Three years later, the Norwegian Leprosy Act was passed. This law ordered lepers to live in precautionary isolation away from their families. In 1856, there were 2858 lepers living in Norway. By the turn of the century, only 577 lepers were left; and that number plummeted to 69. By 1930 the spectacular discoveries of science allowed Norway to control this disease, but the precautions had been written down by Moses almost 3,500 years earlier.*[79]

Fortunately, leprosy can now be controlled by antibiotics, so that there is no longer a need to quarantine lepers. However in the time of the writing of the Old Testament, God's prescription was the most effective and humane way to prevent the spread of this disease.

Let us now look at another commandment found in the Law of Moses. This one is in Numbers chapter 19. Here one finds the command from God that anyone who touches the body of a dead person was to be declared as unclean for seven days. In addition, they were to be unclean until several precisely specified hand and body washings had been completed. Even the person who aided in the cleansing was required to wash himself. As in the provisions with regard to skin diseases, these rules may seem harsh. Those who served the families when loved ones died were segregated from human contact for some time.

The Law specifically prescribed the use of water containing ash and hyssop for the washing. The minerals in ash in combination with oil from the hyssop plant makes a kind of soap. Even more impressive, it just so happens that the hyssop plant, a type of marjoram which grows in the Middle East, contains in its oil about 50% carvacrol. The chemical name of this compound is 4-isopropyl-2-hydroxytoluene. This is an organic compound almost identical to the commonly used antifungal and antibacterial compound thymol. It has been shown to be very effective against both bacteria and fungus. Therefore, water, ash and hyssop combine to make a powerful natural antibiotic soap. Is it reasonable to believe this was just luck on Moses' part?

$$CH_3$$

OH

$$H_3C \qquad CH_3$$

THE CHEMICAL STRUCTURE OF CARVACROL, A POWERFUL ANTIFUNGAL AND ANTIBACTERIAL AGENT.

It is interesting to note that the stringent practice of hand washing between the touching of patients and especially after touching of dead bodies was only introduced to "modern" medicine by the work of the Hungarian doctor Ignaz Semmelweis in the 1840s and 1850s.[80] Semmelweis worked at that time in a hospital in Vienna in which 13% of the maternity patients died in the hospital. No wonder women back then preferred to have their children at home! These depressing statistics were typical numbers for hospitals at that time. Semmelweis noted that a typical practice for the doctors in his hospital was to perform autopsies on the patients who had died the previous day before immediately proceeding to examine their gynecological patients. Today, of course, we understand how deadly this can be, but it should be noted that the concept of infectious disease, germ theory, was not introduced to the world or proved by modern science until the mid-nineteenth century by the work of the likes of Pasteur, Lister and Semmelweis. Semmelweis ordered that all doctors performing autopsies must wash their hands thoroughly before working with live patients. The death rate dropped to one fifth what it had been.

IGNAZ SEMMELWEIS. HERO OF GYNECOLOGICAL MEDICINE.

Semmelweis eventually observed that even contact with one maternity patient after touching another live patient could result in infection, so he further ordered hand cleansing in chlorine water between obstetrical examinations. The mortality rate dropped to less than 1%; a thirteen-fold decrease. Semmelweis could have referred to Leviticus chapter 12 at this point where women who give birth are declared to be "unclean" for seven days. It is now known that the nature of childbirth, which opens the circulatory system of the mother to outside infection, makes it a particularly dangerous practice for doctors to move from one maternity patient to another without a very thorough cleaning of hands. This remains true for several days after childbirth. The Bible prescribes seven days. Thanks to modern science, obstetricians do not need to wait seven days between examinations. Nevertheless one can infer that if medical doctors had used procedures derived from Leviticus, millions of unnecessary deaths could have been prevented.

It is an interesting side note that the work of Semmelweis was not easily accepted by the medical establishment of his day. He was ridiculed by many of his peers in the medical community. He was persecuted so strongly that he was fired from the hospital where he did his original work. Even after publishing convincing proof of the effectiveness of hand washing, he was scorned by his peers. Semmelweis was finally committed to a mental institution where it was reported that he died of a blood infection.

Semmelweis was not the only proponent of germ theory to be persecuted. The great French chemist Louis Pasteur demonstrated by experiment that specific species of bacteria are responsible for specific illnesses such as anthrax and smallpox. He also used the germ model to infer the existence of viruses, leading to a vaccine for rabies. Despite successes in curing diseases such as anthrax, his germ theory was vigorously opposed. One of his opponents, Guerin, even challenged him to a duel.

But there is more! Let us look at Leviticus 17:13-14.

> *Any Israelite or any alien living among you who hunts any animal or bird that may be eaten must drain out the blood and cover it with earth, because the life of every creature is its blood. That is why I have said to the Israelites, "You must not eat the blood of any creature, because the life of every creature is its blood; anyone who eats it must be cut off."*

Quite apart from the obvious health dangers in eating blood unless it is very thoroughly cooked, one finds an interesting statement here. "The life of every creature is its blood." The function of blood in carrying life-giving oxygen as well as many other nutrients to the cells of the body was not understood until the nineteenth century. The discovery of white blood cells and their role in the immune system is also relatively recent.

What makes the wisdom in the Law of Moses striking is the fact that "bad blood" was one of the chief (incorrect) diagnoses of medical science for all kinds of symptoms right up until the mid-nineteenth century. Medical doctors theorized that the cause of many diseases was poisons spread through the body by the blood. They reasoned that removing some of the bad blood using leaches or scalpels would relieve the symptoms of infections. The red stripes of the barber's pole represent a common practice of barbers as professional blood-letters from the Middle Ages right up to the nineteenth century. A study of the record of the treatment leading up to the death of George Washington shows an unusually large number of bloodlettings, prompting some to suggest that he may have actually died principally from a loss of blood. We have learned from science that the blood is the carrier of white blood cells, the body's principal means of protection against all kinds of disease. Bloodletting never helped anyone to recover from infectious disease. If only medical practitioners had taken the opportunity to read the Bible on this subject: "The life of every creature is in its blood." This statement in Leviticus is literally true. God was trying to protect his people so that they would not be overcome by "any of the diseases I brought on the Egyptians" (Exodus 15:26). Once more, the amazing wisdom of the Bible from a medical perspective is made clear.

Another commandment in the Old Testament which had positive health implications for the Jews was the circumcision of their male children. This practice was instituted a few hundred years before the time of Moses, during the lifetime of Abraham. In Genesis 17:12 one can read:

> *For the generations to come every male among you who is eight days old must be circumcised, including those born in your household or bought with money from a foreigner—those who are not your offspring.*

There are two points to be made here-first is the command to circumcise all males-second is the command to circumcise on the eighth day. Circumcision is a painful process! Why would God have had his people go through this? From a theological point of view, God established circumcision as a seal of the covenant he was making with his people. There were spiritual implications in circumcision, but it just so happens that there were health benefits as well.

Whether to circumcise or not is a matter of debate among the medical community today. Because of the level of daily hygiene, the need for this procedure has been reduced dramatically in most parts of the world. However, in a culture such as that of Israel over three thousand years ago, personal hygiene was certainly not up to the level available to most people today. In Old Testament times, people went extended periods without bathing. The warm, damp area behind the male foreskin is an excellent breeding ground for all kinds of bacteria and fungi. Consider the advantage to God's people in this practice, both for preventing the spread of sexually transmitted diseases, and for preventing any of a number of common infections.

God could have commanded his people to take a bath every day, but that would have been impractical, especially as they wandered in the desert for forty years.

There is another medical advantage to circumcision. In 1932, Dr. A. L. Wolbarst of New York reviewed the records of 1,103 cases of cancer of the penis.[81] Not one of these cases was a Jewish patient. considering the proportion of Jewish men in New York, the fact that none of the cancer patients was Jewish was an astounding revelation. In fact, cancer of the penis is virtually unknown among Jewish men. Up until 1975, only six cases of this disease among Jews were recorded.[82]

Perhaps there is some sort of genetic resistance to this type of cancer among Jews. Statistics show that circumcision is a factor, independent of whether the person is Jewish. Three large studies have shown that of 521 cases of cancer of the penis, none of the subjects had been circumcised.[83]Noting that roughly half the male population of the risk-group was circumcised, this provides a statistically convincing case for the efficacy of circumcision in preventing this rare, but often fatal disease, whether or not one is of a Jewish background.

Did God institute circumcision of males for these health reasons, or did he have in mind only the theological implications? That would be hard to say since it is never specifically referred to in the Bible as beneficial to health. Whatever the case, there is clearly a pattern emerging when we look at the laws given to the Jewish people. When the Jews followed the commands of the Bible, they were protected from all kinds of diseases. I think it is safe to conclude that this is not coincidence. It continues to build on the evidence that the Bible is inspired.

It is interesting to note that circumcision is much safer if performed on infants. In our modern culture, when older boys are circumcised, typically due to inability to retract the foreskin, the operation requires either general anesthesia, with its attendant risk of death, or a local anesthetic, which has been known to cause impotence. On the other hand, circumcision of an infant is a fairly simple and safe procedure. Within the first three weeks of birth, circumcision causes pain, of course, but the symptoms disappear immediately after surgery. On the other hand, adults experience pain for at least a week.

There is still one detail of the commandment to discuss. Why circumcise on the eighth day? While circumcision of a male child on the second or third day in a hospital setting is completely safe today, for the Israelites this was not necessarily the case. It has been noted by pediatricians that the risk of hemorrhage for children increases dramatically from about the second to the sixth or seventh day of life. After this point, the risk drops dramatically. In a hospital, under proper care, circumcision between the second and seventh day of life is unlikely to lead to major harm: but in the conditions of surgery prevalent in the times of the Old Testament, the implications are significant.

Let us look at the science of blood clotting as it relates to infants. Upon birth, the level of vitamin K in a baby is similar to that of its mother. However, the body does not produce its own supply of this nutrient. Bacteria present in the intestines produce vitamin K, releasing it into the body. Infants are born without the required bacteria in their intestines. It takes a few days for the bacteria to build up to the point that a safe level of vitamin K is reestablished. This is important because the body requires Vitamin K to produce the protein prothrombrin. The molecule prothrombrin is a required part of the blood clotting mechanism. Today, because of the research on vitamin K levels, doctors give shots of this important vitamin to newborns.

The science of prothrombrin and infants has one more interesting fact relevant to the biblical command. Studies show that once vitamin K levels come up, the level of prothrombrin peaks out significantly above normal levels for a couple of days. This fact is illustrated in the figure below.

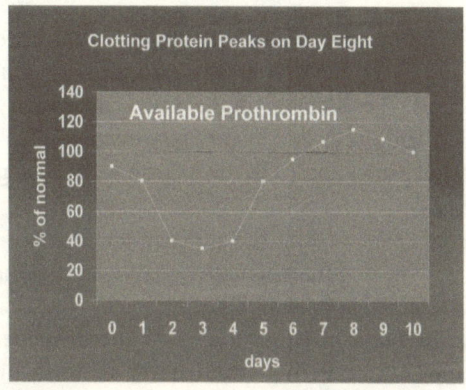

FIGURE 6.[84]

Prothrombrin levels in infants peak out at about the eight or ninth day. The fact is that according to scientific research, under the circumstances prevailing in ancient Israel, the safest day in the life of a male Jew to be circumcised was on about the eighth day.

Abraham clearly did not have access to this data, nor any way to generate it. Why did he tell the people of Israel to circumcise on the eighth day? Or even if someone is a thorough skeptic who will not even admit that Abraham existed, how can such a person explain that this is in the Bible? Perhaps the skeptic will claim that it is just luck or coincidence. How many coincidences will need to be pointed out before this argument becomes irrational? Let us not forget that not only does the Bible contain great medical insight, it is also missing such dubious medical advice as the six-oil formula to eliminate baldness which is found in the Ebers Papyrus.

Another case of advanced insight in the Pentateuch is found in Leviticus 18. Here we find laws against incest. Specifically, the Jews were commanded not to marry or to have sexual relationships with close relatives. This would include aunts, uncles, and cousins. Incest was a common practice of the day, continuing right up to modern times. Again, there may be additional reasons that God forbade this practice, but it just so happens that children born from a union between close blood relatives have shown a significantly higher incidence of genetic disease. Moses did not say why to avoid this type of behavior, but for the Jews who followed these decrees, much disease and heartache was avoided.

Scanning through the Old Testament will reveal a list of commands which led to the emotional and physical well being of the Jews. One discovers in Leviticus 7:22-25:

> *Do not eat any of the fat of cattle, sheep or goats... Anyone who eats the fat of an animal from which an offering by fire may be made to the Lord must be cut off from his people.*

It would be interesting to have data on how much lower the rate of arteriosclerosis and death due to heart disease was among the Israelites who obeyed this decree. The discovery of the direct correlation between animal fat consumption and death due to coronary heart disease is a recent one, but God provided protection to his people from this, the greatest killer in the Western world.

In Proverbs 23:20 we find the admonition, "Do not join those who drink too much wine or gorge themselves on meat." Both admonitions are good health advice, as has been well documented. Note that the Bible does not forbid consumption of either meat or wine in moderation. Meat in small proportions can be an important part of a healthy diet. The medical jury is still out on whether wine in moderation is harmful, or possibly even beneficial to health, but clearly much wine is extremely injurious to both mental and physical health.

Most of the commands listed so far are unique to the Bible. No other ancient religion or traditional medicine gave similar advice. All these Biblical laws show great medical wisdom. By contrast, God's commandments concerning sexual relationships, are not unique to the Bible. However, they provide still more evidence of the wisdom and practical nature of this great book in bringing health and happiness to anyone who will follow it. God specifically forbids homosexuality (1 Corinthians 6:9,10, Leviticus 18:22 and Romans 1:26,27), prostitution (1 Corinthians 6:9,10), adultery (Proverbs 5), and any kind of sex outside of marriage (Galatians 5:19).

There is a pervasive belief in modern society that an open attitude about sexual lifestyles is a healthy thing. The media portray the significant minority in America who still accept the biblical teaching that sex outside of marriage is wrong as narrow minded and mean-spirited. The mainstream of our culture believe that sexual experience before marriage, preferably with more than one partner, is a good thing—leading ultimately to greater sexual fulfillment. Experience tells us, however, that the opinion of the majority does not equal truth. Trust is an essential key to a healthy marriage relationship. There is a huge benefit to be reaped for those who delay sexual gratification until a commitment to a lifelong relationship has been sealed. Much disease and emotional hurt would be avoided if people obeyed the guidelines for sexual behavior in the Bible! The emotional benefit (let alone the spiritual benefit) to human lives would be incalculable.

Obedience to the Biblical teaching in this area would yield benefits to our physical health as well. Sexual promiscuity is certainly nothing new. Homosexual and heterosexual prostitution was at the heart of many ancient religions. The list of sexually transmitted diseases, including gonorrhea, syphilis, hepatitis and AIDS seems to be always increasing. These diseases would be wiped out in short order if people only had the wisdom and self-control to obey God's commands. Like the Israelites, We, too, can avoid many of the diseases of those around us if we follow God's commands.

In conclusion, God was not playing the part of a cosmic politician-promising much but delivering little-when he promised Israel that if they would obey his commands he would not bring on them any of the diseases of the surrounding cultures. However, God's principal interest was not in the physical health of his people. He was much more interested in their spiritual well being. For a person who is willing to adopt the Bible as their spiritual PDR, God has left many marks of inspiration, not the least of which are the Old Testament commandments relevant to medical science. The evidence from medical knowledge in the Old Testament is very impressive. If the only evidence for the Bible was its lack of harmful, non-scientific medical advice common in the time of the Old Testament, that alone would be strong testament of biblical inspiration. Combine this with the undeniable benefit of so many commands in the Old Testament, including knowledge which was unavailable apart from divine revelation, and the case for inspiration becomes strong indeed.

FOR TODAY

1. *Do you believe the health-related commands which were given to Israel were primarily intended to protect the people's health, or do you believe God gave the commands for other reasons, and they just happened to be good for the Hebrew nation's health?*

2. *Can you think of any laws in the Old Testament which would have been bad for the Israelite's health?*

3. *We made a little fun of the rattlesnake fat cure for premature grayness. Can you think of any modern-day health claims, which have proven to be more or less equivalent to using rattlesnake fat?*

4. *Can you think of any reasonable argument to refute the claim that God's plan for circumcision on the eighth day provides evidence for the inspiration of the Bible? Try to do this, even if you are inclined to believe the argument.*

RECOMMENDATION

Prepare a list of health-related commands in the Old Testament. Next, divide the list into those which would still be in force under the New Testament, and those which would no longer be laws for Christians. Finally, ask yourself which of the Old Testament commands would still give us health benefits, even with our modern medical technology. Do you see a pattern?

74 S. E. Massengill, *A Sketch of Medicine and Pharmacy* (Bristol, Tennessee: S. E. Massengill Co., 1943), 16.

75 C. P. Bryan, *The Papyrus Ebers* (New York: D. Appleton, 1931).

76 I would like to acknowledge several of the ideas in this section are inspired by a book I highly recommend to interested readers. It is S. I. McMillen, M.D., *None of these Diseases* (Old Tappan, New Jersey: Power Books, 1984).

77 Lewis Ginsberg, *The Legends of the Jews* (Philadelphia: Jewish Publication Society of America, 1956), 23.

78 George Rosen, *History of Public Health* (New York: MD Publications, 1958), 62-63.

79 S. I. McMillen, M.D., *None of These Diseases* (Old Tappan, New Jersey: Power Books, 1984), 22.

80 Risse, G.B., Semmelweis, Ignaz Philipp. *Dictionary of Scientific Biography* (New York: Charles Scribner's Sons, 1970-1980), *Medical historians and Semmelweis."* Journal of Medical Biography, London, May 1994; volume 2, No. 2, 84-88..

81 A. L. Wolbarst, *Circumcision and Penile Cancer,* Lancet, 1, (1932), 150-153.

82 E. Leiter and A.M. Lefkovits, "Circumcision and the Penile Carcinoma," *New York State Journal of Medicine,* 75, (1975), 1520.

83 C.W. McMillan, A. E. Weis and A. M. Johnson, "Acquired Coagulation Disorders in Children," *Pediatric Clinics of North America,* 19 (1972), 1034.

84 Graph courtesy of Mark Ottenweller, M.D.

CHAPTER 8

ALWAYS BE PREPARED TO GIVE AN ANSWER TO EVERYONE WHO ASKS
YOU TO GIVE THE REASON FOR THE HOPE THAT YOU HAVE.

1 PETER 3:15

FACT OR FABLE?

Although the greatest number of references in the Bible relevant to science is in the area of medical knowledge, there are also a number of statements of interest to geologists, biologists, cosmologists and others. These will be discussed in the present chapter.

It has already been pointed out that the scientific sophistication of the cultures surrounding the Hebrews was primitive by any measure. The picture from Greek mythology of Atlas holding up the sky may be interesting to anthropologists and historians of religion, but it cannot be taken seriously from a scientific perspective. Such myths were prevalent even among the Greeks, who were considered universally to be the most advanced of ancient cultures in the application of logic and reason as well as in knowledge of nature. This backdrop of relative scientific ignorance is the environment in which the Old Testament was written. This will help us to judge whether the Bible is of human or divine origin or some combination of the two.

Let us explore the possibility that the Jews were an exception to the rule—that unknown to the world around them; they had a culture which allowed them to acquire accurate understanding of the working of natural laws. Consider this nonbiblical statement from a Jewish writer from the early Roman period.[85]

> *The flood was produced by a union of the male waters, which are above the firmament, and the female waters issuing from the earth. The upper waters rushed through the space left when God removed two stars out of the constellation Pleiades. Afterward, to put a stop to the flood, God had to transfer two stars from the constellation of the Bear to the constellation of the Pleiades. That is why the*

Bear runs after the Pleiades. She wants her children back, but they will be restored to her only in the future world.

Male and female waters? Water flowing out of a constellation? Stars being moved around in the sky? Hmmm.... This passage, represents the kind of thinking found among Jewish writers contemporary with Jesus. Its mixture of astronomy, religion and fable is typical of writers, not only of Judaism, but of the neighboring cultures. This passage is indicative of the kind of material which one can assume would have crept into the Bible if it were written according the wisdom of the Jews at the time. As has already been said, the Bible does not have a large number of statements about the heavens, the history of the earth, world geography and so forth, but it does provide sufficient information to test the hypothesis that its scientific content shows evidence of divine origin. Miracles are recorded in the Bible, but they are presented as miracles, not natural events. Myths and fables with obvious scientific mistakes such as the one quoted above are completely absent from the Bible. This is a big claim, but it can be tested by reading the Bible. I have heard countless times that the Old Testament is myth, with blatant errors of fact in its description of nature. As a scientist, I do not find examples to confirm this claim. Readers who find it hard to accept this ought to study the Old Testament for themselves.

Here is a passage from the Old Testament which might be of interest to a biologist. In Genesis 16:4 one can read concerning Abraham that "He slept with Hagar and she conceived." Probably for the majority of Bible readers, this scripture and its scientific implications would slip right on by. Here the Bible is claiming that conception occurred in Hagar after sexual relationship with Abraham. A possible response would be "no kidding," but it just so happens that it was not generally accepted until the nineteenth century that conception occurs in this manner. The first in the Western world to propose that male and female mammals have "seed" was British scientist William Harvey, who published his theory in 1638. His theory was rejected by the majority of the scientific community. It is an interesting exercise to look at medical textbooks from the eighteenth century complete with diagrams showing how men deposited the already conceived baby into the uterus of the mother. Genesis 16:4 has conception occurring in the mother.

In the Koran, the scripture of Islam, one can read that man deposits the baby into the womb (Sura 16:4, Sura 22:5, Sura 23:14). Because the Koran was written by human wisdom, it reflects the generally accepted beliefs of the time. Again, the Bible reflects accurate knowledge which seems hard to explain given the ideas contemporary to its writing.

What about cosmology? In Job 26:7 it is stated that "He spreads out the northern skies over empty space; he suspends the earth over nothing."

This is an amazing statement. Here one finds the Bible proclaiming that the earth is freely moving in space, not attached to anything else. Simple observation of physical events in the world would cause one to believe that everything falls downward toward the earth. Not surprisingly, using simple human reasoning, the ancients either pictured the earth as a flat plate-like object resting on some larger object or as being the literal center of the universe, with the sun, moon, planets and stars attracted to the earth and circling it once a day. This second idea, called geocentrism, was the dominant theory of intellectuals up until the modern era. Popular religion generally held to ideas like the first. However, the biblical book of Job gets it right.[86] The earth is suspended on nothing. In fact, it moves through the universe under the influence of the force of gravity, primarily from the sun. That is quite an insight for a scientifically ignorant people.

Did anyone else come up with this idea as far back in time as Job? Scholars generally accept that Job is one of the oldest writings in the Old Testament. We cannot attach a definite date to its writing, but it is likely to have been written down before 1000 BC. A few hundred years after the writing of Job, Greek astronomers, Pythagoras, Anaxagoras and Aristarchus among them, did reach this conclusion. However, ancient peoples generally and even the majority of Greeks rejected the notion that the earth moves. More common was ideas such as that contained in the Puranas, part of the scripture/mythology of the Hindu religion. Here we find the statement that the earth is on the back of four elephants on top of a turtle, encircled by a serpent, swimming in a sea of milk.[87] Are the Sutras inspired by God? What about the Vedas or Upanishads; other Hindu scriptures? These questions deserve careful thought, but it should be noted that each of these contain stories as scientifically suspect as the elephant/turtle/milk myth. Another common misconception of the ancients was that the sky is basically like a bowl, with all the celestial objects moving at the same distance from the earth across the circumference of this bowl. The scriptures of Jainism (a religion native to India) go a bit further to describe different levels of the heavens, with different celestial objects revolving at different distances from the earth. Obviously, none of these ideas bear any resemblance to the facts about the universe. The reason is that they are of human origin.

Concerning the stars, one can read in Jeremiah 33:22 "I will make the descendants of David... as countless as the stars of the sky..." This statement is part of a poetic passage, making it wise not to read too much into it. Nevertheless, the Bible is stating that the stars cannot be counted. Again, this may seem like an obvious point, but the number of stars in the sky was the subject of debate in the Near East in Jeremiah's time (about 580 BC). Greek philosophers, including Democritus, speculated and debated over the total number of stars. In about 420 BC Democritus was the first person known to have proposed that the Milky Way is actually unresolved stars, and that therefore there are an inconceivable number of stars in the universe. Actually he was the second, counting Jeremiah.

About the earth itself, one can read in the Bible in Isaiah 40:22 that the earth is round (the Hebrew word can also be translated "sphere"). Most who thought about such things at the time of the writing of Isaiah (about 750 BC), believed the earth was flat. In about 525 BC, the Greek mathematician and mystic Pythagoras (famous for the Pythagorean Theorem) was the first person known to have claimed that the earth is a sphere. The first, that is, if one is to ignore Isaiah. In about 150 BC, Eratosthenes, a Greek living in Alexandria, measured the circumference of the earth, using a combination of experiment and mathematics. He was accurate to within about ten percent.[88]

By the way, to clear up a common misconception, although the uneducated people of Columbus' day may have believed in a flat earth, the majority of intellectuals in the fifteenth century believed, along with Pythagoras and Erastosthenes, that the earth was spherical. Columbus did not have to convince Queen Isabella that the earth was round; he just had to convince her that the voyage was a good financial investment. To do so, he claimed that the spherical earth was smaller than most in his day believed, and that therefore China was just a few thousand miles to the west. However, Isaiah, writing two thousand years before Columbus was ahead of his time. The point is not so much that Isaiah was more advanced than Pythagoras but that the Bible, to the extent that it reflects scientific knowledge, appears be consistently correct. By contrast, let us look at the Koran. The scripture of Islam was written over the twenty years or so before the death of Mohammed in the year 632 AD. Mohammed claimed to be a prophet of God. If the claim is true, then the Koran should be accurate to the extent that it can be compared to scientific knowledge. In the Koran it is claimed that the sun and stars revolve around the earth (Sura 21:33) This would be in agreement with the Greek Ptolemaic concept of the universe prevalent in Mohammed's time, called the geocentric theory. The only problem is that it is wrong. The reason the sun and stars appear to circle the earth is that the earth is spinning on its axis. This should cause one to question the scientific accuracy of the Muslim scripture.

Another interesting passage in the Koran records a piece of the sky falling and killing someone (Sura 34:9, Sura 52:44). This story reflects the assumption that the stars are imbedded in a crystal sphere, which was the most common cosmology of the ancients. In Sura 15:18 it is stated that shooting stars provide protection from evil spirits. In Sura 12, one can read about the eleven planets. In Sura 18:9-19 we find a story of a group of boys who fell asleep in a cave with their dog. They woke up three hundred years later and left the cave. This would make for an interesting fable if it weren't for the fact that it is recorded as if it were a true story in the scripture of one of the world's major religions. The Koran has King David making an iron coat of mail (Sura 34:11). This is both a historical and a scientific anachronism because the making of steel armor had not yet been invented. Chain mail armor was invented in about the first century BC. To the ancients, the cause of rain was a mystery. Where does the rain come from? Why is it that the rivers continually flow into the sea but the sea does not ever overflow? It is an interesting exercise to explore some of the fables and myths produced by ancient cultures to explain this phenomenon. The Greeks invoked the gods to explain the production of rain. Aristotle proposed that sea water was desalinized underground and reemerged as spring water. In Amos 5:8, it is stated that it is God "who calls for the waters of the sea and pours them out over the face of the land." Also, we find in Job 36:27 the statement that God "draws up the drops of water, which distill as rain to the streams." In other words, the Bible describes a cycle which begins with water evaporating from the surface of the earth, condensing, and distilling back to the earth, only to evaporate and return to the atmosphere again. The correct explanation of this process, called the hydrological cycle, gained general acceptance by the scientific community in the West in the late seventeenth century. The first to publish a correct theory of evaporation and condensation was the French scientist Pierre Perrault in 1674. The Bible attested to this fact, over two thousand years before scientific investigation led to the correct answer to this basic question. Skeptics claim that the Bible is a book written by scientifically ignorant people in a scientifically ignorant age. Instead of ignorance the Bible communicates superior insight.

Another interesting piece of information in the Bible relates to shipbuilding technology. It is found in Genesis 6:15. In the story of the flood, God told Noah to build a large ship to save his family and animals from the great flood to come on the earth. God prescribed to Noah the dimensions of the ark. The ark was to be 300 cubits long by fifty cubits wide by thirty cubits high. It just so happens that the thirty to five to three ratio of length to width to height for the construction of large ships has been found, both from long experience of oceangoing nations, and from engineering principles, to be the ideal dimensions for a balance of large volume, stability and speed in the building of ships of commerce. It is not clear that the ark needed to be built for speed, but large volume and stability were definitely important qualities. Historically, the Hebrews have never been an oceangoing people. From the time of Abraham all to the way to the period of the kings, the Israelites lived away from the ocean. This fact makes it difficult to imagine how the writer of Genesis got the ideal dimensions for a large ship right. Could it be that God had a hand in providing this knowledge? Some who attempt to undermine the Bible have tried to find passages which reveal its scientific errors. They claim that the kinds of obvious mistakes such as those taken from the Koran and the Hindu Puranas in the section above are also found in the Bible. The criticisms tend to fall into two categories. They either claim as scientific error events which the Bible writers clearly identify as miracles, or they take statements from poetical passages out of context.

As an (example) of the former, skeptics have referred to the parting of the Red Sea as a biblical scientific mistake. There certainly is no natural explanation for the Red Sea spontaneously parting (despite efforts of some to find one). However, the dividing of the Red Sea is unquestionably described as a one-time supernatural occurrence, not a natural event. The Bible writers never portray the parting of the Red Sea as being the result of a natural phenomenon. If they had, perhaps one could argue that this is a scientific error. The parting of the Read Sea is only a scientific "mistake" if one assumes up front that miracles have never occurred. This would be to commit the logical fallacy of begging the question. As an (example) of a supposed biblical scientific error which in reality is simply a misinterpreted poetical passage, look at Isaiah 11:6-9. In this scripture, Isaiah prophesies that "the wolf will lie down with the lamb, the leopard will lie down with the goat" and "The infant will play near the hole of the cobra." This is a poetic and prophetic reference to the future kingdom of God, written in the apocalyptic style, common to Hebrew literature. In God's kingdom, all kinds of people who would never have come together because of deep-rooted class, ethnic or nationalistic hatred will join hands in one family. It is not a prediction that cobras will suddenly make good pets. The claim that Isaiah 11:6-9 is a scientific blunder shows a lack of understanding of the context and meaning of the scripture.

Another unreasonable criticism of the scientific accuracy has been taken from 1 Kings 7:23. Here the diameter of a circular bowl in the temple is given as ten cubits, while its circumference is quoted as thirty cubits. Using a more precise value for the number "pi," the author of 1st Kings should have said the circumference was 31.415 cubits, but apparently he rounded off a bit. It seems unreasonable to use the biblical author's rounded off dimension as evidence of a scientific/mathematical mistake.

In conclusion, some speculate that the Bible, and especially the Old Testament, is a collection of legends and myths. The common stand of scholars is that the Bible is the product of the imagination of a scientifically ignorant people. Let me respond to this charge with a rhetorical question. Which myths are you referring to? I have a PhD in chemical physics and I have read the Bible through a number of times. I fail to find any blatant scientific error. (one paragraph please)When the teachings of the Bible are compared to those of non-biblical Jewish writers, to other ancient writings or to the scriptures of other religions, one finds a contrast so striking as to be unexplainable. Unexplainable, that is, unless one allows for the possibility of the inspiration of the Bible.

This book which the skeptic claims is the product of scientifically ignorant writers, is in fact laced with accurate claims of a scientific nature. This ought to cause an open-minded person to question the validity of the atheistic/humanistic criticisms of the Bible. Go ahead, be skeptical. Good idea. Do not assume anything to be true unless the evidence speaks for itself. If a person decides to study through the Bible with a sincere heart and an open mind, he or she will eventually "accept it not as the word of men, but as it actually is, the word of God, which is at work in you who believe" (1 Thessalonians 2:13). Not only that, but if Bible believers are intellectually honest enough to question their own beliefs about the scientific accuracy of the Bible, they will not be disappointed by the exercise. Their faith will be deepened, leading to convictions which will allow them to weather the storms of life.

FOR TODAY

1. *Read Psalm 74:12-14. Would this represent a scientific "blunder" in the Bible? Why or why not?* What about Jonah 1:17 and 2:10?**

2. *Playing devil's advocate with one of the arguments in this chapter, how might you attempt to defend the Hindu account of the turtle and the milk etc.? What about the Koran's mention of eleven planets?*

RECOMMENDATION

Locate a copy of the Koran or find the purana referred to in the text of this chapter. Apply the same standards you used in question number one above to one of the claims in this chapter of scientific error in the scriptures of other religions.

* Author's answer: In the first case, Psalm 74 is a poem. The writer is using poetic license to make a point about God, not to present a scientific argument that some sort of sea monster exists. In the second case, what happened to Jonah is clearly presented as a miraculous event. Could anyone survive in the belly of a huge fish for an extended period of time? I would have to say no. That is why what God did for Jonah is such a great miracle. One which Jesus said prefigured his three days in the tomb (Matthew 12:40), an event which science certainly cannot explain.

85 Lewis Ginsberg, *The Legends of the Jews* (Philadelphia: Jewish Publication Society of America, 1956), 76.

86 In analyzing Job 26:7, the reader should bear in mind other passages in the book such as Job 9:6, in which an earthquake is metaphorically described as God making the earth's "pillars tremble." Bear in mind that Job 9:6 appears to be metaphorical, while Job 26:7 does not. Job is a book of poetry, written in a dramatic style. It is not a systematic treatise on cosmology. It is wise to look at scientific content in Job with some caution. Nevertheless, Job 26:7 is in striking agreement with our present knowledge of cosmology.

87 From the eighth canto of the *Bhagavata Purana.*

88 It may be a mistake to make a very strong conclusion from Isaiah 40:22, since the Hebrew word has an ambiguous meaning, and the point of Isaiah is spiritual, not scientific. Nevertheless, the Bible does not have anything equivalent to the turtle/elephant/milk story. In any case, whether round or spherical, Isaiah gets it right.

CHAPTER 9

IT IS MERE RUBBISH THINKING AT PRESENT OF THE ORIGIN OF LIFE.
ONE MIGHT AS WELL THINK OF THE ORIGIN OF MATTER.

CHARLES DARWIN, FROM ORIGIN OF SPECIES, 1857.

WHERE DID I COME FROM?

There are a number of important questions about the relationship between the Bible and science which remain to be addressed. Some of these strike at the heart of the issue. We will now begin to address some of these very controversial topics.. Among the questions still to be asked are the following:

1. What about evolution?
2. What about Adam and Eve and the origin of man?
3. What about the flood of Noah?

All these questions have been mentioned already, but they deserve more attention. The first two, being closely related, are covered in this chapter. The scientific implications of the flood will be covered in chapter ten.

EVOLUTION

No question which brings together science and the Bible has generated more controversy and even outright animosity than the question of the evolution species and the related question of the origin of man. The issue pits atheists against creationists. It divides deists from theists and science teachers from school boards. The debate is not only between polar opposites; even within the Christian community there has been heated disagreement over how to deal with the question of evolution. Some believers see evolution as God's way of creating various species. Others see the theory of evolution as Satan's instrument to destroy belief in God. The makers of bumper stickers have made a good profit from the Darwin versus Jesus debate. Non-believing scientists declare "evolution is a fact," even when they are well aware that science does not have the ability to discover "the truth," but can only create consistent models. On the opposite side sit the young earth creationists who insist adamantly that creation is a scientific theory which should be given at least equal treatment in public schools with evolution. For some, their goal is to remove evolution from the curriculum and replace it with the young earth theory.[89]

Probably the most famous battle in this ongoing war was the Scopes "monkey" trial in Tennessee in 1925. The teaching of evolution in public schools was at issue in this trial. It pit the aging orator William Jennings Bryant, who defended special creation, against Clarence Darrow, who argued for the teaching of evolution. Darrow won the legal battle, allowing evolution to be taught in schools in Tennessee for the first time. In another showdown in 1968, the U.S. Supreme Court reached a decision in the case of Epperson v. Arkansas which struck down an Arkansas law forbidding the teaching of "the theory or doctrine that mankind ascended or descended from a lower order of animals." In these cases and several others, politicians, creationists, scientists and religious leaders have fought for control of the secondary school curriculum related to the origin of species and of man. Is the science of young-earth creationism of the same quality as mainstream science on this question? The answer is no, it definitely is not. This is at least part of the reason the cases above were "lost."

More recently, supporters of Intelligent Design have attempted to force equal treatment of design alongside a completely materialist concept of evolution. In this context, a materialist is not a person who seeks material possessions. The materialist believes that the only allowable explanations for phenomena are those which use natural, physical laws. He or she rules out *a-priori* supernatural causes. Skirmishes in the battle over Intelligent Design include the "Scopes II" trial in Dover, Pennsylvania as well as the well-publicized hearings before the Kansas State Board of Education in 2005. The "science" of Intelligent Design is on much stronger footing, but it remains to be seen where these trials will lead. Stay tuned. Intelligent Design arguments will be more thoroughly explained in this chapter.

SETTING THE STAGE

We will begin our treatment of the theory of evolution with a careful definition of the theory and the issues it raises. Next, the evidence in support of this theory will be discussed. Following that, a possible alternative way of thinking about the origin of species will be presented along with a discussion of how all this relates to the contents of the Bible.

The discussion of evolution has been left to a separate and later chapter of the book for two reasons. First, although evolution and its relationship to the Bible is a very interesting subject, it seems that the debate over evolution is not central to the themes of this book-the existence of God and the inspiration of the Bible. As to the existence of God, it has already been shown beyond a reasonable doubt that both the universe and life were created. Yes, there is a God. Whether God created just one life form at some distant point in the past and let it "evolve" from there according to the wisdom of his natural laws, or whether God created all the life forms visible today only a few thousand years ago-either way, God created life, and there is a God!

The fact is that the theory of evolution explains, not how life came to be in the first place, but rather how existing species have changed over time. Evolution is not a theory of origins, it is a theory of change. The original existence of life is a miracle, plain and simple. How much created life has changed through evolution is to be discovered principally through studying fossil and genetic evidence.

As to how it relates to inspiration, evolution is not directly addressed in the Bible. Outside of the first chapter in Genesis, the origin of species is not discussed. The relationship between Genesis 1 and evolution will be dealt with presently, but it can be broadly stated that the issue of evolution is not strongly connected with questions about biblical inspiration.

The second reason evolution was left for a later chapter is that, although I am a trained scientist, my personal expertise is in physics and chemistry, not biology. The origin of the universe is a question of physics primarily, while the origin of life is a question mostly of chemistry. Evolution is a question principally of biology. Although I have read more than a dozen books on the subject, the reader may want to take into account the fact that I am not an expert on evolution when reading the following.

Life was created by God. As stated above, the theory of evolution provides a model to explain how the original life form or forms have changed since their creation to produce the myriad of life forms that exist on the earth today. In the words of Charles Darwin from his book *Origin of Species*:

> *It is mere rubbish thinking at present of the origin of life. One might as well think of the origin of matter.*

The origin of the first life-forms, whether they were one-celled or very advanced-whether there were many created species or one, the evolutionist will have a difficult time ultimately deciding. This is because evolution is not a theory of origins, rather it is a theory of change. We can see from the quote above that Darwin was well aware his theory could not explain the origin of life. In fact, in *Origin of Species*, Darwin allowed for the possibility that a number of original species were created.

A DEFINITION

The modern theory of evolution is very different from that originally proposed by Charles Darwin in his 1859 classic, *On The Origin of Species by Means of Natural Selection, or the Preservation of Favoured Races in the Struggle for Life*. Darwin's original theory did not include a mechanism by which information is passed from parents to offspring. This question was solved by Gregor Mendel in the 1860's with his phenomenological theory of genetics. A molecular explanation of heredity was provided by James Watson, Francis Crick and Rosalind Franklin in 1953, with their discovery of the structure of DNA. This was soon followed up by the discovery of the genetic code and an understanding of the mechanism of DNA replication, transcription and translation into proteins.

Darwin had a workable theory of how various available traits in existing species were selected to create new species, but he had no explanation of how the variety of traits among which nature selected came about in the first place. Biologists have since proposed natural mutations of DNA to explain the creation of new genetic traits, although the efficacy of natural mutation to the evolution which is observed is hotly debated. The modern theory of evolution is so far beyond Darwin that it is called neo-Darwinism.

In order to begin our discussion, let us ponder the following statement of the theory of evolution, with all the implications required for the materialist to be able to accept it:

> *The original one-celled life form, through mutation and subsequent genetic variation, under the influence of natural selection has produced all the life forms which now exist or have ever existed on the earth.*

This claim is either true or it is not. It will either hold up to scientific criticism and the evidence or it will not. We will examine how well this statement agrees with the evidence, along with its relationship to statements in the Bible.

EVIDENCE FOR EVOLUTION

First let us peruse the evidence in support of the theory of evolution. In order to honestly critique evolutionary ideas it is absolutely essential to understand the evidence which underlies the theory. Contrary to the impression some like to create, there is a wide range of data to support evolution. There are three principal categories of evidence which can be used in support of the theory of evolution. They are:

1. Genetics.
2. The fossil record.
3. Empirical observations of evolution.

This is an oversimplification, but sufficient for a starting point. Contrary to popular belief, it is genetics rather than fossils which supply the strongest evidence in support of evolution. Those who seek to "disprove" evolution typically attack the evidence from the fossil record rather than that from genetics. They also tend to downplay or are unaware of recent observations of evolution in the laboratory. The goal here is not to attack or even to disprove evolution. However, any attempt to do either should discuss the genetic evidence in support of evolution.

The basic idea of genetics is that each generation of a species inherits its traits from its parent or parents through the DNA molecules contained in its chromosomes. This has strong evolutionary implications. When biologists analyze the DNA in mammals they find that all mammals have similar DNA, providing strong support for the idea that the different species of mammals are all genetically related, and therefore perhaps all evolved from some original "mammal."

The logical implication of evolution is that species which are closely related by descent should have similar DNA. This law, although perhaps not perfectly adhered to, generally proves true. For (example) the DNA in chimpanzees has about a 98-99% similarity to that of humans. Logically (at least according to the logic of evolution), crocodiles should have DNA less similar to that of humans than chimpanzees to humans. On the other hand, ostriches should have more similarity in their DNA to hummingbirds than to lobsters. When the DNA evidence is examined, although there might be some interesting surprises, the general implications of evolution for genetics prove true.

To those who are emotionally tied in to the idea that Adam and Eve were a special creation (the author would count himself among them) this sort of information may incite a reaction. Facts are facts, however, and the fact is that studies of the DNA in plants and animals, at least on the surface, are consistent with the theory of organic evolution. The argument on the other side is that we measure closeness of descent in the evolutionary "tree" by the DNA similarity and then turn around and use the similarity of the DNA as evidence of common descent. The argument may have a degree of circularity in it. Perhaps a creator, creating similar species, used similar DNA. The experts will argue over details, but the fact remains that genetic evidence strongly supports the idea of evolution of species.

The second category of evidence used to support the evolutionary model is the fossil record. Fossil evidence was particularly important to Darwin's original work partly due to the fact that he did not use genetic evidence to support his theory. The science of genetics was first presented by Gregor Mendel in 1865, and first published by him in 1866. It is an irony of science history that genetic theory existed during Darwin's life, yet as far as we know he never heard of Mendel's work. Mendel worked in obscurity and his work was ignored by the scientific community until the beginning of the twentieth century. So although he believed in heredity of traits, Darwin did not use genetics to support his conclusions. However, Darwin did refer to the evidence from the fossil record. He also used as evidence the apparent adaptation of living species to their environment. His most famous (example) was the fourteen species of finches on the Galapagos Islands. To quote Darwin:

> *The great principle of evolution stands up clear and firm, when these groups of facts are considered in connection with others, such as the mutual affinities of the members of the same group, their geographical distribution in past and present times, and their **geological succession**. It is incredible that all these facts should speak falsely. He who is not content to look, like a savage, at the phenomena of nature as disconnected, cannot any longer believe that man is the work of a separate act of creation*[90] (emphasis added).

By "geological succession," Darwin means from fossil evidence. Darwin is claiming here, and evolutionists have followed his lead, that when one looks at the fossil evidence, one will find a gradual change from more ancient species to more modern ones. This is illustrated by the familiar evolutionary family tree which will show mammals and birds evolving from reptiles, which in turn evolved from amphibians, which evolved from fish and so forth back to the most ancient single-cell ancestors.

Creationists have cried foul at this point, but not just creationists. Legitimate science has often and consistently called into question this claim that the fossil evidence supports evolution of humans and other higher animals from one-celled organisms. They ask for evidence of missing links and certain hard-to-imagine in-between evolutionary forms. A statement of the famous orator William Jennings Bryan given at the Scopes trial, although perhaps a bit overstated, will represent this view:

> *Today there is not a scientist in all the world who can trace one single species to any other, and yet they call us ignoramuses and bigots because we do not throw away our Bible and accept it is proved that out of two or three million species not a one is traceable to another. And they say that evolution is a fact when they cannot prove that one species came from another, and if there is such a thing, all species must have come, commencing as they say, commencing in that one lonely cell down there in the bottom of the ocean that just evolved and evolved until it got to be a man. And they cannot find a single species that came from another, and yet they demand that we allow them to teach this stuff to our children, that they may come home with their imaginary family tree and scoff at their mother's and father's Bible.*[91]

The question of succession of species and the related question of missing links is a difficult one, but the evolutionists defend their position as follows:

Yes, it is true that the succession of separate families of species cannot be demonstrated in the laboratory, and yes it is true that significant "gaps" in the fossil record exist. Nevertheless, with the passage of time and as the body of evidence increases, new data consistently tends to fill in the gaps and to support the general claims of evolution. If the theory of evolution were without any validity, then one can assume that as evidence is collected it would tend to make the theory less and less believable. The converse is true. With increasing fossil evidence, the theory of evolution has in general become more plausible, not less. With regard to the fossil record, Darwin predicted a very slow and gradual change over great periods of time. The data simply does not agree with this prediction in general. The pattern which paleontologists detect is cycles of very rapid, seemingly almost instantaneous change on a geological time scale, followed by millions of years of very slow drift. To explain the discrepancy between the predictions of Darwin and the data, neo-Darwinists such as Stephen Jay Gould and Niles Eldridge created the theory of punctuated equilibrium in the 1970s. They proposed that some mechanism or set of causes which we still do not completely understand results in occasional periods of very rapid evolution.

This idea, designed to help the theory to agree with the data, remains controversial in the scientific community, both because it is not demonstrated by experiment and because it suffers from a somewhat vague mechanism. The third category of evidence which supports the theory of evolution is empirical studies of relatively simple plants and animals which have been observed to "evolve." Such experiments take two forms. One involves studying apparent rates of drift between closely related species that even young-earth creationists can agree are related by descent. The other kind of experiment involves observing actual mutations in the laboratory which produce a positive change for the species in the environment studied. In one such experiment, biologists have experimented with bacteria which perform a certain reaction only in oxygen-poor environments. When these bacteria are exposed to oxygen-rich environments, a mutation which allows them to repair oxygen-related damage is seen to occur. In one study, two hundred bacterial generations (involving billions of bacteria) were sufficient to observe a positive mutation.[92] So far, such evidence is only observed in very simple life such as bacteria and viruses. It is certainly possible to argue about whether such change can successfully be scaled up to explain the evolution of higher life forms. However, those who claim that successful evolution caused by random mutation has not been shown in the laboratory are in error. Others respond to evidence of actual evolution by beneficial mutation by saying that microevolution happens, but that macroevolution has not been shown in the laboratory. The problem with this criticism is that the distinction between micro and macroevolution is arbitrary, and by definition, it is not fair to ask a biologist to demonstrate "macroevolution" in the laboratory because such gross changes, if they occur by natural process, will presumable take tens of thousands or even millions of generations.

Remember that there are significant questions to be asked of the evolutionary theory, which we are about to do. However, to summarize this brief exposition on the data in support of evolution, we have observed the following.

1. There may be some fine points to argue over, but in general the genetic evidence supports the theory of evolution.

2. The evidence from the fossil record can be reasonably interpreted either as generally supporting the theory of evolution or as creating a major problem for the theory. Time and evidence has both filled in some of the "gaps" and made it more clear than before that some sort of instantaneous or extremely rapid changes have happened.

3. Experimental evidence validating what some might call microevolution by random mutation has now been observed in the laboratory. Whether or not these findings can be scaled up to explain evolution from single celled organisms to advanced species is an open question.

The fact is that the chief predictions of the evolutionary theory are more or less consistent with known fact. As data continues to come in, rather than providing more reason to doubt evolution, it tends to support it. Notice the word *tends* is used here, because it will be shown that there is a significant body of evidence which calls into question many of the assumptions of the evolutionary theory.

PROBLEMS WITH THE DARWINIAN MODEL

Having covered how the evidence can be used to support he evolutionary model, let us now bring up some of the difficulties in the evidence used to support evolution. The theory itself has "evolved" to deal with some difficult questions. One of the problems for evolution is finding a mechanism for genetic change over time which agrees with the data. How do new species come about? How does a species with 46 chromosomes evolve from a more ancient predecessor with 34 chromosomes? The theory of change by adaptation to the environment assumes genetic variety in a population and "natural selection" of the traits most suited to the specific environment. The question is where does this variety come from?

Geneticists propose natural mutations in a species as the source of variations in the gene pool. Mutations do indeed occur, but the vast majority of them are not beneficial to the organism. The probability of a single mutation being beneficial has been estimated as low as one in a million. Since mutations are virtually always either harmful or neutral, critics of evolution by natural processes claim that they cannot possibly explain how simple, one-celled organisms evolved to higher species. It is a matter of simple statistics and numbers. Mathematicians who have tried to estimate the probability of advanced species evolving from simpler ones have struck a consistently negative note.

It is relatively easy to imagine how statistics will allow for the world population of a particular species of mosquito, with its short life span and huge population to evolve around a particular environmental difficulty through mutation. It is more difficult to imagine a species of whales, numbering in only the thousands using mutation to survive an environmental change. The time between generations of bacteria is on the order of hours, for mosquitoes it is weeks, for whales it is several years.

The amount of genetic change (i.e. positive mutations) involved in changing from one species to another is far greater than that required to respond to a single environmental change. It was stated above that apes are approximately 98-99% similar in genetic material to humans. What was not mentioned is that there are about four billion base pairs in the human genome. Using that number, even a change of one percent in genetic information would require forty million beneficial or at least non-harmful genetic changes through mutation. How long would this take to happen? For a species with about twenty years between generations and with a world-wide population which was probably less than one million until fairly recently, can random mutation achieve this level of positive or neutral change in DNA in, say a few hundred thousand years? How many generations would be required, and how many simultaneous changes can happen at once? For the fully materialistic theory of evolution to be supported, these questions must be answered. This is where current models, demonstrated rates of mutation and mathematics converge to raise serious questions about the efficacy of random processes to explain evolution from bacteria to dolphins. One scientist who has applied mathematics to study the theory of evolution is Sir Fred Hoyle, a professed agnostic. Hoyle has attempted to model the probability of beneficial mutations along with estimations of the number of simultaneous beneficial mutations required for species to evolve from one another. He concluded that:[93]

> *The general scientific world has been bamboozled into believing that evolution has been proved. Nothing could be farther from the truth.*

In the same book, he makes the bold statement regarding his study of mutations and their relation to speciation, "These conclusions dispose of Darwinism."

Another physicist, H. S. Lipson, performed similar calculations, which were published in the *Physics Bulletin*.[94] He concluded that:

> *We must go further than this and admit that the only acceptable alternative is creation. I know that this is anathema to physicists, as indeed it is to me, but we must not reject a theory that we do not like if the experimental evidence supports it.*

Lipson is not at all a creationist, but his willingness to make a statement like this openly is admirable. He is simply stating that the level of improbability for the evolution of species by today's models forces him to at least admit the possibility of special creation.

Evolutionists, of course, have devised models which attempt to explain how this process occurs. The fact is, however, that the means by which genetic diversity occurs and its relationship to natural selection is still very much in doubt. Evolutionary theory has proven to be very flexible. Historically it has been adapted in response to whatever evidence has been discovered. Nevertheless, a convincing model to explain the origin of genetic diversity is still lacking.

This brings out a significant point about the theory of evolution. It is by its very nature impossible to prove or to disprove evolution. The theory uses data from the distant past to explain events of the distant past. Despite the confident claims of evolutionists that the theory is "proved," in the end, the evolution of birds from dinosaurs is not a repeatable experiment. The process, if it occurred, certainly cannot be demonstrated in the laboratory, so the normal method scientists use to verify a scientific theory is not available.

On the other hand, evolution can never be disproved scientifically either. Because it is a theory primarily about the past, the proponents of evolution need only adapt the theory as well as possible to fit the available data from the past . Both philosophically and practically, evolutionists cannot prove that their model is an accurate description of the past. It is worth remembering that a great number of evolutionists are committed to the theory at least in part because they have assumed, before even beginning the investigation, that every phenomenon has a natural, rather than a supernatural explanation. One popular book on the debate over evolution is *Darwin on Trial* by Phillip Johnson. This is an excellent book with an attention-grabbing title, but the fact is that Darwin will not be found guilty beyond a reasonable doubt, at least by scientific method.

Whether or not random mutation can explain the genetic change which is observed is very questionable. Questionable, that is, if we do not make the mistake of assuming before we ask the questions, that random processes *must* be the answer.

THE CAMBRIAN EXPLOSION AND OTHER EVIDENCE

There is another significant problem in the evidence which props up evolutionary assumptions. When one looks at the fossil record, one finds information *dramatically* in contradiction to what would seem to be the logical implications of the evolutionary theory—slow and fairly gradual change of species. In fact, the fossil record shows evidence of *extremely* rapid change on a geological time scale. When the fossil record is examined, species seem to make great leaps of change in what seems to be zero time geologically. In some cases, species even appear seemingly out of nowhere morphologically in virtually zero time, followed by long periods with very little change.

Upon a careful examination, the fossil record does show some long periods of relatively small and gradual change, consistent with the broad idea of the evolutionary theory. However, at certain times in the past, events have occurred after which as much as ninety percent of all species have disappeared, followed by dramatically new species seeming to appear almost as if out of nowhere from an evolutionary perspective.

The most famous of these dramatic appearances of new species is called the Cambrian explosion. To quote from an article entitled The Big Bang of Animal Evolution:[95]

> *Nevertheless, compared with the context of the 3.5 billion years of all biological history and the roughly 570 million years since the start of the Cambrian, the phyla do seem to have appeared **suddenly and simultaneously**. For that reason, some paleontologists refer to the Cambrian "explosion"... This evidence seems to confirm that there was a spectacular evolutionary radiation in the early Cambrian... [the] Cambrian explosion was characterized by the **sudden** and roughly **simultaneous** appearance of many diverse animal forms almost 600 million years ago* (emphasis added).

There it is. Although some slow and gradual change does seem to occur when the fossil record is viewed (for example, there is reasonably good evidence from fossils of primitive elephant-like species evolving over millions of years into mastodons, wooly mammoths and modern elephants), the evidence shows that many of the most significant changes in life forms on the earth have occurred in what appear to be geologically sudden and simultaneous events. As noted in the quote above, all the animal phyla with hard parts arose during this Cambrian explosion. In the subsequent 550 million years, no new hard body part patterns have appeared. The explanation of this sudden explosion of entirely new phyla remains as a mystery to those who assume random mutational processes are the only option. The fossil record seems to imply a small grove of evolutionary trees rather than a single tree reaching back to the first life form. This is the kind of data which led Gould and others to propose the theory of punctuated equilibrium. The problem with this is that in the case of the Cambrian explosion, reasonable preceding species appear to be non-existent.

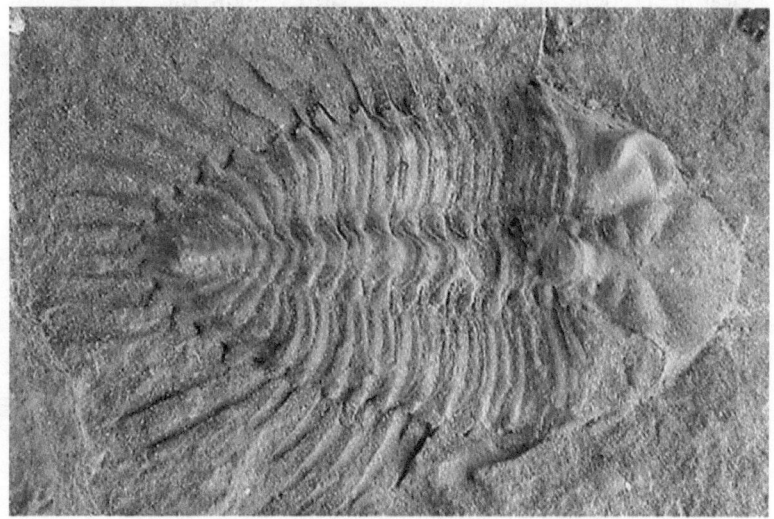

(FIGURE 9.1) TRILOBITE FOSSIL, ONE OF THE MILLIONS OF LIFE FORMS THAT EMERGED DURING THE CAMBRIAN EXPLOSION.

The Cambrian event is not unique, although it is the most striking one discovered so far. As early as the eighteenth century, paleontologists noticed a dramatic, quantum shift in the fossil record which occurred at the end of the Paleozoic era, about 251 million years ago. Again, a sudden change is noticed which was so rapid that it has been estimated to have occurred within thousands of years or even less. In this, the greatest of the "mass extinction events," as much as 95 percent of all species disappeared, both from water and land. At the same time, many radically new species appeared suddenly in the fossil record. Five mass extinction events are now recognized in the fossil record, including the one which probably wiped out the dinosaurs 65 million years ago. It should be noted that this is not an idea from paleontologists on the fringe of the field. This is a thoroughly documented finding of which all evolutionists are well aware.

Of course, supporters of evolution attempt to explain the data. To quote the above-mentioned article:[96]

> *Evolutionary biologists are still trying to determine why no new body plans have appeared during the past half a billion years... One idea worth entertaining is that evolution occurs more slowly today than it did when the earth was young... I have argued that at least part of the answer may depend on the evolution of commitment to a developmental program... In response to natural selection pressures, developmental programs may evolve to restrict the degree of change in successful body plans. We can only speculate about what genetic mechanisms might permanently set development...*

This is an article by a main-line evolutionist. The proposal is astounding! The rate of evolution is said to be variable. Evolution may have a "commitment to a developmental program." The author should be given leeway in using familiar terminology to describe an unfamiliar occurrence, but this is surprising language for an evolutionist to use to say the least. Evolutionists see evidence of a development program. It would certainly seem reasonable to assume that there is a planner at the head of the development department. In fact, the lack of transitional forms in the fossil record between species has prompted Stephen Jay Gould, who was one of the most respected evolutionists of our day, to make the following statements.[97]

> *New fossils almost always appeared suddenly in the fossil record with no itermediate links to ancestors in the older rocks of the same region.*

> *The extreme rarity of transitional forms in the fossil record persists as the trade secret of paleontology. The evolutionary trees that adorn our textbooks have data only at the tips and nodes of their branches; the rest is inference, however reasonable, not the evidence of fossils... We fancy ourselves as the only true students of life's history, yet to preserve our favored account of evolution by natural selection we view our data as so bad that we never see the very process we profess to study.*

Gould was definitely not a believer in creation, but he points out that the fossil evidence is in dramatic contrast to the natural predictions of the evolutionary model as it is normally used.

It can be predicted that evolutionists will devise a model, however speculative, to explain the facts. The question is, does the completely materialistic model of the origin of the species serve as the best model to explain the data? In the final analysis it does not.

Life was created. As stated before, the only question is whether God created one original life form or many. Even Darwin speculated that there may have been a number of different original species. The evidence above speaks strongly for the idea that God has created different life forms at different times. The evidence points to various divergent species appearing "suddenly and simultaneously" at different points in the past. Here the hand of God can be seen. The picture created by scientific evidence is consistent with the creation of different species at different times, followed by a slow and gradual evolution of these species from that point forward.

Although the model of multiple specie-creations is consistent with the fossil evidence, it can be predicted that it will not find its way into biology textbooks any time soon. This is partly because of the atheist/naturalist bias of the textbook writers. The non-believer assumes that a miraculous event cannot happen, therefore they will not give serious attention to this model, no matter how compellingly the evidence supports it. There is a less sinister reason the creation model will not be found in mainstream textbooks. This has to do with the nature of science. A scientist who is open to this idea might struggle to put it into her science text because a creation event is something science does not know how to deal with. Even a scientist who believes in multiple strands of creation followed by evolution might mention it in class, but not include it in a textbook. An idea which invokes supernatural forces is not strictly "science."

The evidence from the fossil record pointing to nearly simultaneous massive destructions and creations of species is not the only area that has caused many evolutionists to take a good hard look at their models. Another kind of evidence which classical evolutionary theory struggles to explain is the existence of complex systems in living things for which it is extremely difficult to conceive how random mutations could assemble such systems. A case in point is the eye of the trilobite, a very primitive and relatively simple species (by comparison to humans) which appeared right at the Cambrian explosion. Some trilobites were blind, but some had an incredible eye. Unlike the flexible lenses in the eyes of mammals, the upper half of the eye of the trilobite was formed of a very hard crystal of the mineral calcite. In this part of the eye, a large number of separate mini-crystals were stacked together in such a way that they produced a perfect focus at the back of the eye, where apparently there were nerve receptors to receive the image. To make this even more amazing, the lower part of the lens was composed of the hard organic material called chitin, which also had a shape that could focus light at the same point as the upper part. This amazing double lens had the property of eliminating what physicists call spherical aberration. Spherical aberration is a problem which spherical lenses have in producing a focused image. Even the human eye has this problem, but not the wonderfully designed eye of the trilobite.

The question to be asked is how many beneficial mutations had to occur for this eye to form where there was no eye before? Surely it would involve thousands of mutations. For this eye to function, the genetic code had to be created which could produce the enzymes capable of synthesizing and forming the calcite crystals in precisely the correct shape, along with separate genetic information which could make the compounds responsible for constructing the chitin part of the lens. Not only that, but unless the beneficial genetic mutations (hundreds or thousands of them) which could produce the nerve cells to detect the light happened simultaneously, what good would all these supposedly beneficial mutations forming the two lenses be?

Remember that the trilobite appeared in the fossil record suddenly on the geological scale with no obvious predecessor. It did not just have a new eye, it had a very large number of other new features. How did this happen? Perhaps it is unfair to ask the evolutionist for a single, complete explanation, but the idea of many thousands of coordinated beneficial mutations (which would not even be beneficial unless they occurred in parallel) begs an explanation of some sort. Again, according to the fossil record, such changes must happen very rapidly. A noted evolutionist, Gordon Rattray Taylor, said concerning the eye of the trilobite:[98]

> *By what conceivable chance could the trilobite have accumulated the one material in the universe-namely calcite-which had the required optical properties, and then imposed on it the one type of curved surface which would achieve the required result?... We are still reeling at the improbability of this.*

Taylor was at one time the chief science advisor for the BBC. He was not a believer in special creation at all, but rather an evolutionist. However, his studies led him to believe that the Darwinian model simply cannot explain the evidence.

It is interesting to note what Charles Darwin said in *Origin of Species* concerning the origin of the human eye:

> *To suppose that the origin of the eye, with all its inimitable contrivances for adjusting the focus to different distances could have been formed by natural selection, seems, I freely confess, absurd in the highest possible degree.*[99]

He was quoted later in life as saying "The eye gives me a cold shudder." There are a great number of other systems in living things showing signs of "irreducible complexity" which can be mentioned.[100] Many of these require such a great number of simultaneous beneficial mutations that evolutionists find themselves grasping for terms such as "positive evolutionary principle" or "evolutionary plan" to describe them.

Considering such evidence, and knowing that the fossil record in places such as the Cambrian explosion shows massive and sudden appearance of new species, seemingly out of nowhere, the open minded person is forced to search for a radically different model from the current Darwinian or neo-Darwinian evolutionary theories.

ANOTHER MODEL

The author will conclude that the most reasonable explanation of the fossil record is that the Creator has created a number of different species at different times in the past. After creating these species, it appears that God has allowed them to "evolve" gradually into the forms which may be observed today. A majority of scientists will obviously resist this model because it invokes a supernatural explanation, but it seems to be the best model that can explain the data.

This rather bold claim brings up a question. If one accepts this model, it is reasonable to ask why the Creator would spend hundreds of millions of years creating life as we now see it. Does this mean he is not really so powerful? If the creation of human beings was the ultimate goal, why did God stretch creation out over billions of years? It seems that an omnipotent Creator could have made more efficient use of time. A statement by the author Kenneth Miller may be helpful here.[101]

Whatever God's characteristics, impatience is not one of them. A genuine believer trusts not only in the reality of the divine, but also in its wisdom, and sees history, indirect, comic and tragic, as the unfolding of His plan. There is no religious justification for demanding that the Creator hold to a certain schedule, follow a defined pathway or do things exactly according to our expectations.

There seems to be a parallel between how God intervenes in human history and in natural history. The pattern in both cases is that God normally allows things to proceed freely and in a natural way. In the history of his people, as recorded in the Bible, God intervened miraculously only very rarely, *and for definite reasons*. In biblical history, God intervened miraculously in dramatic ways only during the times of Noah, Moses, Elijah/Elisha and Jesus. In each case, new revelation was being given to mankind. It is possible to view the fossil record in a similar way. God intervened in natural history only rarely, allowing "natural" forces to work their slow progress for almost all of natural history. One can only speculate about why God chose to create the world over such a long period of time, using a mixture of divine and natural processes. Similarly, one can only speculate why God allowed thousands of years of human history to proceed without intervening to bring salvation to humanity sooner.

If one allows for the supernatural intervention of God in the formation of species to explain the sudden appearance of new species, then what about the more gradual type of evolution which is observable from the fossil record? If extremely rapid changes and sudden appearances of species has a divine explanation, is it reasonable to conjecture that God has a hand in every step of the process of evolution? Perhaps God influences even the most minute but favorable genetic change. Admittedly, this is speculation, but the question seems to be not so much whether or not God has intervened in the origin of species, but rather how much and how often he intercedes.

Argument by analogy amounts to speculation, so we should be very cautious. However, let us for a moment extend the analogy used above. Biblical history describes God dramatically intervening in the natural course of human history only very rarely and then only for a reason. Having said that, does God also intervene in less dramatic ways in human lives all the time? As Paul said to his Athenian hearers, "From one man he made every nation of men...and he determined the times set for them and the exact places where they should live. God did this so that men would seek him and perhaps reach out for him and find him, though he is not far from each of us." (Acts 17:26-27). This is a theistic not a deistic God. God is intervening in subtle ways in the spiritual world all the time.

Yet, God allows human nature to work as it will in most things. Can this teach us about how God works in the evolution of species? Remember that we are now in the area of nearly pure speculation, but it seems to be in the nature of God to keep his "finger" in things. Does a proper reading of the Bible allow for theistic evolution? Is this the most reasonable (though admittedly by definition not scientific) explanation of how species change? By this model, God created different species at different times for reasons knowable only to him. He also keeps his hand in nature, sustaining the gradual, "natural" process of evolution. Let the reader decide.

The first life was created by God (chapter four). Although we cannot say it is proven conclusively, scientific evidence points to various divergent species being created at different times. These species were created according to a "developmental program." Apparently, they were created according to a common genetic pattern as well. Although different created species have different DNA molecules, they all have much in common in their genetic code because they were created according to a pattern.

This model is consistent with the thinking of many early evolutionists. Typically, they hesitated to speculate about the origins of life. At one time Darwin proposed the idea of a number of different original species from which evolution occurred. Darwin was not the only early evolutionist to discuss the idea of multiple species being created. An early evolutionist, Frederick Temple, said:

If we begin, as it were, at the other end and trace things back-wards from the present, instead of forwards from the remote past, it cannot be denied that Darwin's investigations have made it exceedingly probable that the vast variety of plants and animals have sprung from a much smaller number of original forms.[102]

Here the author saw an unspecified number of original forms. It was only when later evolutionists attempted to come up with a theory which was avowedly naturalistic—one which did not necessitate invoking a divine creator-that this idea of multiple original forms came to fall out of favor. Given the most recent fossil evidence, it is time to recall the multiple original form idea to the evolution debate.

This brings us back to Genesis chapter one. The Genesis account of creation involves different species being created at different times ("days"). "So God created the great creatures of the sea and every living and moving thing with which the water teems, according to their kinds, and every winged bird according to its kind" (Genesis 1:21). Given the evidence already shown in this book, it is not surprising that the account in Genesis is consistent with the model proposed above, which in turn is consistent with the best scientific evidence available today.

CONCLUSION

In summary, the Bible clearly describes God as the creator of the universe and the creator of life. Regarding the origin of individual species, the Bible says precious little. Young earth creationists try to create the impression that the evolutionary theory is a paper tiger which will fall apart with the slightest scientific scrutiny. This is simply not the case. The data available from science is, on the whole, consistent with evolutionary model. However, when one looks closely at the proposed mechanisms for genetic change and at the fossil record, one will discover that the form of evolutionary theory to which the materialist ascribes struggles to explain the evidence. It would be unwise to declare flatly that the materialist version or evolutionary theory is absolutely proven wrong. We have also been admonished by Augustine to hesitate when we impose debatable interpretation of scripture on our theories about nature. However if one does not reject divine operation out-of-hand, a model more consistent with the evidence emerges. The evidence from science is consistent with a model of special creation of different species at different times in the past, along with a gradual change over time by "natural" processes which may or may not be guided by the hand of God. There is a sense in which this model is not "scientific" in that it invokes supernatural events. However, to exclude divine influence *a priori* is not intellectually honest. This model of special creation plus gradual change is consistent with the evidence from science, it is consistent with the biblical picture of God, and it is consistent with the Genesis creation account.

THE ORIGIN OF MAN

The second question to be discussed in this chapter is the origin of man. Did human beings evolve from apes or are we a special creation of God? This question is closely related to the question of evolution already discussed. This was the real issue behind the Scopes monkey trial.

It has already been shown that life was created. We have also seen that the fossil evidence is most reasonably explained by a model which includes special creation of species along with gradual change of species over time. But what about man? Did we evolve from an ape which began to walk upright about four million years ago, or were Adam and Eve created "out of the dust of the ground?" There does not seem to be much middle ground on this one. This is a highly charged emotional question for many people. The first question which should be asked is what does the scientific evidence tell us?

Most of us have seen the pictures from one of the National Geographic articles on the evolution of man. They show a series of species, beginning in the fairly remote past, gradually standing more erect, acquiring a more pronounced forehead and possessing a larger brain. The next-to last picture in the series is the Neanderthal (also known as Neandertal), followed by the Cro Magnon, modern man. The implication is clear. A statement from the National Academy of Sciences brings out the full implications of this picture.

> *Studies in evolutionary biology have led to the conclusion that mankind arose from ancestral primates. This association was hotly debated among scientists in Darwin's day, before molecular biology and the discovery of the now abundant links. Today, however, there is no significant scientific doubt about the close evolutionary relationships among all primates or between apes and humans. The "missing links" that troubled Darwin and his followers are no longer missing. Today, not one but many such connecting links, intermediate between various branches of the primate family tree, have been found as fossils.*[103]

This statement is an overstatement of the facts, but it typifies the view of many scientists, especially those who are atheists.

So what are these "links," and what do they suggest? To answer these questions we will contemplate the current status of the fossil evidence. In Darwin's day there was no direct evidence that man evolved from apes. In *Origin of Species*, Darwin did not even mention the origin of man, perhaps because of lack of hard evidence or perhaps out of reticence to bring more than the necessary criticism on his ideas. It was fifteen years after the first edition of *Origins* that Darwin chose to address the issue in his book, *Descent of Man* (1871). Here, Darwin came out decisively for human evolution from apes, based on faith in his theory as a whole and on the similar anatomical form of apes and humans. He had no fossil evidence for human evolution. This situation has changed dramatically in the past one hundred years with the discovery of early human and pre-human fossil remains which have been proposed as links between ancestral apes and humans.

One proposed link is the fossil species known as *Australopithecus afarensis*. This species and its cousins *africanus, boisei* and *robustus* are conjectured to have lived from about four million until about one million years ago. The most famous afarensis find is known as Lucy. This fossil discovery was announced in 1976. It is missing a skull, the most important part of the skeleton for making comparisons to human features. Since the discovery of Lucy, over three hundred fossil finds have been classified as being *afarensis*. Most of these are fragmentary—a part of a jaw or a few teeth and the like. However, in 1992 a nearly complete skull identified as *afarensis* was discovered. This *Australopithecus* species was about four feet tall. Evidence suggests they walked upright a significant part of the time. They had a brain size of between 400 cc and 500 cc, compared to modern humans with a brain size of about 1350 cc.[104] For comparison, modern gorillas have a brain size of about 500 cc. Other proposed links have been discovered and identified as distinct from *Australopithecus afarensis*. These include *Homo erectus*, proposed to have lived from about one million to a few hundred thousand years ago. This species had an average brain size of about 850 cc. Another distinct species has been identified as "archaic" *Homo sapiens*, proposed to have lived from a few hundred thousand years ago until about two hundred thousand years ago. The distinctions between these species are hotly debated among anthropologists, and it can be assumed that the current labels will change with time as new discoveries are made.[105]

On a more solid footing is the more recent species, *Neanderthal*. Specimens identified as *Neanderthal* have been dated from about two hundred fifty thousand years in the past to about forty thousand years ago (these numbers are debated as well). Unlike the species mentioned above, there is a wealth of evidence concerning *Neanderthals*. Hundreds of skeletons have been identified. Most recent of all are the fossils known popularly as *Cro Magnon*. Most anthropologists would concur that *Cro Magnon* is modern *Homo sapiens*. In other words they are people.

So what about the evidence? As one looks at the skeletal remains, one sees ape, ape, ape, people, and people. The first three species named above were all clearly apes. They all had arm hand and leg features of apes. The major distinction between these apes and modern chimpanzees and gorillas is that their hip structure implies that they moved about largely by walking upright. Anthropologists debate even this conclusion. They all had brain sizes about one third to one half that of modern humans, the same size, more or less, as modern apes. On the other hand, *Neanderthal* had brains on average slightly larger than modern man's. They had significantly different muscle structure and facial bone structure, but if dressed up carefully, they could pass as modern man. They used fire, made tools and built simple living structures.

It is time to relate the evidence to what is found in the Bible. Biologists claim that modern man is the end product of gradual evolution from a half-ape/half-human ancestor. What does the Bible have to say about this? To answer the question, one must return to the book of Genesis. The creation of Adam and Eve is recorded in Genesis chapters one and two. "So God created man in his own image, in the image of God he created him." (Genesis 1:27) "And the Lord God formed man (Adam) from the dust of the ground and breathed into his nostrils the breath of life, and man became a living being." (Genesis 2:7)

According to the Bible, man is a special creation. A straight forward reading of Genesis seems to preclude the possibility of humans evolving from apes. It is hard to imagine interpreting these scriptures any other way. Luke assumed Adam was a real person (Luke 3:38). Paul used Adam as a prefigure of Jesus (Romans 5:14, 1 Corinthians 15:22,45). How are we to understand the biblical account in the light of scientific knowledge? Can they be reconciled?

Some, in an attempt to reconcile the Bible with the scientific evidence, have taken the creation story of Adam and Eve to be an allegory which describes in the most general terms the creation and fall of man. In other words, they take the creation story in Genesis to have no basis in physical reality. Given the scientific reliability of Genesis chapter one and given the historical reliability of the Bible in general, this seems inconsistent with what we know of the Bible. Besides, the inspired writers of the New Testament clearly did not think Adam and Eve were allegorical figures. It seems reasonable to reject this theory (but to remain open-minded).

Others have speculated that God took an already-evolved, intelligent being (presumably modern *homo sapiens*) and imbued that creature with spiritual qualities to make man in his own image. In other words, some believe that Adam and Eve were the first humans to have a soul and a spirit. This would be consistent with what God said in Genesis 1:26; "Let us make man in our image, in our likeness..." If true, it would also resolve any perceived contradiction between the scientific evidence and the Bible. The problem with this interpretation is that it certainly disagrees with a straight forward interpretation of Genesis one and two. "And God formed man from the dust of the ground and breathed into his nostrils the breath of life, and man became a living being" (Genesis 2:7). Let me say personally that I do not agree with this interpretation. I reject it, not for scientific reasons but because this interpretation seems to be in conflict with what I see to be the most obvious way of understanding how Genesis was written. Genesis describes actual special creations which are consistent with scientific evidence and I see no reason to change approach when we come to Adam and Eve.

However, it is wise to not be dogmatic on this point. We have seen some good advice from Galileo, Thomas Aquinas, Augustine and others (see chapter one) to avoid forcing a particular interpretation of the Bible with regard to natural events. History tells us that believers have forced a particular personal interpretation onto their understanding of evidence from the natural world, only to be proven wrong. Humility and charity with regard to opinion seems advisable in this case.

Without dogmatically rejecting the possibility that God made an evolved being into humans by planting a soul into Adam and Eve, let us present an alternative which preserves the straight forward understanding of Genesis and which does not contradict the Bible. It has already been shown that life was created. It has also been suggested in the previous section using evidence from the fossil record, that God has created many different species at different times. It is not a great stretch to imagine that God created mankind. In other words, the most reasonable way to interpret Genesis one and two is to conclude that Adam and Eve were a special, miraculous creation by God.

There is a very important point to be made about this however. The bottom line is that belief in mankind as a separate supernatural creation of God is based principally on faith. The strongest reason to believe the creation of man was by miraculous means is because the Bible says so. Remember that it is important for us to separate what is believed by faith from what is believed primarily because of the evidence. A conviction that the Bible is inspired by God leads to a conviction about heaven. There is no scientific evidence for heaven. Confidence in the inspiration and therefore the authority of biblical scripture leads to faith that Jesus Christ will come back some day. It is also part of the reason to believe the Adam and Eve account.

It is true that the evidence from paleontology points to ape, ape, ape, man, man. It is possible to interpret the data from anthropology to be consistent with the Biblical account. However, let us be honest about the evidence. It is not ridiculous or absurd to interpret the evidence from the fossil record to imply evolution of human beings. Perhaps a more careful look at the evidence by those who do not assume only materialistic causes is justified. Many times scientists have ended up red-faced because they were not sufficiently skeptical about unproved theories. Nevertheless, the fact is that as evidence has been accumulated, it has lent more credence, not less, to the claim of the evolutionists in this area. Although the ascent of man from apes is far from proven, it is not an outrageous leap from the evidence either. In fact I would be so bold as to admit that if it were not for what is recorded in the Bible, I would probably have accepted the evolutionist's conclusion about the origins of man. The theory of the evolution of man from apes is a virtual religion to many anthropologists. Their zeal may cause them to be overconfident in their claims. Nevertheless, let it be said one more time. Although the evidence from science allows for special creation, it certainly does not *demand* it. The principle reason for believing in the special creation of Adam and Eve is faith in the reliability of the Bible.

In summary, one is left with an unproven theory of human origins by evolution. As with any theory about things in the past, it remains unproven, but there is certainly enough supporting evidence to make it believable. One is also left with a Biblical claim that Adam and Eve were a special creation by God. This claim does not conflict with the scientific evidence. Acceptance of the Biblical claim that man was a special creation amounts to a belief in the supernatural—a belief that science cannot explain every event that has ever occurred. For reasons too numerous to list, I believe the Bible is inspired by God. I believe in the Biblical account of creation of mankind.

FOR TODAY

1. *What ideas about evolution and the origin of man did you bring in to reading this book? Have any of these beliefs changed? Why?*

2. *Do you believe the special creation model of the origin of species and of humans should be taught in science classes on an equal footing with evolution? Why or why not?*

3. *Whether you believe in it or not, can you summarize the evidence which supports the theory of evolution in a few sentences?*

4. *How does evidence from the fossil record, such as that of the Cambrian explosion relate to the question of the origin of species?*

5. *Assuming that you accept the account of Adam and Eve do you believe the account because of evidence to support it, or because it is recorded in the Bible and you have faith in the accuracy of the Bible?*

89 For an example of this agenda being applied, a bill was passed by the Arkansas state legislature in 1981 legislating the teaching of creation science in public schools. Creation science was defined in this bill (Arkansas Statute 590) as:

(It) means the scientific evidence for creation and inferences from those scientific evidences and related inferences that indicate: (1) Sudden creation of the universe, energy and life from nothing. (2) The insufficiency of mutation and natural selection in bringing about development of all living kinds from a single organism. (3) Changes only within fixed limits of originally created kinds of plants and animals. (4) Separate ancestry for man and apes. (5) Explanation of the earth's geology by catastrophism, including the occurrence of a worldwide flood. (6) A relatively recent inception of the earth and living kinds. This legislation was later found to be unconstitutional.

Points one through three can be supported from science, and perhaps point four as well, but points five and six are what makes this a "radical agenda," at least in the opinion of the author.

90 Charles Darwin, *The Descent of Man*, 1871.

91 William Jennings Bryan, July 16, 1925. From the Scopes Trial, Dayton, Tennessee.

92 E. C. C. Lin et al., "Evolution of an *Escherichia coli* Protein with Increased Resistance to Oxidative Stress," *Journal of Biological Chemistry*, 273 (1998), 8308-8316. A summary of examples of both types of evidence mentioned above is found in Kenneth R. Miller, *Finding Darwin's God* (New York: HarperCollins Publishers, 1999).

93 F. Hoyle and N. C. Wickramasinghe, *Evolution from Space* (New York Simon and Schuster, , 1981).

94 H. S. Lipson, *Physics Bulletin*, 30, 1979, 140, H. S. Lipson, *Physics Bulletin*, 31, 1980, 138, and H. S. Lipson, *Physics Bulletin* 31, 1980, 337.

95 Jeffery S. Levinton, "The Big Bang of Animal Evolution," *Scientific American*, November 1992, 84.

96 Ibid. 87, 90.

97 Stephen Jay Gould, "Evolution's Erratic Pace," *Natural History*, Vol. 5, May, 1977, 12, 14.

98 Gordon Rattray Taylor, *The Great Evolution Mystery* (London: Taylor, Secher and Warburg, 1983), 98. Many similar examples are mentioned in this book.

99 Taken from the sixth edition (1872) of *On The Origin of Species by Means of Natural Selection, or the Preservation of Favoured Races in the Struggle for Life*. Charles Darwin, Everyman's Library (London: :J.M. Dent & Sons:,1928) 167.

100 A good treatment of this subject can be found in Alan Hayward, *Creation and Evolution* (Minneapolis: Bethany House Publishers, , 1995), 13-53. Also see Michael J. Denton, *Nature's Destiny* (New York: The Free Press, 1998), chapters 13-15.

101 Kenneth Miller, *Finding Darwin's God* (New York: HarperCollins Publishers), 245.

102 Frederick Temple, *The Relations Between Religion and Science* (London: Macmillan and Company, 1884).

103 *Science and Creationism: A View from the National Academy of Sciences*, (Washington DC.: National Academy Press, 1984).

104 Numbers from Henry McHenry, "Tempo and Mode of Human Evolution," *Proceedings of the National Academy of Science*, 91, 6780-6786, 1994.

105 A series of *National Geographic* articles present some of the evidence discussed here in a very readable form. These include articles in the September 1995, January 1996 and March 1996 issues.

CHAPTER 10

THE FIRST TO PRESENT HIS CASE SEEMS RIGHT, TILL ANOTHER
COMES FORWARD AND QUESTIONS HIM.

PROVERBS 18:17

WILL IT BE FIRE
NEXT TIME?

The last major subject we will examine is the Flood. Chapters six through eight of Genesis describe a great flood of seemingly worldwide scope. If the flood is historical, when did it happen? When the flood happened, was it truly a world-wide flood? Maybe the story is just an allegory, or perhaps less argumentatively, perhaps it is a parable about the nature of man and how God feels about sin. Those not familiar with the flood account should read Genesis six through eight before continuing. To sum it up, a few quotes from Genesis are provided that illustrate the nature of this flood as described in the Bible.

> So the LORD said, "I will wipe mankind, whom I have created, from the face of the earth—men and animals, and creatures that move along the ground... For forty days the flood kept coming on the earth and as the waters increased they lifted the ark high above the earth... The waters rose and covered the mountains to a depth of more than twenty feet... Everything on dry land that had the breath of life in its nostrils died... Only Noah was left, and those with him on the ark (Genesis 6:7; 7:17,20,22,23).

A few questions present themselves immediately. What is the meaning of the statement that the mountains were covered to a depth of more than twenty feet? Does it mean a total depth of twenty feet of rain, or that literally the highest mountaintop was twenty feet under? What about "Everything on dry land" dying? Does that mean all species had at least some members perish in the flood, or does it mean every member of every species (except those in the ark) was killed? Is there evidence this flood actually happened?

A number of explanations of the Biblical account have been offered. The skeptics argue that this is just another of the myths in the Bible—further proof that the Bible was written by a scientifically ignorant people. They scoff at the idea of God speaking to Noah, and laugh at the thought of him building such a huge boat and just waiting around for all these animals to show up at his door. To be honest, if it were not for the overwhelming evidence for the inspiration of the Bible, a small part of which is already presented in this book, the skeptic would have a very good point. This is clearly something that does not happen every day. It is not within the normal range of animal behavior for them to travel great distances and voluntarily enter a boat with other species. In fact it would be downright miraculous. Surely, however, the evidence of the divine origin of the Bible is sufficient to encourage one to look more closely.

At the other extreme, we have already seen that some in the young-earth creationists' camp believe not only that the flood described in Genesis happened but this worldwide flood explains the majority of the sedimentary deposits on earth. In other words, creationists use a single catastrophic flood to explain the presence of nearly all the sedimentary rock on earth. They also claim that the biblical flood can explain virtually the entire fossil record, with its trilobites consistently lying below the early amphibians, which, in turn managed without exception to settle in the flood mud below the dinosaurs. In this same flood, the dinosaurs always settled into layers of sediment below the great mammals. All this entropy-defying miraculous sorting occurred in one great cataclysmic event, producing sedimentary deposits as much as 80,000 feet deep. No more needs to be said about this. Others have proposed pseudo-natural (i.e. pseudo-scientific) explanations of the flood. One such attempt is called the canopy theory. Canopy theorists claim that the water which fell to the earth in the flood was held in the atmosphere of the earth in a water "canopy" prior to the deluge. According to this theory, once Noah and his family entered the ark, the entire water canopy fell to earth over a forty-day period, causing the flood. There is no conceivable natural explanation for how all this water could be held up in the atmosphere. If sufficient water to cover the earth by many feet were somehow held in the upper atmosphere, in defiance of the law of gravity, it would block enough sun light to kill most plant life. Besides, if the water fell from the sky during the flood, where did it go afterwards? Did it evaporate back into the canopy? If so, why is it no longer in the sky? The theory makes no logical sense at all as a "natural" explanation.

Still others, seeking a natural explanation of the flood, have proposed the local flood theory. They claim that there was a massive flood, but that it only affected the immediate area of Mesopotamia. According to this model, all life in Mesopotamia was wiped out, but the rest of the earth was relatively unaffected. Somehow the water piled up over this one region without spilling over to neighboring regions. It is conceivable that one could justify this interpretation of the Genesis flood using legitimate biblical hermeneutics. There are instances in which Bible writers use the phrase "all over the world" metaphorically to refer to events which they knew did not literally affect the whole world. Acts 24:5 is a case in point. However, if we study Genesis chapters six and seven, we find a flood which is not only world-wide, but one which lasts for hundreds of days. There is no scientific explanation for water piling up hundreds of feet for months on end in Mesopotamia without gravity causing the water to subside and spread to other regions. The local flood is no more "natural" and no less miraculous than a worldwide flood. There is no physical evidence for a massive local flood, and this interpretation certainly seems to run counter to what is said in Genesis. We would do well to not take this flood theory seriously.

These explanations are weak attempts to make the flood "scientific".[106] Let it be put simply: if the flood described in Genesis occurred, it was nothing short of a miracle. The flood cannot be explained by science any more than the resurrection of Jesus from the dead or his predicted return to judge the earth by fire. These are not natural events. Any attempt to read these as something other than the miraculous intervention of God is doomed to fail. As is written in 2 Peter 3:6-7,

By water also the world of that time was deluged and destroyed.
By the same word the present heavens and earth are reserved for fire,
being kept for the day of judgment and destruction of ungodly men.

There is no conceivable *scientific* explanation for the flood, just as there will be no natural explanation of earth's future destruction by fire. These are supernatural acts of an omnipotent God in response to the moral condition of mankind.

According to the Bible, the flood occurred, not because of some natural law, but because of man's sin. It is stated in Genesis 6:6-8 that "The Lord was grieved that he had made man on the earth, and his heart was filled with pain."

Having said this, there is some evidence that a worldwide flood did indeed happen several thousand years ago. We will look at some of this evidence. In fact, if the flood occurred, it seems reasonable to expect that some remnant physical evidence would remain. We will ponder what one can expect to observe if the flood of Noah actually happened. However, let it be remembered that although there is some tantalizing evidence to support belief that a world-wide flood did indeed occur, ultimately belief in the Genesis account of the flood is based principally on faith in the Bible.

Like Peter said, we know by faith that Jesus will return in judgment. This faith is based on the reality that God has already judged the earth by water.

First, what physical signs would be left behind by a flood such as that described in Genesis 7? If the Genesis flood occurred, then one can assume that the water rose to significant heights over the course of forty days. Presumably there would have been a signigicant amount of erosion. Bear in mind, though, that once the flood covered a particular area, the erosion would stop, as water would no longer be flowing downhill. How much erosion would such a flood cause? Would it be enough to carve canyons hundreds of feet deep through solid rock? The answer is that a single flood, no matter how great, could not cause this kind of erosion.

The question is whether the Genesis flood would leave unmistakable signs to be discovered thousands of years later. Such a flood would cause erosion, but no more erosion than might normally have occurred in a few years or at most a few hundred years in any one place. Mud layers would be left behind by the flood, but probably no more than a few feet or at most a few tens of feet. After all, the material loosened by a flood-even a massive one-would mostly only redistribute the topsoil and some relatively loose rock. There is not enough topsoil available to leave hundreds of feet of sediment anywhere, even if the flood were worldwide.

In point of fact, if one looked for signs of a world-wide flood which occurred several thousands of years ago it is not clear that any sign would be left behind about which one could say: "Aha! There is solid proof that the flood described in Genesis occurred." The flood described in Genesis would probably not leave behind a smoking gun.Thinking carefully about the nature of the flood described in the Bible leads one to conclude that there would be no absolutely clear-cut physical evidence that the flood occurred, assuming that God miraculously produced and later miraculously cleared away the water. So what evidence is there that this flood actually occurred?

Probably the strongest evidence for a worldwide flood is in the records of cultures across the globe. Nearly every ancient culture has a record of a great flood. Cultures with a flood story include the Hindus, the native cultures of Burma and of New Guinea, the Aborigines of Australia, as well as the inhabitants of New Zealand. Also, there are records or stories of a great flood among the Incas and the Aztecs as well as a number of tribes in North America. In addition, we have flood accounts from the Greeks, the Babylonians, the Japanese, the Hottentots in Africa, the ancient Celts in Western Europe and the Sumerians in Mesopotamia. The Sumerians are one of the earliest great civilizations. Inscriptions show that they dated their dynasties from before "the flood" and after "the flood." In fact, when Sir Leonard Wooley excavated the ancient Sumerian city of Ur, he found an eight foot thick layer of mud and debris at the bottom of the city, below which flints and other relics of the stone age were found.

The list could continue. In the majority of ancient cultures, on every inhabited continent, a story of a massive flood can be found. Interestingly, the stories are almost universally of a world-wide flood. Many mention a single person or family surviving by either building a boat or going to the highest mountain peak. Scholars have claimed that the Genesis account was borrowed from the Babylonian or Sumerian flood story. Surely they cannot claim that the Aztecs and the Aborigines in Australia borrowed their stories from the Babylonians as well.

What is the source of all these stories? They seem to have so much in common, yet many of them originated in divergent cultures in parts of the world between which there was no known contact. It is not unreasonable to conclude that they are a record of an actual event in the remote past. Not unreasonable, that is, if one admits the possibility that a miraculous event, one which violates the laws of nature, can occur. No other great planet-wide event of the past left such an indelible mark in human memory that it was recorded in cultural histories across the world. However, let us be honest about this. The flood stories do not provide physical proof of the sort acceptable to scientists, but their consistency is tantalizing evidence.

There is another piece of evidence worth mentioning. Although the flood may not have left an unambiguous sign on dry land, there is evidence of a dramatic drop in salinity in the ocean in the not-too-distant past. Geologists drilling core samples on the continental shelf of the Gulf of Mexico in the late sixties and early seventies made a surprising discovery. When analyzing the oxygen isotope ratios in the discarded shells of planktonic foraminifera in these cores, they found that there was a sudden and dramatic lowering in the salinity of the Gulf of Mexico about 11,600 years ago, followed by a gradual increase in salinity to more normal levels. In the words of Cesare Emiliani, one of the geologists who studied the samples:

> *We know this, because the oxygen isotope ratios of the foraminifera shells show a marked, temporary decrease in the salinity of the waters of the Gulf of Mexico, it clearly shows there was a major period of flooding from 12,000 to 10,000 years ago. There is no question that there was a flood, and there is also no question that there was a universal flood.*[107]

Emiliani is one of a number of scientist who studied these samples. Among them are James Kennett of the University of Rhode Island and Nicholas Shackleton of Cambridge University. By the way, Emiliani and the others do not conclude that this flood was the one recorded in the Bible, but their findings are interesting.

There are a few questions about the flood story in Genesis that a thinking person will raise. Let us anticipate some of them. According to the account in Genesis, the flood wiped out all people except Noah and his family. How then, the skeptic might ask, did this story survive in all these ancient cultures? How did the ancient languages, cultures and even racial features in various parts of the world survive? To answer this question, speculation is required. Perhaps the flood affected the entire earth, but did not literally wipe out all human and animal life everywhere. How do we interpret the twenty feet of water in Genesis seven? Perhaps the flood had world-wide effect but left remnants of life scattered around the world.

Continuing in this vein, a thoroughly literal reading of the Genesis flood account implies that members of every one of the millions of species on the earth were on the ark. The skeptic might legitimately ask whether Noah sailed past Australia to drop off the kangaroos, koalas and duck-billed platypuses, since they clearly could not survive hopping or waddling back to Australia. Unfortunately, there is no ready and convincing answer for these questions. Certainly God could miraculously recreate these species. Again, the flood could have been universal, but not literally complete in wiping out every single member of every species. Possibly Noah and his family only carried local species in the ark, and God preserved others from destruction through means he does not explain. The account in Genesis only specifically mentions domesticated animals. It is simply impossible to be sure about these things. The wise person will keep an open mind and avoid being dogmatic concerning questions left open in the Bible.

As a side note, some groups have claimed that remains of the ark have been discovered on Mount Ararat in eastern Turkey. A thorough analysis of the supposed evidence for the discovery of the ark has been published.[108] To summarize, there is no credible evidence that the ark has been discovered on Mount Ararat or anywhere else. Genesis 8:4 has Noah and his family coming to ground in "the mountains of Ararat." This may be near present-day Ararat or it may be in the Urartu Mountains in present-day Iran in the region around Lake Van. In any case, the ark almost certainly settled at the foot of such mountains, not on the top of one of the peaks. Besides, wooden objects almost never last 5000-10000 years. As my friend Douglas Jacoby has pointed out,[109] "Besides, would not the ark have been a valuable commodity? Rather than abandon it, surely it is more realistic to expect that Noah and his sons would have made good use of the wood for structures, tools, fuel and the like."

In conclusion, some things about the flood are clear and some are not. First, the Bible, with all its marks of inspiration, records a flood with universal effect. The inspired writers of the New Testament mention the flood as a matter of historical fact. Second, there is a nearly universal record across the world of a great flood, some with features remarkably similar to those described in the Bible. Third, there is also some evidence from geology that a worldwide flood did indeed happen. It will never be possible to clear up every question which might be asked about the Genesis flood, because it happened in the distant past, but the Bible believer can be confident that the flood happened. Remember, though, that belief in the flood as described in Genesis is based partially on the evidence, but also largely on faith in the reliability of the Bible. Worrying about the depth of the water, the number of animals or the extent of the destruction seems to miss the point. This flood serves as God's advance notice that he will return to judge the world. A wise person will devote their energy to preparing for the second day of judgment; this time by fire.

> *By water also the world of that time was deluged and destroyed.*
> *By the same word the present heavens and earth are reserved for fire,*
> *being kept for the day of judgment and destruction of ungodly men*
> *(2 Peter 3:6,7).*

FOR TODAY

1. *Do you believe the flood recorded in Genesis actually happened? Why or why not?*

2. *In this chapter it is claimed that a worldwide flood would not leave behind a "smoking gun In other words, it is not clear that a great (colossal or worldwide) ancient flood would leave behind unambiguous physical evidence. Does this sound like a reasonable claim to you?*

3. *Do you think that genuine Christians can disagree over the nature and extent of the Flood?*

106 A more recent theory along these general lines is the "Hydroplate Theory." This interesting proposal suggests the floodwaters were stored in giant underground reservoirs,. When they were suddenly released in a cataclysmic event, the flood was triggered. However, this hypothesis falls into the same category as the others. A well-written description of this theory can be found in Walt Brown, *In the Beginning* (Phoenix: Center for Scientific Creation, 1995, www.creationscience.com).

107 Taken from Cesare Emiliani, "Ancient Temperatures," *Scientific American*, 198, (1958), 54-63.

108 Rex Geissler and B. J. Corbin, *The Explorers of Ararat* (Highlands Ranch, Colorado: Great Commission Books, 2000) .

109 Douglas Jacoby, *Genesis, Science and History* (Billerica, Massachusetts: Discipleship Publications International, 2004), 209-222.

A Closer Look at the Laws of Thermodynamics

In chapter four the application of the laws of thermodynamics to the question of the origin of life was introduced. The arguments in that chapter can stand on their own. However for those with some scientific background legitimate questions can and have come up which deserve a more thorough treatment. The author has been asked the questions raised in the the following section many times, both in personal conversation and in Q&A sessions at public presentations. The discussion below tends more toward the abstract and the mathematical, which is why it was left for an appendix. Readers with a strong background in chemistry and physics have probably already anticipated some of the arguments to follow. It is hoped that further discussion will also be helpful for those with less science background who are willing to wade through some admittedly tougher material.

Could life have been created by a "natural process"? Can the materialist assumption be upheld in view of what we know about living things and about the nature of entropy? We have already used qualitative arguments to say no. Let us now be more quantitative. The first law of thermodynamics, simply stated, is as follows: "In any process, the total energy of the universe is conserved." In other words, for any natural process, energy may change forms or move from one place to another, but the total energy content in the universe is constant. No single scientist is given credit for discovering this law. Recognition is shared by French mathematician Sadi Carnot and the brewer and physicist James Prescott Joule. In the 1820s Carnot studied the theoretical efficiency limit for heat engines. Joule's experiments in the 1840s on the mechanical and electrical equivalency of heat are so important that the metric unit of energy is named after him. By the middle of the nineteenth century, this first empirical law of thermodynamics was thought to be more or less proven by the scientific community.

The first law of thermodynamics can be applied to energy conversions such as in the combustion of gasoline. When gas is burned, chemical energy in the molecules is converted to heat and light. The amount of heat and light energy produced will exactly equal the amount of chemical energy used up, assuming no other forms of energy are involved. If the heat produced is harnessed in an internal combustion engine, the chemical energy will be turned into heat (lost out the muffler and the radiator as well as due to friction with the road and the air), into mechanical energy to move the car, and into electrical energy to run the lights, the stereo and so forth. In any case, the total amount of energy produced will exactly equal the total energy used up. This law has been extensively confirmed by experiment.

Another conservation law was discovered about forty years before the conservation of energy. The law of conservation of mass was established through some very elegant experiments done by the chemist Antoine Lavoisier in the late 18th century. It can be stated as follows: "In any natural process, the total mass of the universe is conserved." In other words, in any process which can occur matter is neither created nor destroyed.

In the year 1905, Albert Einstein threw a wrench into this neat set of conservation laws with his theory of special relativity. In a paper published that year he proposed that matter can be converted into energy and energy into matter. This fact is expressed in the famous equation $E = mc^2$. This law states that the amount of energy created (or used up) in a process is equal to the amount of mass used up (or created) in the process times the square of the speed of light. The conversion of matter into energy is demonstrated in nuclear fusion or fission, in which atoms are built up or split apart releasing huge amounts of energy. In normal chemical reactions, the amount of energy involved (E) is so small the amount of mass change (m) is too small to be measured by any standard mass-measuring device, which explains why the law of conservation of mass was accepted for so long. A combined law may be expressed in a more general first law of thermodynamics as follows: "In any process, the total mass and energy of the universe are conserved."

The first law of thermodynamics amounts to a mathematics of natural processes. It does not predict whether a particular process can happen; only the result in terms of energy if it does. For this reason, the first law is not the crucial one to help us decide whether life was created or began by natural processes. To illustrate this, let us apply the first law to a rock balanced on the edge of a cliff. If it were to leave the edge of the cliff, it is easy to predict what would happen-it would fall! Knowledge of the laws of thermodynamics is not needed to predict this. However, one can apply the first Law to this event by describing what happens in terms of energy. When the rock falls, gravitational potential energy is turned into kinetic energy as the rock accelerates. Some of the energy is lost as heat due to friction with the air. What happens to the kinetic energy when the rock hits the ground? The answer is that it is turned into heat (as well as a little bit of sound energy). If a person quickly went and felt the ground where the rock hit, it would have gotten just a little bit warmer.

This is where the limitations of the first law of thermodynamics become clear. There is nothing in the first law which precludes all the heat energy in the ground coming together and spontaneously causing the rock to be thrown off the ground, up into the air, and back up onto the cliff. One knows intuitively that this process is impossible, but the first law of thermodynamics cannot explain why. If a film was seen showing a large rock suddenly rising off the ground into the air and landing in a delicately balanced position on top of a cliff, the viewer would know instinctively that the film was being run backward. Some processes in nature are only spontaneous in one direction and not in the reverse direction. Well, not quite. If a person used intelligence and planning, he could pick up the boulder and carry it up to the top of the cliff, replacing it in its original position. This apparent exception to the law of spontaneity will be revisited later.

The case above reveals the fact that in nature certain events simply do not happen spontaneously. Remember the example used in chapter four of an old building being demolished, producing a cloud of dust and a large pile of rubble. It is obvious that the pile of rubble and cloud of dust could never spontaneously join themselves together to reform a building with all the pipes soldered together and all the bricks laid straight, cemented in position, etc. This would be absolutely impossible. Don't forget, though, that buildings do exist. They require an intelligent creator, willing to plan carefully and work hard in order to bring the different components into a carefully ordered state.

The principle by which scientists predict whether processes can occur spontaneously or not is the second law of thermodynamics. Nothing in the first law precludes the possibility of the blown up building being recreated spontaneously out of its dust and rubble. However, the second law of thermodynamics can be used to predict that this process is not possible.

The second law of thermodynamics is more abstract than the first. It is difficult to state it in a way easily understood by the uninitiated. One of the earliest statements of the second law is as follows. "Heat flows spontaneously from hot to cold objects, but not from cold objects to hot objects." In other words, if you put a hot rock into cold water, the rock would cool off, while the water would get hotter. It is impossible for the hot rock to absorb heat out of the cooler water, causing the cold water to get even colder. It is tempting to say in response, "I did not need some scientist to tell me that." This is true. However, using this law in the form of an equation, the French physicist Sadi Carnot was able to predict that it is impossible to create a perpetual motion machine—one whose sole function is to convert heat into mechanical energy with 100% efficiency. The work of Carnot and others to improve the efficiency of steam engines by applying the laws of thermodynamics to the problem contributed greatly to the industrial revolution in the nineteenth century.

A later formulation of the second law is that of Claussius. This statement is of relevance to chemistry, and therefore to the question of the origins of life. It can be stated as follows: for any spontaneous process, the entropy of the universe increases. Loosely stated, entropy is a measure of randomness or freedom of motion. In quantitative terms, the entropy of a process is the heat of that process, done in a reversible way, divided by the absolute temperature of the process. If the temperature is not constant while a process occurs, calculus must be used to define entropy.

In any case, Claussius gave us a more general rule to predict whether a process will occur spontaneously. A process which creates more order (entropy) in the universe will not be spontaneous. To illustrate, let us list a few processes which increase entropy. In doing so, we will see that the concept of entropy is more intuitive than one might expect. For example, when ice is melted, the molecules of water change from a state in which they are fixed in position to one in which they move about freely with random motion. This increased freedom of motion implies that the entropy of liquid water is greater than that of ice. Similarly, when water is boiled, entropy is increased because the water molecules are no longer attracted to one another in steam as they were in water, allowing for more freedom of motion.

Clearly, blowing up a building dramatically increases entropy. On the other hand, the creation of a large building with so much "order," with all the bricks lined up just right and all the wires attached at the right places requires a very large decrease in entropy. It therefore will not happen spontaneously. (Do not forget, though, that with sufficient external input of energy by an intelligent creator, buildings can be built. More on this later.)

What about chemistry? Large molecules such as DNA, proteins, complex lipids and sugars are in a very low state of entropy. Creating these macromolecules from smaller ones (a necessary process in order for life to be created spontaneously) involves a large decrease of entropy. The great decrease in entropy is due to two factors. First, such molecules reduce the freedom of motion of hundreds or even thousands of atoms by bonding them together. Second, entropy is decreased because of the great degree of order in the three-dimensional structure of the molecules. In order for an enzyme molecule to function, entropy must be reduced in a few ways. First, several atoms must be bound together in just the right way to form the separate amino acids. Second, dozens or hundreds of amino acid molecules need to come together spontaneously. The correct number of each of the twenty naturally occurring amino acids have to be joined in exactly the right order for the enzyme to work. In addition, the three-dimensional shape of the chain of amino acids must be in a very specific arrangement for the enzyme to function. If the primordial soup from which life is supposed to have been created contained any besides the twenty correct amino acids (and it unquestionably would have), they would have to be excluded from the structure. This too requires a decrease in entropy.

Even if by chance a large, complex, ordered thing such as a DNA molecule or an enzyme were somehow to come to exist in apparent violation of the second law of thermodynamics, the same law could be used to predict that the molecule, if subject to the vagaries of the environment, would soon fall apart. It would decompose to smaller, more random chunks of molecule, with more entropy. This is why, as mentioned earlier, Nobel prize-winning chemist Melvin Calvin said that when looking at ancient sediments under bogs, they do not even look for proteins or polysaccharides (sugars), because it is a matter of common knowledge that these molecules are not stable.[110] Why materialists theorize that these molecules slowly built up and evolved into more and more complex structures over great periods of time in some ancient earth environment seems to be beyond explanation. It is also beyond the second law of thermodynamics.

It is tempting to say, "case closed" on the spontaneous origin of viable protein molecules, given that such molecules have very low entropy. However, it is not quite that simple. Processes which decrease entropy do in some cases occur. When water is frozen entropy decreases. Apparently, under the right conditions, ice can be created out of water, even though this results in a decrease in entropy. This raises some more questions. Under what conditions can entropy decrease locally? Do the conditions which allow ice to form make it possible for large biomolecules to be produced spontaneously? More importantly, living things clearly do exist and they certainly have very low entropy. Aren't they violations of the second law of thermodynamics? In order to approach these questions, a more detailed investigation of the second law of thermodynamics is required.

The ice-from-water example will provide a good illustration. It turns out that the statement of the second law of thermodynamics given above, although correct, needs to be put more carefully to be useful. This is true, because entropy can decrease in one place, as long as it increases somewhere else at the same time but by an even greater amount. As noted when water freezes the entropy of the water decreases. However, if the temperature is low enough, when the heat leaves the water to go into the environment (such as in your freezer), it increases the entropy of the environment even more than it decreases the entropy of the water. When objects absorb heat, their entropy increases. Consider a situation in which as some water freezes, the change of entropy in the water is $\Delta S = -10$ entropy units. (S is the conventional symbol for entropy) If the environment increases in entropy because of the heat it absorbs from the water by $\Delta S = +15$ entropy units, then the total entropy change for the process is $\Delta S = -10 + 15 = +5$ entropy units. In this case the total change of entropy of the universe is positive, and the water will freeze spontaneously.

The fact is that below zero degrees centigrade (32 degrees Fahrenheit), the total entropy change for water to turn to ice is positive, and water freezes spontaneously. Above zero degrees centigrade the total entropy change for water to freeze becomes negative and water will not freeze. Therefore a scientist can predict the freezing point of water to be zero degrees centigrade, based on the second law of thermodynamics.

Evidently, the simple fact that a process has a negative entropy change is not a sufficient predictor of whether or not it will be spontaneous. In order to make this concept useful for one trying to predict whether a process will be spontaneous, one can describe four possible scenarios, as listed in the table below.

Scenario	ΔS system	ΔS surroundings	Spontaneous?
1	positive	positive	yes, always
2	positive	negative	yes, only at high temperature
3	negative	positive	yes, only at low temperature
4	negative	negative	

A process which fits into the first scenario will definitely have a total entropy change which is positive, so it will definitely be spontaneous. A process described by the fourth scenario will definitely have a negative total entropy change and it will therefore definitely not occur spontaneously. Whether a process described by case 2 or 3 is spontaneous depends on the temperature. Water freezing to form ice falls under scenario 3, so it can occur, but only at sufficiently low temperatures. An example of scenario 1 would be paper burning to form carbon dioxide and water. This is a spontaneous process. A process which fits scenario 4 is to chemically combine carbon dioxide and water to form paper. This process requires absorption of heat from the environment, making the entropy change of the environment negative. It also requires the formation of very complex cellulose molecules, making the entropy change of the system negative. The conclusion is that paper will not form spontaneously under any circumstances no matter how much heat one puts into a mixture of the proper gases. No matter how long one waits, it will never happen!

The same criterion can be applied to the supposed pathways by which Carl Sagan, Melvin Calvin and others claim life came into existence by a spontaneous process. The chemical reactions by which the basic molecules of life (carbohydrates, lipids, proteins and nucleic acids) are created from simpler building blocks all absorb heat from the environment; therefore they have a negative entropy change in the environment. They all result in a decrease in entropy in the molecules as well. This falls under scenario 4 described above. Because the formation of biomolecules both absorbs heat and decreases entropy, one can conclude that molecules such as enzymes will never be produced in usable quantity spontaneously out of a soup of simple molecules even if one waits indefinitely. This argument applies to the spontaneous production of a usable quantity of just one functioning enzyme molecule. It is a great leap from this point to even begin to propose the production (simultaneously and at the same place) of thousands of different molecules of lipids, carbohydrates, proteins and nucleic acids-all coming together to form a unit which is able to ingest food, grow, and reproduce.

But there is still one more question to be answered. This is probably the hardest one to deal with of all. Clearly paper exists, and it has rather low entropy. Despite the second law of thermodynamics, it is undeniable that living things exist as well. Even if God created living things, does not the very continued existence of living things constitute a violation of the second law of thermodynamics? Don't living things have to make proteins, nucleic acids and so forth, with very low entropy, in apparent violation of the second law? It is time to answer this intriguing question.

How can life exist with its extreme amount of order-with its unaccountably low entropy? The answer is that all living things have an *energy-fixing mechanism*. In other words, all living things have the ability to derive usable energy from their environment, and to use that energy to decrease entropy (for example to synthesize large, ordered molecules). A living thing has an extremely complex set of metabolic pathways; a series of chemical steps controlled by enzyme molecules which it uses to turn food into the raw materials (sugars, fats or amino acids) for metabolism, eventually converting the energy in food into such energy-storing molecules as ATP (adenosine triphosphate). The energy stored in these molecules, used in an intelligent way, allows the living cell to synthesize large protein and nucleic acid molecules-those molecules which allow a living thing to eat, grow, reproduce and think, etc.

The bottom line is that if energy is used in a carefully controlled way, it can be used to reduce entropy locally at the expense of increasing entropy globally. This is demonstrated in a refrigerator. A refrigerator moves heat from a cold place to a hot place. At first glance this would be in direct violation of the original statement of the second law above. However, the second law allows for the possibility of energy from outside a system being used to decrease entropy locally, if it is incorporated into a system in a carefully controlled way. The point to be made here is that refrigerators do not create themselves. It takes a thinking, planning designer to create a device such as a refrigerator. The same is true, except to an inconceivably greater degree, in the design of a living thing.

Remember the boulder which fell off the cliff in an earlier illustration? It is possible for a being with a purpose in mind to take the boulder, carry it up the hill, and place it balanced precariously at the edge of the cliff. Of course, such a process would involve the one carrying the boulder back up the hill to increase the entropy of his or her environment at the same time. This simple example illustrates the problem nicely. Imagine trying to pump a lot of energy into the boulder at the bottom of the cliff in some sort of random fashion. Perhaps by some amazing accident, the energy could conceivably cause the rock to be thrown up into the air, landing at the edge of the cliff, but it is incalculably more likely to destroy the rock. Energy incorporated into a system with out intelligent flow of that energy is very limited in what it can accomplish.

One of my favorite subjects is biochemistry. In studying this subject one gets a glance at the overwhelming chemical complexity of even the simplest living system. This sort of thing, with its great order (and very low entropy), is made possible because a very intelligent designer created a chemical system which can incorporate food energy in such a way which allows the system to synthesize the very chemicals which allowed it to incorporate the food in the first place. Which came first, the chicken or the egg?

This brings the argument to the last stand of the materialists as they attempt to save the religion of scientism which excludes the possibility of a transcendent creator. They claim that if sufficient energy were available (possibly from sunlight, or from thermal vents in the ocean), given the right building blocks, and sufficient time, entropy could be reduced enough in some local environment to spontaneously produce a living thing. Given our description of how a refrigerator works, this almost sounds plausible.

(FIGURE 10.1) ILLUSTRATION: AN (EXAMPLE) OF ENERGY CREATING DIS-ORDER, NOT ORDER. AN EARTHQUAKE CAN DESTORY AN ENTIRE CITY IN JUST A FEW MOMENTS.

In fact, if sufficient energy is input into a system in a non-intelligent way, *thermal entropy* may be reduced, but *informational entropy* cannot. The distinction between the two types of entropy may be defined by analogy. This is shown by an explosion such as the one which occurs in an internal combustion engine. This explosive energy can be used to compress a gas (decreasing the thermal entropy), which ultimately moves a piston in the engine, causing a car to move up a hill (a process normally not spontaneous because it decreases the gross amount of entropy). Another example of energy being used to decrease thermal entropy is in a refrigerator. Here either electrical or chemical energy is used up to carry heat from a cold to a warm place, decreasing entropy locally.

None of these illustrations involve a decrease in *informational entropy*. Consider a room with a pack of playing cards randomly distributed on the floor. Now, picture a backward vacuum cleaner pointed at the cards as a source of energy. It could be used to push all the cards into the corner, decreasing the "thermal entropy." However, it could not be used to place the cards into four separate piles of hearts, clubs, diamonds and spades. It could also not be used to build a house out of cards. The likelihood of the backward vacuum cleaner creating a house of cards is zero. Energy can only be used to build a house of cards or to create neat stacks of cards sorted by suit if the energy is directed by design. Simply throwing energy at a system will never decrease the informational entropy of that system to a significant degree. The fact is that thermal energy always tends to decrease information.

The refrigerator provides another case in point. A refrigerator can be used to reduce entropy. It uses up electrical energy to reduce thermal entropy. However throwing a bunch of energy at the raw materials needed to produce a refrigerator could never result in the production of a refrigerator. There is no way that one could take a pile of iron ore and crude petroleum (as well as all the other raw materials required to build a refrigerator), and then simply add energy and wait long enough for a refrigerator to result, with the bolts turned into the proper holes, the belt on the motor and so forth. Instead, a designer is required to direct the flow of energy needed to create the refrigerator.

There is no way around this fact of nature. Nature does not create information by itself. Materialists, intent on preserving belief in the random creation of life, simply avoid the unavoidable requirement for a great decrease in informational entropy in order for life to be created. One exception to this rule is Belgian chemist Ilya Prigogine, who received the Nobel prize for his work on non-equilibrium thermodynamics. He discussed the distinction between reducing thermal and informational entropy as it relates to the origin of life.

> *Needless to say, these simple remarks cannot suffice to solve*
> *the problem of prebiological order. One would like not only to estab-*
> *lish that the Second Law (S>0) is compatible with a decrease in the*
> *overall (system) entropy (S<0), but also to indicate the mechanisms*
> *responsible for the emergence and maintenance of coherent states.*[111]

Prigogine and his co-author Nicolis point out that it is not enough to show that overall system entropy (what I am calling thermal entropy) can be reduced by inputting energy. The question to be asked is how did "prebiological order" or "coherent states" come to be? Scientists have no answer to this question, or they refer to "chemical evolution" and "sufficient time" as the explanations. This amounts to hand-waving. Use of these nice-sounding terms does nothing to change the fact that more and more energy and more and more time will always yield an increase in informational entropy, not a decrease. Information simply does not gradually increase in nature without an intelligent injection of energy.

Humans are quite good at creating objects with low informational entropy. Such objects illustrate the general rule that intelligence or design is required for energy to be used to create information. Consider a blank cassette tape. It contains magnetic material which, when the tape is bought, is randomly oriented (high entropy). When an electric signal proportional to the sound of a musical instrument is run through the record head, the magnetic field on the tape is unrandomized (low informational entropy), producing sufficient order that it is able to cause music to be played back when the magnetic signal is read. Does anyone believe that the applying magnetic energy to a tape at random could ever produce a piece of music, with a rhythm, lyrics and so forth? The answer is an emphatic "No!" This would require a large reduction in informational entropy. It could only be done by intelligent design.

Even the simplest living organism is much more complex and has inconceivably more order than a house of cards or even the cassette tape of a musical piece. In other words, the probability of a backward vacuum cleaner being applied to a pile of playing cards producing a well-designed house of cards is far greater than the chances of a prebiological soup producing even one usable gene, never mind all the thousands of proteins, carbohydrates, nucleic acids and lipids needed to produce a living thing.

In fact, the probability of a house of cards being built by a backward vacuum cleaner is not just small; it is zero. Even if by some amazing coincidence all the cards just happened to be in the right position to form a house at some instant in time, the very vacuum which created the house in the first place would instantaneously destroy it. This is another reason the proposal of scientists that an unlimited amount of energy could create a large degree of informational order is illogical. The large amount of energy required to decrease the entropy in a chemical system (or a group of cards) would very quickly randomize that information, even if it were instantaneously produced.

There is the rub. The secret ingredient of all probability arguments for believers in non-transcendent creation of life is time. Remember, however, that "sufficient time" does not change the argument about information in the slightest. Very unlikely events will have their probability increased by waiting. If one plays the lottery ten million times, the probability of winning goes up. However, impossible events, such as those that grossly decrease informational entropy without the intervention of a creator, will not become more possible with time. To illustrate, the probability of a very large asteroid hitting the earth this year is extremely low. However, it can be predicted that in the time span of a billion years, this very small probability will increase to the point that the event actually becomes likely over that very great time span. Picture the reverse process, the impossible one. Imagine running an asteroid collision backwards. In other words, imagine trillions of dust particles, small rocks, many huge boulders as well as millions of gas particles spontaneously joining themselves together to become a giant asteroid, which then lifts itself off the surface of the earth to be hurtled back into space. This is an impossible event, whose probability will not grow with time. The same concept applies to the formation of life without a creator.

This brings us back to our last problem. In view of the need to reduce informational entropy, how does life maintain itself? Living cells are able to break the law of information production because they already contain information. The information essential to life is contained in the DNA. This information is able, intelligently, to direct the synthesis of proteins, carbohydrates, lipids and, most significantly, the reproduction of the information for the next generation of cells. Without the pre-existent information in a cell, such processes are impossible.

How much information are we taking about? Let us take as our model the same *e. coli* bacteria mentioned previously. The genome of bacteria is far smaller than that of humans, involving hundreds of millions of base pairs as opposed to some four billion. The genome of *e.coli* is 4.6 million base pairs. For the sake of argument, let us allow that the simplest primitive life contained as few as two million pieces of information. This is equivalent to a book of about one thousand pages. Could the ink of two million letters, commas, periods and spaces, thrown randomly at a pile of paper, be expected to produce a book that makes sense? This is literally impossible. But even the illustration of letters placed at random on a page is far too simple, as a living thing has levels of order and information above and beyond the simple two million pieces of information contained in the nucleic acids. Remember, the first living thing had to simultaneously contain both the DNA with its two million pieces of information *and* the proteins which, conceptually, would have been formed by that DNA. The proteins in this accidental cell need to be the correct ones so that the DNA which forms them can in turn be formed by the proteins. Add to that the information contained in the lipids, carbohydrates and so forth, and one begins to see the enormity of the problem. Besides, the world in which life is supposed to have formed was far less amenable to the formation of information than our model of a piece of paper at which we throw letters.

A great number of additional problems with the formation of life by random natural process could be mentioned. Hopefully the point has been made. It is tempting to quote statistics and probabilities, such as the probability of making a particular chain of protein out of a random sample of amino acids, or the probability of excluding other extraneous molecules at the same time and so forth. Throwing out extremely small numbers and multiplying them to produce even smaller numbers could go on ad infinitum. In the end, the informational requirement reduces the probability of even a single usable molecule of DNA being produced to zero. The interested reader will find a good reference which covers both the probability arguments and the informational entropy concept more thoroughly in paper by Walter L. Bradley.[112]

In summary, the laws of thermodynamics imply that life could never have happened by natural processes. No amount of scientific fast talk will change this fact. The reason many scientists cling to the natural explanation for the origin of life is either a lack of sufficient understanding of the relevant scientific laws or, more likely, an unwillingness to give up the preconception that natural laws alone explain everything that ever has happened or ever will happen. Yet great amounts of information can only be created by a system which already contains information. Life requires an intelligent creator.

110 Melvin Calvin, *Chemical Evolution* (Eugene: Oregon State System of Higher Education, 1961), 34.
111 G. Nicolis and I. Prigogine, *Self-Organization in Non-equilibrium Systems* (New York: John Wiley and Sons, 1977), 23.
112 Walter L. Bradley, "Thermodynamics of the Origins of Life," *Journal of the American Scientific Affiliation*, June 1988

THEOLOGY AND PHILOSOPHY OF SCIENCE

The Confessions of St. Augustine (New York: Penguin Books, 1963)

Augustine, *The Literal Meaning of Genesis:* Eng. trans. in Ancient Christian Writers, no. 41 (New York: Newman Press, 1982)

Francis Bacon, *Novum Organum* (Peru, Illinois: Carus Publishing Company, 2000)

Henry Blocher, *In the Beginning* (Downers Grove, Illinois: Intervarsity Press, 1984)

Rene Descartes, *Discourse on Method* (London: Penguin Books, 1999)

Immanuel Kant, *Critique of Pure Reason* (Cambridge, UK: Cambridge University Press, 2000)

Wade Rowland, *Galileo's Mistake* (New York: Arcade Publishing, 2001)

SUGGESTED BOOKS BY CREATIONISTS WHO ACCEPT THAT THE EARTH IS ANCIENT

Michael J. Behe, *Darwin's Black Box* (New York: The Free Press, 1996)

William A. Dembski and Michael J. Behe, *Intelligent Design: The Bridge Between Science and Theology* (Downer's Grove, Illinois: InterVarsity Press, 1999)

Michael J. Denton, *Nature's Destiny* (New York: The Free Press, 1998)

Kenneth R. Miller, *Finding Darwin's God* (New York: HarperCollins Publishers, 1999)

Hugh Ross, *The Fingerprint of God* (New Kensington, Pennsylvania: Whitaker House, 2000)

_____, *The Genesis Question* (Colorado Springs: NavPress Publishing Group, 1998)

Gerald L. Schroeder, *The Science of God* (New York: Broadway Books, 1998)

Ian Stewart, *Life's Other Secret* (New York: John Wiley and Sons, 1998)

John Clayton, *The Source: Eternal Design or Infinite Accident* (South Bend, Indiana: Does God Exist? 1990)

Suggested Books from the Young-Earth Creationist Perspective

Walt Brown, *In the Beginning* (Phoenix: Center for Scientific Creation, 1995)

Alan Hayward, *Creation and Evolution* (Minneapolis: Bethany House Publishers, 1995)

Henry M. Morris, *Scientific Creationism* (El Cajon, California: Master Books, 1974)

_____ and Gary E. Parker, *What is Creation Science?* (El Cajon, California: Master Books, 1987)

Bernard Ramm, *The Christian View of Science and Scripture* (Grand Rapids: Eerdmans, 1954)

Jonathan Sarfati, *Refuting Compromise* (Green Forest, Arkansas: Master Books, 2004)

John C. Whitcomb and Henry M. Morris, *The Genesis Flood* (Phillipsburg, New Jersey: Presbyterian and Reformed Publishing, 1961)

Suggested Books from an Atheist or Agnostic Perspective

John Desmond Bernal, *The Origin of Life* (London: Weidendorf and Nicholson, 1967)

Melvin Calvin, *Chemical Evolution* (Eugene, Oregon: Oregon State System of Higher Education, Eugene, 1961)

Charles Darwin, *The Descent of Man* (New York: Penguin Books, 2004)

_____, *On the Origin of Species by Means of Natural Selection, or the Preservation of Favoured Races in the Struggle for Life* (New York: Random House, 1979)

Richard Dawkins, *The Selfish Gene* (Oxford, UK: Oxford University Press, 1989)

_____, *River Out of Eden* (New York: Basic Books, 1995)

Niles Eldredge, *The Monkey Business* (New York: Washington Square Press, 1980)

_____, *The Triumph of Evolution, and the Failure of Creationism* (New York: W. H. Freeman and Company, 2000)

Stephen J. Gould, *Rocks of Ages* (New York: Ballantine Publishing, 1999)

Jeffery S. Levinton, "The Big Bang of Animal Evolution," *Scientific American*, November 1992, p. 84

GENERAL

Walter L. Bradley, "Thermodynamics of the Origins of Life," *Journal of the American Scientific Affiliation*, June 1988

S. I. McMillen, M.D., *None of these Diseases* (Grand Rapids: Fleming H. Revell Co, 2000)

Ronald Numbers, *The Creationists* (Berkeley: The University of California Press, 1992)

John Oakes, *Reasons for Belief: A Handbook of Christian Evidence* (Spring, Texas: Illumination Publishers, 2005)

John Oakes, *Field Manual for Christian Apologetics* (Spring, Texas: Illumination Publishers, 2011)

John Oakes/David Eastman, *That You May Believe* (Spring, Texas: Illumination Publishers, 2011)

Douglas A. Jacoby, *Compelling Evidence for God and the Bible* (Eugene, OR: Harvest House, 2010).

All of the books and audio teaching series
by Dr. John M. Oakes are available at
www.ipibooks.com

www.ipibooks.com